FROGS

TO MY WIFE

THE AUSTRALIAN NATURALIST LIBRARY

Frogs

MICHAEL J. TYLER

Collins SYDNEY · LONDON

Also in the Australian Naturalist Library

© MICHAEL J. TYLER 1976

First published 1976 by William Collins (Australia) Ltd
Type set by Queensland Type Service Pty Ltd, Brisbane
Printed by Dai Nippon Printing Co. (Hong Kong) Ltd

ISBN 0 00 211442 9

Contents

ACKNOWLEDGMENTS

Photographic plates were contributed by D. Anstis: Pl 3 upper; Marion Anstis: Pl. 1 upper, Pl. 2 upper, Pl. 4 upper, Pl. 9 lower, Pl. 11, Pl. 12 lower, Pl. 16 lower, Pl. 17–18; Stanley Breeden: Pl. 2 lower, Pl. 4 lower, Pl. 9 lower, Pl. 13 upper, Pl. 15; Dale Cavill: Pl. 8 lower; Barry Craig: Pl. 20 lower; Barry Douetil: Pl. 5, Pl. 20 upper; Alan Easton: Pl. 1 lower, Pl. 14 upper, Pl. 19 lower; Harry Ehmann: Pl. 9 upper; Graeme Gow: Pl. 14 lower; Angus Martin: Pl. 8 upper; Greg Miles: Pl. 18; the late F. J. Mitchell: Pl. 18, Pl. 19 upper; Fred Parker: Pl. 12 upper, Pl. 13 lower; Bohdan Stankewytsch-Janusch: Pl. 3 lower, Pl. 6–7.

Illustrations

Text Figures

Preface

AT PRESENT scarcely anything has been published for the naturalists interested in Australian frogs, and absolutely nothing at all upon the vast number of interesting frog species in New Guinea. There are really two major deficiencies in this literary void: firstly a book providing information about the lives of frogs, enabling them to be appreciated as living animals and, secondly, one designed as a field guide for identification. These two objectives are quite different, and my book is concerned only with the first one, which is just how frogs strive, thrive and stay alive.

Unfortunately there are still a number of fairly substantial gaps in our knowledge, and many of the vital studies on aspects of breathing, feeding etc. have been undertaken overseas on foreign species. There isn't really any reason to suppose that Australian and New Guinea frogs are any different in the way in which they function, but until confirmation is available we remain uncertain. More significantly, it means that it is still necessary to make reference to foreign species.

Just what should be regarded foreign is not as easy to decide as one might imagine. The Australian fauna has close affinities with the fauna of New Guinea, and with more remote islands further east such as New Britain and the Solomon Islands. In terms of similarity we find a close kinship between Australian animals and those on these islands. For this reason it is unrealistic and unreasonable to pursue an isolationist policy and the outlying islands' faunas have been included in this book.

One or two actions require comment. The first is my failure to use the subspecies names of frogs denoting geographic races. It doesn't imply that I fail to recognize that these races really are different from one another. However, the fact is that for the beginner two Latin names strung together can be pretty off-putting, even in this the shortest form. I would be very sorry to dampen any latent enthusiasm by adding to these the third. Hence, depending where it comes from, the giant tree frog is known to specialists as either *Litoria infrafrenata militaria* (New Britain and New Ireland) or *Litoria infrafrenata infrafrenata* (New Guinea and Australia), but for us *Litoria infrafrenata* will do for both.

Secondly the Latin names of particular kinds of animals quoted in many of the works I refer to have changed over the past few years. When quoting early works I felt it would be simpler to use the current going name for the species and not mention the former one which was actually used. It sounds a trifle dishonest, but to act otherwise would have introduced numerous digressions of explanation at quite inappropriate points in the text, so breaking the sequence of the presentation.

My indebtedness to friends and colleagues really is considerable. In the early stages of preparation the senior member of the Editorial Committee, Professor H. G. Andrewartha, provided extremely useful and most constructive criticisms of style which profoundly influenced preparation of remaining chapters. Dr S. J. Edmonds, Miss L. M. Angel and Mrs P. M. Thomas (Department of Zoology, University of Adelaide), and Dr L. Bennett of the South Australian Institute of Technology all gave valuable advice for the chapter on parasites. Mrs C. Houston, formerly of the South Australian Museum, located and drew my attention to numerous publications containing references to Aboriginal associations with frogs.

For some extremely interesting and often quite bizarre frogs from Queensland, and detailed notes about their habits, I am indebted to Mr C. Corben and Mr G. Ingram of Brisbane, whilst Miss J. Covacevich and Mr M. Archer of the Queensland Museum generously let me examine an illustration from the manuscript of their paper on *Bufo marinus*.

The vast majority of the figures were prepared or redrawn by Adrienne Edwards of the South Australian Museum. Her patience in the face of dubious, inaccurate and oscillating advice bore testimony to sympathetic appreciation of the instability of those who elect to study frogs. Figures 14 and 15 are the work of Marion Anstis.

For permission to reproduce figures published elsewhere I am indebted to the University of Missouri Press (Fig. 5), the American Museum of Natural History (Fig. 10), the American Association for the Advancement of Science (Fig. 22), the Linnean Society of New South Wales (Fig. 34), the Commonwealth Scientific and Industrial Research Organisation (Fig. 6), the Royal Society of South Australia (Figs. 29 and 33), and the Canadian Journal of Science (Fig. 23).

Photographic plates were provided by Barry Douetil, Bohdan Stankewytsch-Janusch, Marion Anstis, Harry Ehmann, Fred Parker, Ann Mitchell, Barry Craig, Angus Martin, Greg Miles, Dale Cavill, Graeme Gow and the Queensland Museum.

The manuscript was expertly typed by Mrs E. McDonaugh, Miss C. Burford and Mrs L. Kingston.

Finally I would like to express my gratitude to my wife Ella for her encouragement and support.

1 Introduction

THE WORDS 'frog' and 'toad' are popular terms that permit us to distinguish what we may regard to be different types of animals. It is highly likely that when we refer to a toad we invariably have a mental image of an ugly, warty-skinned creature living in a dark, damp place away from water, whereas we tend to call a frog anything that doesn't look like a toad. Hence we tend to be more liberal in our concepts of frogs, visualizing smooth or slimy-skinned animals usually living in water, and yet we also recognize all of the tree dwellers as 'tree frogs'. Most of us are fairly sure in our own minds that we are correct in distinguishing these animals in this sort of way, and what we are really doing is considering it worthwhile to have separate names for what appear to us to be quite different animals.

This distinction between the frog and the toad has been used in the English language for several centuries. Similarly the French have used the words *grenouille* for frog, and *crapaud* for toad, and the Germans *frosche* and *kröte* in exactly the same way.

When early anatomists began to dissect these animals they found that the most well-known European frogs (species of *Rana*) differed from European toads (*Bufo* species) in the way in which the bones of the two halves of the shoulder girdle were joined in the middle of the chest. In *Rana* the bones are fused together in the middle at the central sternum bone, whereas in *Bufo* the two halves are not fused and immovable but are free and joined only by an overlapping of cartilages in such a way that they can move apart slightly (Fig. 1). The herpetologist George Boulenger thought that this feature was of such importance as to merit placing all of the families of frogs into one group, and the toads into another, and to use names for the groups based on this difference. For the frogs he coined the word Firmisternia from the Latin words *firmus* (firm) and *sternum*. Arcifera, for the toads

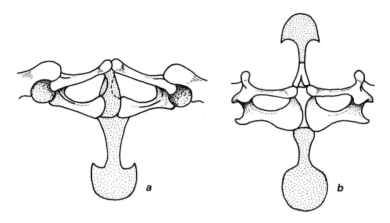

FIG. 1 Shoulder girdles of *a*. the cane toad *Bufo marinus* and *b*. the frog *Rana papua*.

referred to the bow-like form of cartilages at the junction of the halves, and was derived from *arcus* (a bow) and *fero* (I bear).

These terms are still used, but recently zoologists have woken up with a start, and have virtually asked: 'Why should we arbitrarily pick on one character from amongst many, and attach such importance to it?' In fact, our era of trying to set to rights examples of racial and sexual inequality in man has a parallel in scientific thinking, to the extent that many zoologists are most reluctant to admit that they attach particular importance to or favour any feature used in classification more than another. All features are equal until proved otherwise.

As it happened, discord between the technical division of animals into the Arcifera and Firmisternia by Boulenger's followers, and the popular concept of frogs and toads was almost immediate. It happened that the creatures that in Australia we call tree frogs have an arciferal (toad-like) bone arrangement. Certainly there were a few zoologists who proceeded to call all tree frogs 'tree toads', but this practice never gained very much support.

Within Australia there are only seven species of Firmisternia, all of which are found only in remote portions of northern Australia, and most are so rare that few people have ever seen them. This means that if we attempted to seek a harmony between Boulenger's classification and popular terminology, the vast majority of our animals should be called toads. It would be ludicrous to suggest a change in the way in which Australian naturalists recognize frogs and toads, and I would be the last person to recommend it.

In this book I am drawing no distinction between frogs and toads unless there is real benefit to be gained from it. Therefore I call almost all of them 'frogs', and any statement about a frog can be assumed to apply equally well to the few species that are popularly called toads. Rare exceptions are all references to the introduced 'cane toad' (*Bufo marinus*) where it would be most confusing to call it a frog, and to other popular names, such as the Holy Cross toad *Notaden bennetti*.

There are some small species of the genus *Pseudophryne* which have warty skins and short legs and which, in true toad-like fashion, prefer to walk if they can possibly avoid the more energetic exercise of jumping. These are commonly called 'toadlets', and they were in fact originally, but erroneously, thought to be closely related to *Bufo* and regarded as members of the family Bufonidae. My use of 'toadlet' is confined to quoting common names.

Frogs are members of a major group or Class of vertebrate animals called the Amphibia. What really distinguishes them from other vertebrates is their double life. The tadpole which hatches from the egg is obviously larval and immature; in due course it transforms rapidly into the adult form of a frog, which usually lives on land. Frogs constitute a separate and easily definable sub-group or Order of the Class Amphibia called the Anura, and in scientific texts they tend to be referred to simply as 'anurans'. The principle feature that distinguishes the Anura from other amphibian Orders is the absence of a tail in the adult stage. The tail persists in the adults of salamanders and newts (Urodela), also in creatures resembling large salamanders and called sirens (Gymnophiona), and in legless, wormlike amphibians (Apoda). What has happened to produce the difference that distinguishes the Anura, in their structure, from other groups in the Amphibia is that frogs have become more highly adapted to life on land. Over a long period of time in their evolution the tail became progressively shorter, perhaps because it was more of an encumbrance than a structure of any benefit. Hence in the frogs that inhabit the world today the tail has been completely lost and there is little if any trace of this structure at all. However, the fact that tadpoles possess tails is virtually a testimony that the modern frogs have evolved from an ancestor that possessed one as an adult. The Anura is the only amphibian Order found in Australia and New Guinea.

The task of distinguishing frogs and of classifying them into a supposedly natural system of families and genera would be much easier if the living frogs around us differed from one another to a greater extent than they actually do. The fact is that there are not many features that are unique to one group or to another, and so to define families and genera it is necessary to refer to a large number of different characters, such as the nature of the vertebrae, bones forming the skull, etc. etc.

The actual ways in which frogs differ reflect adaptations to particular ways of life, so that simply by looking at a frog we should be able to interpret some details about its mode of life. For example how it moves and where it probably lives. For this reason a study of the external features of an animal can be designed to provide a method of seeking what are really biological clues.

When taking just a very brief look at a frog we tend to assess its size, the shape of the head and the body, the length of the hind limbs, the texture of the skin and the colour. Size is normally expressed in millimetres as the distance between the tip of the snout and the cloaca (vent). This is therefore the total length of head plus body. Most frogs in Australia and New Guinea fall within the range of about 25 to 75 mm, but the extremes are 5 mm for many young juveniles to 250 mm for the adults of some of the particularly large species that are to be found in New Guinea. Hence in Australia and New Guinea are to be found some of the smallest and largest frogs in the world.

The shape of the head and body, and the length of the limbs are not determined independently but are directly associated with one another. I mean by this that frogs with slender, elongate bodies invariably have long heads with prominent, tapering snouts, and exceptionally long hind limbs. When the body is squat, and possibly even circular in shape, the legs are always very short.

Elongation produces the streamline form so suited to jumping great distances. *Litoria nasuta* of New South Wales (Plate 5) is an example of aerodynamic perfection and is known most appropriately as the rocket frog. Such elongate frogs lie fairly close to the ground; they are timid and tend to leap for cover when disturbed. In contrast the squat-bodied frogs have short limbs because their body form does not lend itself to agility. They sit with a much more erect posture; their jumping ability is limited to cumbersome and most ungainly hops and some don't jump at all but walk on all fours.

Skin texture is difficult to interpret in terms of adaptation. As a broad generalization it is true to say that the warty, dry-skinned creatures tend to inhabit places that are fairly dry in summer, and very few of them live close to water. Warty frogs tend to be grey, brown or occasionally even yellowish, but never bright green. Uniform green coloration is confined to tree-dwellers although there are many tree frogs sporting other colours.

Looking at the head in detail it will be noticed that the eyes and the nostrils are positioned virtually on the top of the skull (Fig. 2). The forehead and the high skull of other vertebrates such as mammals has evolved to accommodate development of a large brain. Frogs with their very small brains (described as 'an apology for a brain' by an expert in such matters) retain a rather flat head, but in water they at least have the advantage of being able to see and breathe whilst the remainder of the head and the body are submerged and so hidden from view.

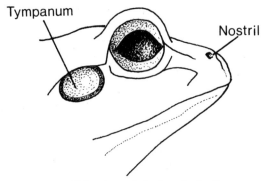

FIG. 2 Side view of the head of a frog.

Although the eyes may give the impression of looking out on opposite sides they are actually inclined very slightly towards the front. The extent to which the eyes are inclined inwards varies with the overall shape of the head but, as a rough guide, the snout can be considered a blind spot: an area that the frog cannot scan. Certainly frogs are also physically incapable of seeing anything directly in front of their snouts. This is well demonstrated by watching them feeding, for if there is a food item directly in front of their snouts they tend to turn the head to one side, seemingly preferring to have a really good look with one eye. Many lizards behave in exactly the same way.

The shape of the pupil of the eye is frequently mentioned in classifications of frogs. When constricted, as occurs in bright illumination, the frog pupil has a distinctive shape: usually in the form of a vertical or horizontal slit, a rhombus or a diamond (Fig. 3). None have the circular pupil characterizing man. The light from a small torch shone at the eye of a frog from a distance of a few centimetres will cause the pupil to constrict to its characteristic shape within about fifteen seconds. The practical value of information on constricted pupil shape is demonstrated in the family Hylidae, for the two Australian genera, *Litoria* and *Nyctimystes*, can be distinguished from one another on the basis of this character alone. In *Nyctimystes* the pupil always assumes the form of a vertical slit, whereas in *Litoria* it is a horizontal slit or occasionally rhomboid-shaped, but never vertical.

In his classic work on the evolution of the eye Sir Stewart Duke Elder (1958) has demonstrated from studies on many vertebrate animals, that vertical shape of the pupil is normally associated with inner structural changes that equip the animal for sight in

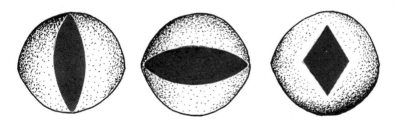

FIG. 3 Differences in the shape of the constricted pupil of the eye.

conditions of poor illumination. For frogs it therefore seems that this particular form is the height of perfection for nocturnal life.

The colour of the iris surrounding the pupil is highly variable from species to species and can often bear an elaborate and quite beautiful pattern. However, its usefulness in classification lies in the fact that similarities in iris colour and pattern can provide a good indication of close relationships amongst species. This certainly isn't true in all instances, but there is one group of species of *Litoria* which share a reddish or reddish-orange iris, and from other shared characters they are known to be closely related to one another.

Just behind the eye there is usually a circular disc called the tympanum or tympanic membrane (Fig. 2). This structure is the outermost portion of the ear and, in its classical form, the tympanum resembles the taut membrane of a drum. From species to species it varies considerably in its size and it may be partly or completely hidden from view by the surrounding skin. It is occasionally lacking altogether, for there are a few genuinely earless frogs such as the southeastern Australian Bibron's toadlet, *Pseudophryne bibroni*. Because earless frogs are not deaf but respond to sound it is assumed that the bones of the skull must provide adequate sound transmission to the auditory nerve.

All frogs have only four fingers on each hand, for the true thumb has been entirely lost. Some species do have a bony spine called a prepollex jutting out near where the thumb should be (Fig. 4). However, this is not a rudiment of a thumb but a supplementary structure that may have evolved to assist males in the process of grasping their partners during the process of mating.

Much can be learned from a study of the hand of a frog, and in fact what can genuinely be called palmistry is of considerable value in classification. The hand also reflects the sort of life that the frog leads. If it is used for grasping, the first finger tends to be splayed away from the others much like our thumb. The tips of the fingers are broadly expanded into flattened discs in tree frogs, whilst burrowers usually have short cylindrical fingers.

On their undersurfaces the joints between the finger and toe bones are often marked by the presence of raised pads of tissue termed subarticular tubercles (Fig. 4). Their function is un-certain, but they probably bear much of the friction involved

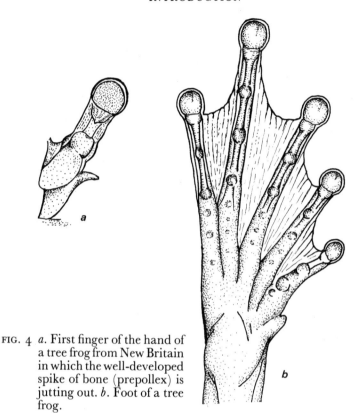

FIG. 4 *a*. First finger of the hand of a tree frog from New Britain in which the well-developed spike of bone (prepollex) is jutting out. *b*. Foot of a tree frog.

during activities such as walking, jumping and grasping. The tubercles indicate the joints of the bones which vary in number from finger to finger. The outer two fingers usually have four bones and the inner two fingers have three. These bones are particularly tiny so that they usually have to be examined by means of X-rays or by a modern treatment that enables the soft tissues to be rendered transparent, and the bones stained deep red with alizarin dye. This procedure reveals valuable information such as whether the bone at the tip is unmodified, has a knob-like form, is claw-shaped, T-shaped or Y-shaped. The classification to a particular family may depend upon details such as whether the bones at the end of the fingers meet to form a simple joint, or whether they are separated by a disc of cartilage or bone.

Many tree frogs have a thin membrane of webbing linking the fingers. It is by no means common to all of them, but in Australia the presence of any at all can enable a frog to be identified to the family Hylidae with assurance.

The foot with its five toes provides just as many aids to classification and clues to the habits of the possessor. Webbing between the toes occurs in all of the hylid tree frogs but is most highly developed in frogs which spend their entire lives in and around water. However, there are frogs that completely lack such webbing and yet swim magnificently and obviously manage perfectly well without it.

Almost all of the burrowing frogs dig with their feet and not, as one might suppose, with their hands. To assist this function several species have developed a spade-like tubercle on the inner edge of the foot. It is the type of structural detail that enables us to interpret something about a frog's habits.

Throughout the world there are probably about 2550 species of frogs known to science at the present time. Gorham (1963) estimated the total number (from his examination of the literature up to 1958) as 2300, but at least 250 have been found and named in the intervening years and there is no question that many more undoubtedly await discovery. In terms of actual numbers and diversity of species it is quite clear that the richest frog faunas are to be found in the tropical and subtropical zones.

What are considered to be the most primitive frogs exist today only in cooler climates, for the family Leiopelmatidae is restricted to New Zealand and to parts of the U.S.A. The New Zealand representatives are the most numerous and yet consist of just three species of *Leiopelma*. They are thought to be primitive for a number of reasons of which one is the presence of nine presacral vertebrae (vertebrae in front of the sacrum forming the hump in the back), whereas other frogs have eight or even fewer as a result of a fusion of adjacent bones. This feature is considered primitive simply because frogs are believed to have evolved from animals that had longer bodies. Hence a major evolutionary change would involve shortening the spine by reducing the number of bones in it. For example *Triadobatrachus* (Fig. 5), a fossil amphibian that lived over 200 million years ago in Madagascar and which is thought by some zoologists to be the sort of aquatic

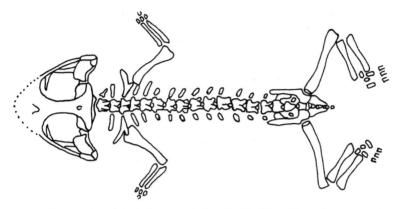

FIG. 5 Reconstructed skeleton of the fossil *Triadobatrachus*, a tailed amphibian about 25 cm long. It lived about 200 million years ago, and possibly resembles the ancestor of modern frogs (after Estes and Reig 1973).

animal from which frogs evolved, had sixteen presacral vertebrae. Another primitive feature which has been retained by *Leiopelma* is a very short muscle with an incredible name of unrivalled length: the caudalipuboischiotibialis. This muscle is thought to be a tail-wagging muscle, inferring that the adult frog has been left with the means of wagging something that it no longer possesses. Irrespective of the merits of the argument that leads us to accept the theory of the proposed function of this muscle, the New Zealand Government has recognized the uniqueness of *Leiopelma*. The Government enforces stringent regulations to protect the strange frogs of this genus and so ensure, as far as man is able, that it will not become extinct.

Leiopelma and *Ascaphus*, which is the North American representative of the Leiopelmatidae, may not really be members of the same family. We lump them together because there are features that are shared only by them, and recognize the family as a unique one because these same features are not shared by any other frogs. However, it is quite possible that many millions of years ago all of the frogs that inhabited the world had these characteristics. Just because they are now common to *Leiopelma* and *Ascaphus* may not be sufficient reason for including the genera in the same family.

It all sounds rather confusing, but this is genuinely the present situation of frog classification: a state of confusion and amicable controversy. Each year new schemes of frog classification are introduced by zoologists, involving recognizing some groups of genera as new families, and suppressing the recognition of other families by placing the genera they contained in other existing families. In some cases the proposals follow fresh interpretation of old knowledge, and in others the introduction of new information. Anyone interested in reading more about this topic should refer to the collection of papers presented at a symposium held in Kansas City in 1970, and now available in a volume published in 1973 and edited by James Vial.

Classification is nothing more than the arrangement of animals into groups and so involves the recognition of genera and families into a cohesive system. It isn't just an arbitrary system but a means to an end, being an organization of the species in the animal kingdom in a way that will show the evolutionary hierarchy of animals. We use comparable systems of classification in our daily lives, and understanding the basis of other systems of classification equips the naturalist to approach the problem of classifying frogs.

We can compare the classification of the Order Anura (all frogs) to another group of things around us which are loosely termed automobiles. It may help a little to give this group a Latin-sounding name, so we'll call it the 'Automobilia'. Within this Order Automobilia we recognize the existence of different families for which we use names such as Utility, Sedan, Estate, etc. Within the family Sedan we have several genera such as *Holden*, *Chrysler*, *Ford* etc., with species corresponding to the models produced in different years.

It is worth pointing out that when we identify cars the accuracy of our efforts depends partly upon the extent of the opportunity (a glimpse as the species flashes past, or a detailed study when it is quietly at rest at the kerbside), and partly upon our own previous knowledge and expertise.

Unlike frogs, cars evolved after the arrival of man upon the earth, but their rate of evolution has been phenomenal. The original ancestral stock is a species called *T* of the genus *Ford*. The genus has flourished, but it is only as a result of the concerted efforts of a few ardent conservationists that the species *T* has not become extinct. I believe that very few individuals are now to be found in their natural habitat.

If for the very first time we were suddenly faced with identifying and classifying all of the things called cars, I don't doubt that there would be a few errors. There would perhaps be arguments about whether a recently discovered gas-driven vehicle merited erection of a new family, and whether the members of a genus (manufacturer) were genuinely distinct or should be lumped together with another from which it really could not be separated, because of financial control.

What is happening in zoology is that we are finding that some of our genera should be split and others combined. When this sort of thing happens, the results are usually published in scientific journals that few naturalists are fortunate enough to have access to. It often takes years before there is again any consistency in the use of generic names in the scientific and the so-called popular literature. Naturalists often become frustrated or even annoyed at what often seems an unnecessary step, but the crux of the matter is that changes are needed to correct errors, equivalent to failing to recognize Holden and Chrysler as separate entities.

Changes in the genus classification of frogs therefore affects the scientific names (nomenclature) that we use for them. The name of the species (specific name) may remain unchanged, but it becomes necessary to alter the generic one. It is easier to appreciate that this isn't just the result of a zoologist's whim by looking at a few recent changes, how they were justified and just why the changes were proposed.

An example of a genus being split up into several genera has occurred quite recently. Up to 1972 *Crinia* was thought to contain eighteen species of frogs, but about the only thing that they had in common was their small size. The genus extended throughout the temperate, sub-tropical and tropical zones of Australia and extended into southern New Guinea. In 1971 I examined *Crinia darlingtoni* which had been discovered in the Macpherson Ranges of southeastern Queensland by Dr P. J. Darlington, and described and named in his honour in 1933 by A. Loveridge of the Museum of Comparative Zoology at Harvard University. Loveridge had demonstrated that this was a species previously unknown to science but his description alone suggested an animal quite unlike the species of *Crinia* with which I was familiar. The question in my mind was whether *darlingtoni* could really be grouped together with the other *Crinia* species in one genus. The step taken by Loveridge implied that it was a member of a group of which all of the members had descended from a common ancestor.

In approaching this problem, there is no real set of hard and fast rules for the recognition of genera. Species of frogs are totally unaware that genera exist. However the grouping of species together in a genus implies that the members of that genus are more closely related to one another than they are to any species in any other genus. Although we cannot measure the magnitude of difference that merits, warrants or requires the recognition of genera, it is obviously helpful if we strive to ensure that the criteria employed are similar in each case. If we study a family of frogs, a genus is a useful grouping only in the context of the way in which other genera in that family are recognized and defined.

Through the courtesy of Professor E. E. Williams at Harvard University and Miss Jeanette Covacevich of the Queensland Museum, I was able to borrow specimens of *Crinia darlingtoni* and these proved to be quite unlike the 'norm' for *Crinia*. There were so many features of its anatomy and biology that were not shared by any of the other *Crinia* species, that I believed that *Crinia* would be a more natural group if *darlingtoni* was removed from it. For these reasons I proposed in 1972 that *darlingtoni* be placed in a new genus which I called *Assa*.

Blake (1973) studied the remaining species of *Crinia* and found the need for further subdivision. He believed that they were still a motley group of animals which should be split up into three genera. As a result of his efforts *Crinia* is now a group of only two species, and the remainder are now in genera called *Ranidella* and *Geocrinia*.

Those naturalists who oppose or object to changes of this kind have my sympathy. In fact, the more frequently you use names the harder it becomes to adjust to changes. However, the minor inconvenience has to be weighed against the use of nomenclature in classification. On the one hand we are keen to see stability, or what is really uniformity and perpetuation in the use of names; on the other hand we cannot really afford to ignore, tolerate and perpetuate errors. Thus the changes happening now, simply because zoologists are taking interest in frogs, are providing the foundation of names that will be used and maintained in the future.

There seems to be a good argument for someone to suggest that naturalists should stick to using the colloquial (common) names until there *is* genuine stability. Unfortunately colloquial names have even more drawbacks. For a start one species can have several colloquial names in different parts of Australia. For example, what I call the 'Holy Cross toad' (*Notaden bennetti*) was, and quite possibly still is, called 'Hervy's frog' in western New South Wales. Fletcher (1891) explained that the species gained the name there 'from a fanciful resemblance of the pattern on the creature's back to the letter H, this being Mr. Hervy's sheep brand.' Fletcher himself calls it the 'Catholic frog'.

The usefulness of names has to be judged by the criterion of whether, through speech or written word, we can convey to the listener or reader the precise identity of the animal that we are referring to. Colloquial names serve a valuable purpose in small districts, but it is an obvious advantage if there is national, and preferably universal, uniformity in the use of names. Each State in Australia has its 'bullfrog', but several distinct species bear this name. In fact, there are frogs called bullfrogs in most countries. Despite its weaknesses the system of using Latin names provides the only real hope of ending up with just one name for each kind.

One of the most common sources of former major errors of frog classification arose from what is really the evolution, on different continents, of animals that look alike. Most continents have frogs that are almost totally aquatic, other species that live near water, and yet others in trees or deserts. Certainly there are instances in which frogs that are closely related to one another really do extend across several continents, dominating a particular type of environmental niche. On other occasions the similarity in external form is superficial and quite misleading because the basic good design that is the hallmark of the occupants of a particular niche has evolved quite independently in unrelated frogs.

Amongst the tree frogs and the burrowing frogs there are splendid examples of this convergence in evolution to produce similarity. Thus to assist life in the trees, expanded and usually circular adhesive discs on the tips of the fingers and toes seem to be a prerequisite. The tree frogs of Australia are no different from those of Africa in this respect and, because the discovery of Australian species occurred after similar creatures had been found in Africa, some of the African and Australian species were placed in the same genus (*Hyperolius*). Certainly they do look alike but it is structures such as the discs that emphasize the similarity, for in reality the frogs are not even members of the same family. Life in an African tree is probably not much different from that in an Australian tree and, to achieve the ability to take an option on tree living, the same design evolved on two occasions.

It is difficult to predict what ought to be a good structural shape for a burrowing frog. Nevertheless, it is surprising to find that most burrowing frogs are rather rotund, a shape that can hardly equip them for the actual task of burrowing. It is probably the need to spend long periods underground that dictates the strictly functional form of a water-storage tank (Pl. 2).

In Australia and New Guinea the native frogs are members of four families: the Hylidae, which are mostly tree frogs; the Leptodactylidae, which are principally ground-dwellers; and the Microhylidae and Ranidae, which occupy a very wide variety of moist habitats. Whether or not all of the family names now in vogue will stand the test of time is uncertain because there is mounting evidence that some of the Australian and New Guinea frogs are unique in many ways. Some American zoologists favour the idea of divorcing our leptodactylids from the remainder of the family in South America and uniting them with one genus found only at the tip of South Africa, as a unique family called Myobatrachidae. Similarly they want to put the tree frogs of Australia and New Guinea in a separate family called the Pelodryadidae (Lynch 1973, and Savage 1973). Certainly the frogs of Australia and New Guinea are genuinely unique. With the exception of the tiny microhylid genus *Oreophryne* and the hylid *Litoria* which have entered Indonesian islands from the New Guinea mainland, the ranid *Platymantis* which reaches the Philippines and Fiji, and the cosmopolitan *Rana* which is the sole foreign intruder, our frogs have had little contact with the outside world.

Distributions like that of the Leptodactylidae demonstrate the reason why students of animal distribution (zoogeographers) now take great interest in the recently resurrected theory of Continental Drift. Within the last ten years or so there has been tremendous attention paid to the concept of the southern continents having been once united in a gigantic supercontinent called Gondwanaland. Theories of frog evolution now hinge upon the assumption that there were frogs in various parts of Gondwanaland. These populations became isolated from one another about 110 million years ago as the existing continents split off from the parent land mass, and began to drift apart.

What could assist the theory greatly would be the discovery of fossils of similar frogs in different parts of Gondwanaland. Unfortunately fossils of the necessary age are few in number. In fact most of the fossils found so far are members of existing families in areas where the same families are to be found now.

As for the prehistoric frog fauna of Australia, the only identifiable fossil we possess at present is one small fragment of bone about 13 million years old. It consists of the major portion of the ilium bone of the pelvis. It is about 7 mm long and was found in 1972 by a party of research workers from the University of California and the Queensland Museum. They located it, along with many other broken vertebrate bones, by painstakingly sieving the sands from an old river bed at Lake Palankarinna, north of Lake Eyre in South Australia (Tyler 1974).

Of all of the bones that make up the frog skeleton, the ilium varies most from family to family in the shape of the long portion or shaft, the flanges beneath and above it that fuse it to the other bones of the pelvis, the depth of the depression that forms part of the cup that provides the socket for the ball at the end of the thigh bone, and in many other respects. Because of its variability it is often possible to identify a frog to a particular genus or even a species just by the form and shape that the ilium takes.

The question no doubt is just what this single bone can tell us about the ancestors of our modern frogs. Unfortunately, the answer is: 'very little'. Its most striking feature is a deep groove along the side of the bone. It may not seem a very important character, but it assumes importance because none of the modern frogs with which it has so far been compared have any depression at all. The nature of the bone rules out the possibility of it being a member of the Ranidae and Microhylidae, and in fact it is easier to say what families and genera it cannot be referred to than to identify it with any existing family with any real assurance.

In other parts of the world at least some of the genera that live today have persisted for a long time because they are recognizable in fossils of 13 million years ago, when the frog at Lake Palankarinna perished in its riverbed. At least some of the existing foreign species were living on the earth ten million years ago. The fossil serves as a caution, warning us that the evolutionary history of Australian frogs may be much more complicated than has been appreciated.

2 The Tree Frogs HYLIDAE

MONKEYS ARE so well equipped for life in the trees that the problems that their ancestors overcame in adapting to an arboreal existence tend to be overlooked or ignored. Initially it is difficult to avoid regarding tree frogs in much the same sort of way, for it is because these animals are so perfectly adapted to their chosen habitat that we may fail to appreciate that they evolved from ancestral stocks living on the land. These were creatures that structurally were no better equipped for spending their lives in trees than we are.

In Australia and New Guinea most of the members of the family Hylidae lived in trees and shrubs and are classic examples of what are usually called 'tree frogs'. There remain, however, a few members of the family that climb only occasionally, and spend most of their life on the ground amongst low-growing vegetation. This means that there is a reasonably clear division in this family, with some species which are almost totally committed to spending their lives above the ground and others that have only limited climbing ability and seem determined to retain an option on living on land.

Tree frogs must be able to climb; but, like their terrestrial ancestors, they also spend much time sitting. To be able to climb probably involved much less by way of adaptive changes in structure than was needed to be able to rest in a tree instead of on the ground. They must be able to rest on a vertical surface, or possibly balance upon a slender branch. It doesn't sound particularly demanding, but what is required of a tree-dweller is the ability to distribute the load of the body-weight as evenly as possible. For this reason shape and form of the body has to be such that it can be spread out, and to be fairly flattened in comparison with frogs living on the land. A fat frog with a rounded body would run the risk of toppling backwards off a vertical trunk, or of finding itself hanging precariously upside down from a branch.

Viewed as a group it is true that tree frogs do vary quite considerably in their dimensions, but they tend to conform to a pattern of having relatively flattened or distinctly slender bodies and long limbs. Even the fattest of tree frogs are really restrained in their apparent obesity for they remain capable of flattening the skin of their abdomens, throats and thighs against a smooth surface. The technique involved is well demonstrated by placing any tree frog on a window pane. When it is viewed from the other side you'll be able to see that the skin doesn't simply touch the glass in one or two places but that it is almost entirely in contact with it. The brown tree frog *Litoria ewingi* in Plate 6 demonstrates the technique rather well.

Some tree frogs have quite extensive webbing between their fingers. If the hand is pressed flat against the surface it could probably serve a similar sort of purpose to the loose abdominal skin. However it provides a large and slightly moist area capable of sticking to almost any surface, and for this reason may come into contact on landing from a jump. This webbing is equally important in mid-flight, for Duellman (1970) provides an illustration showing how the Central American tree frog *Hyla miliaria* spreads its fingers so that the hands act as wings enabling it to glide from one tree to another. I have never collected a specimen of the large New Guinea tree frog *Litoria graminea*, but the one that I got nearest to eluded capture by gracefully gliding across a deep ravine. I was unable to get close to it and the light of my torch was inadequate to check the position of the hands. Several other species of tree frogs in New Guinea may be capable of gliding flight.

The circular discs on the tips of the fingers and toes of hylid tree frogs provide another way of increasing the surface area that can be brought into contact with a leaf, branch or tree trunk. However, just below the under-surface of the discs are special glands which secrete an adhesive material. Hence discs do not rely merely upon surface tension for maintaining contact and so they are possibly of greater value to the animal in assisting it to climb up smooth surfaces. There is in fact quite elaborate evidence to show that the adhesive material is released only just when it is needed. Noble and Jaeckle (1928) made a detailed study of the

The north coast green tree frog *Litoria chloris*

Roth's tree frog *Litoria rothi*

Neobatrachus centralis from Alice Springs

2 BURROWING FROGS OF THE DESERT

Notaden bennetti from Queensland

discs on the fingers of a tree frog and found that the outermost cells on the surface of the disc are often shaped like cubes, and that there are normally spaces between them. Stretching from these cells to the bone above are long strands of connective tissue and the glands secreting the 'glue' are located in the middle of these strands.

Immediately the tree frog rests in a vertical position with its discs pressed against rock, bark or similarly hard material, the pull exerted away from the discs is transmitted through the connective fibres. This tightening of the fibres squeezes out the glue and closes up the spaces between the cube-shaped cells, so resulting in a smooth, sticky surface.

Tree frogs have to be nimble to stay aloft, and the overall impression gained from watching them in their natural state is of alert creatures with rather graceful and quite precise movements. When they decide to rest for a while after any period of activity they take great care in arranging the relative positions of their hands, feet and limbs beneath their bodies. The elaborate actions of shuffling their feet until they are quite comfortable is reminiscent of a cat trampling down grass to create a haven exactly to its liking. The resemblance can be carried a stage further, for tree frogs do seem to be neat and tidy creatures living orderly lives. They move amongst foliage with care and superb co-ordination, and so it is a surprise when the image of perfection is completely destroyed when they jump. It is as though they recognize that their lives may depend upon safe arrival on a far branch or leaf. The leap ends in a sort of pancake landing with the legs extended far from the body, and about every portion of the undercarriage striking the surface to ensure that they will not overshoot their target and fall off.

There are tree frogs in most of the Australian State capitals. Some species, such as the brown tree frog of the southeastern States, live in and around the outer suburbs, so that their habits can be watched by city-bound naturalists. In captivity the tree frogs tend to ignore the well-intentioned attempts of naturalists to create 'natural' conditions for them. Despite provision of bark, vegetation and small, leafy shrubs in vivaria (aquarium tanks used for purposes other than for the fish for which they are designed), the frogs inevitably sit on the surface of the glass just beneath the lid. There they stick like limpets, and to examine them you have to use your fingernails to gently prise them away from the glass. It may well be that they would prefer to get much further away from the ground level than is possible in a vivarium. Some of the tree frogs are very rarely seen by man. It is simply that they live above the level of vegetation that we usually brush against or pass through. In fact there are some that live as much as 50 metres above the level of the ground. In Borneo zoologists have constructed special hides in the treetops, like those used by bird-watchers, to enable them to study the special fauna that live there, but, to the best of my knowledge, no comparable observations have yet been undertaken either in Australia or in New Guinea. In southern New Guinea there are reports of a giant tree frog, larger than any yet known to science, which never ventures to the ground. It is said to lay its eggs in water-filled holes in the trunks and it has been seen by the local inhabitants only when large trees have been felled (F. Parker, pers. comm.).

The eventual discovery of this monster tree frog will end the right of another species living in Australia and New Guinea to being known as the largest tree frog in the world. The present title holder is *Litoria infrafrenata* which has a maximum body length of 135 mm. It is a beautiful olive or emerald green frog with a clear white stripe on its upper lip, extending backwards like a gigantic moustache, whilst the back of its thighs are rich crimson. In Australia *L. infrafrenata* is unfortunately to be found only in and around the remnants of rainforest on the eastern coastline of the Cape York Peninsula of northern Queensland, extending south as far as Tully. In New Guinea it is much more abundant and widespread, extending throughout the low-lying areas and on numerous smaller islands to the east and west. On the islands of New Britain and New Ireland situated to the east of New Guinea the frogs differ slightly from those occurring elsewhere, having a little spike of bone projecting out from the side of the thumb.

On the branches of trees or on the fronds of giant palms *Litoria infrafrenata* is completely in its element and is difficult to capture. However, when it ventures to the ground to travel to its breeding site in the swamps and flooded grasslands, the bulky stature and arboreal adaptations are an incredible hindrance to its progress. On the ground it is simply unable to leap sufficiently far upwards to be able to clear any obstacle in its path that is more than a few centimetres high. In addition it becomes hampered by the small leaves, twigs and dirt that stick to its hands, feet and abdomen. Crossing the finely powdered, pumice roads in New Britain the frogs are able to do little more than project themselves forwards for a distance equivalent to the length of their bodies, stopping at frequent intervals whilst they make vain attempts to shake and scrape debris from their limbs and sides. Having picked up a frog there in this plight I later washed it and released it upon the highly polished wooden floor of a house, just to test its jumping ability under more favourable conditions. In four rapid leaps it covered a distance of almost six metres.

Jumping ability varies quite considerably from species to species, and the distance covered in the first bound by the *L. infrafrenata* represented a standing jump equivalent to fifteen times the total length of the head and body of the animal. A man two metres tall has a head and body length of about 80 centimetres and so, to jump with the proficiency of the frog, he would have to clear 12 metres. Actually his maximum is only about 2 metres so that in proportional terms *Litoria infrafrenata* is really jumping about six times the distance that a man can achieve.

Altogether there are about one hundred different species of hylid tree frogs in Australia and New Guinea. They include some of the most beautiful frogs to be found anywhere in the world, with markings ranging from metallic, iridescent gold and sulphur yellow to pink, pale blue and violet. As is the case with the majority of our frogs, they lack common names simply because they are not well enough known by naturalists to acquire them, and the Latin ones can be rather off-putting. Just the same, it is worth examining a few of the Latin names of tree frogs, to establish guidelines that can be used here and elsewhere by anyone curious to find out what these words mean.

In many cases the origin of the words can be established just by looking at the last letter or letters. For example, any specific name ending in *i* is likely to be based on the name of a person. He may have been honoured in this way for being the collector of the first specimens known to science. Thus there are *Litoria coplandi*, *L. glauerti*, *L. darlingtoni* and *L. ewingi*. The ending *-ensis* or even *-iensis* is usually only used for a word based on a geographic place name: *Litoria adelaidensis*, first found at the Adelaide River in Western Australia; *L. amboinesis* from the island of Amboina; *L. booroolongensis* from the town of Booroolong in New South Wales; and *L. louisiadensis* from the Louisiade Islands off the coast of southeast New Guinea. The Latin names for colours have also been used: *Litoria aurea* (golden), *L. caerulea* (blue), *L. nigropunctata* (black-spotted), *L. albolabris* (white-lipped) and *L. rubella* (small, red).

Working out the meaning of most of the other ones requires only a very rough knowledge of Latin. Lacking any knowledge at all isn't a complete hindrance because there are special books listing and translating the names that have been used most frequently for thousands of species of animals.

Perhaps the most striking of all the tree frogs is *Litoria iris* which occurs in the New Guinea highlands and which was named after Iris, the goddess of the rainbow. Girls' names when given to animals often arouse comment. The reason is that a nineteenth-century zoologist established a rather unusual precedent by honouring his current mistresses in this way.

Litoria iris is a fairly small tree frog of slender build, usually within the range of 30 to 40 mm long when fully grown. Its back may be uniform light green, green with a light peppering of tiny black dots or green with large and irregular areas of orange or gold. Beneath it is cream with startling patches of vivid violet on the flanks, and often jet black areas in the armpits (axillae). On the violet areas there are often pale, sky-blue spots, whilst the palms and soles are bright yellow. It has commonly been found on the leaves of shrubs about one metre from the ground, frequently at sides of streams and in appropriately picturesque settings. I once found some amongst low vegetation against an orange background produced by the cascading blooms of the tropical vine, flame-of-the-forest.

This beautiful frog is unique amongst all of our species in laying green eggs on the leaves of trees and surrounding them with large, sloppy masses of clear jelly. The jelly is derived from a coating provided as the eggs pass down the female's oviducts just before they are laid, and one of the really fascinating unanswered questions about this particular species is just where the water comes from to cause the jelly to swell as it does. It isn't just a very minor point of detail, because there is a distinct possibility of there being a delightful example of parallel evolution of a bizarre reproductive habit, between this frog and two unrelated tree frogs in Central America. Pyburn (1970) discovered that as the females of *Phyllomedusa callidryas* and *P. dacnicolor* lay their eggs on leaves, they proceed to empty their bladder contents over them. Each female, with the male still attached to her back, then climbs down to a nearby pool, waits in the water for a while until she has absorbed water through her skin and so refilled her bladder, and then climbs up the shrubs once more to repeat the elaborate and most unusual performance.

What makes the possible parallel of habits between *L. iris* and the *Phyllomedusa* species seem so remarkable is the observation that *L. iris* lays its eggs in numerous small groups. Of twenty-six clumps which I collected in mid-April 1960 the number of eggs per clump ranged from 4 to 37 with an average of 14, whereas gravid females can contain up to 100 eggs. Each female was clearly laying only a small portion of her complement of eggs in any place, and it seemed hard to visualize their being abandoned without first being moistened in some way to ensure their survival.

New Guinea has a greater variety of tree frogs than Australia, including many that are particularly spectacular. *Nyctimystes granti*, with its striking metallic hue, is a good example of the splendid appearance that they can attain. A large frog up to 100 mm long, it has been found on only one occasion since its discovery in 1910. The circumstances of the rediscovery bear mention because they demonstrate how unfair it is that the role played by sheer luck is never mentioned in the list of acknowledgements customarily included in books and scientific articles. What happened was that a geologist who was a member of the Netherlands Star Mountains Expedition of 1959, decided to answer the call of nature whilst he was following a mountain track. He struck off from the paths into the undisturbed vegetation at the side and there virtually sat upon a splendid *N. granti*. Intensive collecting throughout many square kilometres of surrounding countryside by experienced professional zoologists and expert local collectors failed to reveal another.

Nyctimystes species always have a pattern of pigment on their lower eyelids. It is usually in the form of vein-like markings, and there are generally sufficient differences from one species to another for this feature to be a means of helping naturalists identify frogs (Zweifel 1958).

Some of the smaller tree frogs are just as spectacular as the large ones and equally elusive. The pygmy species *Litoria pygmaea* has been found secreted away in neat hiding places, such as the base of the leaves of *Pandanus* where little pockets of water accumulate. There are about thirty specimens in museum collections and the majority of them have been found by chance. Rarely have two or more been taken at one place, and this species remains known from scattered localities, principally in Irian Barat (formerly West Irian, before that Netherlands New Guinea).

Unknown species of tree frogs are still being found with monotonous regularity in both Australia and New Guinea. Amongst the most recent New Guinea discoveries was one subsequently named *L. quadrilineata* because on its brown back there are four longitudinal stripes. There is nothing dowdy about this frog. Its back markings and bright red thighs are features that would attract the attention of any collector, and there is no chance at all that it could be confused with any species previously known and so, perhaps, have been ignored by field collectors. The location of its discovery in March 1973 demonstrates particularly well the point that there probably remains a vast unknown fauna awaiting collection. It was found by Fred Parker, not, as one might imagine, in a remote area far from the beaten track, but on a block of vacant land adjacent to the Post Office in the main street of the coastal town of Merauke. This settlement is the largest and most important on the southern coast of Irian Barat and has been visited by numerous collectors over many years. Some of these collectors probably stayed at the hotel opposite this block of land.

The members of the Hylidae that in their structure are not so well adapted to climbing are on the whole a far less spectacular assemblage of frogs. I am reluctant to talk about them as a 'group', because this word is generally used to imply the existence of a fairly close taxonomic relationship between the members. This isn't always the case, and in fact this, the so-called group of 'ground' hylids in Australia, is a particularly good example. I very much doubt if many of these species are really closely related to one another. One of the attractive possibilities is that amongst the ground-dwelling species of hylids there are some derived from ancestors that never ventured into the trees, and others derived from stocks that were arboreal, but reverted to a terrestrial life. This possibility is unlikely to be resolved until we know a good deal more about such features as the muscles involved in grasping and climbing, and their presence or absence in the ground-dwelling hylids. Possession by some ground-dwelling species of specialized grasping muscles that they don't use to the full, and absence of these muscles in other species would provide the sort of evidence that we need to give some clues about their ancestry.

Amongst the ground-dwelling and partly aquatic hylids there is the rocket frog (Pl. 5), and its close relative, Freycinet's frog. Both of these have a particularly streamlined appearance, and it is difficult to imagine what common name *nasuta* would have had before rockets were invented. Because both of these species are to be found in swamps and streams it can be argued that they are really aquatic frogs, but a number of features lead one to believe that they are best equipped for life on land. For example, the webbing between the toes is somewhat reduced, whereas for the foot to best serve the needs of the aquatic life the webbing should be as extensive as possible to provide the largest possible surface area, like a frogman's flipper.

On the palms and the soles and beneath the digits there are particularly prominent tubercles which are wart-like structures that may possibly reduce wear and tear of the undersides of the hands and feet. Alternatively, by minimizing the area in contact with the ground, they could prevent the hands and feet from sticking to the ground or to debris, and so reduce the chances of hindrance when they jump. There may be other equally plausible explanations for the major functions of these tubercles, but it is difficult to suggest any possible use for them in water.

These two species are quite unlike all other Australian and New Guinea hylid frogs. It is a depressing thought to realize that when one day these two species are placed in a separate genus on their own, the action will have the effect of causing all other current *Litoria* species to change. The reason is that when the genus *Litoria* was first coined by the Swiss zoologist Johann

Tschudi in 1838, he established it specifically for *freycineti*. Over the years we have seen many changes, and now the net result is that all other species have joined *freycineti* in *Litoria*. To show that *freycineti* is so different that it has to be placed in a genus with only *nasuta* to keep it company, involves expelling the remainder and finding a new name for them. This procedure is laid down by international rules governing the naming of animals and helps to keep an orderly and useful system of names.

The sort of problems involved in interpreting with any degree of accuracy the habitat of a frog just from studying the nature of its structure reach a peak when viewing the smallest of the hylids. There are several very small ones not much more than 20 mm long, but the tiniest of all are much like miniaturized *L. nasuta*, and can be fully grown at only 9 mm. Examples such as *L. dorsalis* of southern New Guinea, and *L. microbelos* of northern Queensland have slender elongate bodies, no webbing between their fingers and very little webbing between their toes. Their jumping ability is phenomenal and collectors comment that they act much more like agile grasshoppers than frogs. These species and their near relatives often live in swampy areas for which they seem poorly equipped, but they are so light in weight that they can jump on to fairly small leaves overhanging water, or progress in great bounds upon soggy ground.

One of the small Australian frogs is *L. meiriana*, commonly found in the Northern Territory in the giant inland lakes so inappropriately called rock-holes; it is also known to occur in the far north of Western Australia not far from Kununurra. A few years ago a number were collected in the Northern Territory at the edge of permanent water by a party of anthropologists. The collectors were surprised to note that when the frogs were disturbed they did not jump into the water, as they fully expected them to, but moved away from it, seeking refuge amongst the vegetation on the dry banks.

By far the best known of all Australian frogs is the tree frog *Litoria caerulea*. This is a large (100 mm) green creature which is remarkably tolerant to being handled by humans. To describe frogs as being readily tamed implies a success on the part of the captor, and a virtual conquest over at least the spirit of a wild animal. It would be completely inappropriate to use this term for captive *L. caerulea*, which just seem to possess an amenable disposition. A member of this species doesn't seem at all concerned at being picked up and, if it is handled with care, will simply snuggle down to make itself comfortable on the palm of your hand. There is no doubt that there are basic differences between frog species, with some being exceptionally timid while others, like *L. caerulea*, are almost fearless.

Litoria caerulea has many features that predispose it as a suitable animal for capture as a pet. Not the least of these is its readiness to feed in captivity. It is commonly exhibited in zoos overseas and has been known to live for up to sixteen years. As frog lifespans go that is fairly long, although the records of longevity are held by the toads of the genus *Bufo*, for which the maximum may be as much as forty years.

Litoria caerulea lives in very close association with man and in the moist parts of northern Australia is to be found in house rainwater tanks, toilet cisterns, outhouses and even flower vases. Periodically some of the weekly women's magazines print letters from housewives who have evicted frogs from vases and released them outside, only to find that the frogs soon return to their favourite haunts. This 'homing ability' is at present very poorly understood, but there is no doubt that frogs can locate a spot of their choosing and return to it when transported some distance away. 'Homing' in the wild takes place on a different scale when the males and females of many species migrate to breeding sites. In the case of certain European frogs, Savage (1961) has suggested that each pond has its own distinctive odour, and that the frogs are able to find their way to their particular pond by homing in on a special smell.

Because there are so many spectacular frogs to keep in captivity the less spectacular ones tend to be ignored, with the result that we know little of the lives of quite common animals such as the greyish *L. latopalmata*, and the brown and often rather rough-skinned species *L. inermis*. Almost invariably the drab frogs seem to have something of special interest to repay the observer, but it was only after receiving, quite unexpectedly, a shipment of *L. inermis* from northern Australia that the point was brought home to me.

Shortly after their arrival in Adelaide several of the *L. inermis* simultaneously shed their skins. There is nothing unusual about this event which occurs periodically in frogs and also in reptiles. The apparent co-ordination of the process amongst several frogs probably resulted from an environmental stimulus of some kind such as a sudden change in temperature. However it was because several frogs underwent the process together that I paid proper attention to it for the very first time.

Moulting involves loss of the outermost layer of dead skin tissue, so exposing a perfectly formed fresh layer beneath. In this process of moulting a frog does not passively lose little fragments of dead cells like we do, as demonstrated by the socially undesirable phenomenon of dandruff, but is actually responsible for removing by its own efforts the entire outer covering in one piece.

The *Litoria inermis* gave the appearance of being extremely unwell and it was this that attracted my attention to them. They arched their bodies upwards, opened and shut their mouths, closed their eyes every few seconds, and scraped at their heads and bodies with their hands and feet. They were so preoccupied that it was possible to get very close to them and study this action in detail from close quarters. For example the skin could be seen to move as various muscles beneath the skin were flexed.

What these frogs were achieving was the separation of the old outer dead layer from its new replacement. The hands and feet eventually succeeded in ripping holes in the outer layer which peeled back at the sides. The hands were used to drag and stuff the cut edges into the mouth, and soon the skin was being swallowed like a ripped wet-suit.

Moulting usually takes about an hour to complete and is a remarkable event to watch. In adult frogs it occurs every few days and is likely to be noticed by anyone keeping frogs in captivity.

The golden bell frog *Litoria aurea* of eastern Australia and its relatives in the southeast and southwest of the continent, spend the greater part of their lives in water. They are robust and noticeably muscular animals up to about 90 mm long. The muscles of their hind legs are particularly strong and they can swim powerfully. To the naturalist they would probably rank fairly low in a popularity poll simply because the sharp, triangular heads and darkly encircled eyes give them a rather sullen appearance. Added to this they struggle violently when handled and simultaneously release from their skins a copious secretion of slimy mucus accompanied by an acrid odour, usually resulting, as they intend, in their release. Although they are genuinely timid creatures inclined to panic, they do settle down well in captivity and will eventually take food from your fingers.

Litoria aurea and its relatives are abundant wherever the species occur. They are so commonplace that in Australia their uniqueness in the family Hylidae is rarely appreciated. There are in all about five hundred different species of hylids in various parts of the world, but there is not a single one living outside Australia that in any way resembles *L. aurea*. I suspect that the *aurea* complex of species may be the sort of creatures that are most similar in appearance to the ancestors of the Australian hylids, for they possess jaw muscles and portions of cartilage that have been lost by most other Australian and New Guinea species. The implication is that the other species are anatomically more modified and have changed more radically from the ancestral stock than *aurea* has.

Litoria aurea and its relatives resemble some of the frogs that are members of a genus of another family: the genus *Cyclorana* of the family Leptodactylidae. Unfortunately there is only one clear-cut difference between hylids and leptodactylids and this is that the hylids possess a tiny block of cartilage separating the end bones of their fingers and toes. Leptodactylids lack this block. This feature can be demonstrated only by special staining techniques performed on preserved and skinned frogs, or by cutting extremely thin sections through the fingers, and examining them under a microscope. There is no absolutely foolproof method that enables a naturalist to arrive at an accurate family identification. What we may have to do first is to identify the species to enable us to work out which family it belongs to – a quite ludicrous state of affairs. However, in practice it is only within this one grey area of our present classification that problems of this magnitude exist. is not perpetuated solely through the absence of detailed study by zoologists, but the fact that particular problems of interpretation are raised. However, when the true relationship of *Cyclorana* to the *Litoria aurea* complex is finally resolved, we may well discover the similarity exists because hylids and leptodactylids arose from a common ancestor.

3 Frogs of the Land and Water
LEPTODACTYLIDAE

IN TIME we may well discover that the family of frogs that happen to be grouped together today under the name 'Leptodactylidae', has become a sort of zoological dustbin. The trouble is a very real one, namely that in the past it has been a relatively straightforward task to classify most members of the other families and, if a frog could not be assigned to any of these, there was a tendency for it to be popped into the Leptodactylidae. The result is that we are left today with a diverse group of frogs differing from one another quite strikingly in their appearance, their habits and where they choose to live, and yet are united together in a single family because of what they lack rather than what they possess.

Certainly it is quite possible that modern leptodactylids may prove simply to be derived from ancestors that were adaptable to changes in the environment, and so perhaps exploited to the full any opportunities that permitted them to colonize niches otherwise unoccupied by frogs. This could well explain how they happen to be so diverse in their appearance and habits, but it is of little consolation to the naturalist wanting to know what makes a leptodactylid a leptodactylid. In practical terms the chances are that any frog found in Australia that burrows, or lives on the land or in water and lacks expanded discs on its fingers and toes, is likely to be a member of this family. This general rule will hold good for almost any part of Australia; the exceptions are the Cape York Peninsula of northern Queensland and the northwestern part of the Northern Territory, where there are microhylid and ranid frogs as well as hylids and leptodactylids. In New Guinea leptodactylids are extremely rare.

Amongst the smallest of the leptodactylids are the so-called toadlets of the genus *Pseudophryne* which gain their common name from their warty skins, and which occur almost exclusively in the southern half of Australia. The toadlets are extremely quaint little creatures rarely more than 30 mm long. They have short legs, cannot travel very quickly and hence are very easy to capture. They are usually dull brown or purplish above, and many have large, smooth-outlined areas of intense purple on the under-surfaces of their bodies. Some have vivid sulphur-yellow patterns on the head and sometimes on the body as well, or red or yellow armlets like Boy Scout cubs, whilst the corroboree frog has brilliant yellow stripes along its back (Pl. 3). When there are any bright markings on the toadlets they seem so conspicuous that you can get the impression that the possessor is the victim of one of nature's little jokes. In reality the markings must have some selective advantage to the possessor. They simply wouldn't be there without there being a definite benefit of some kind, but at present we cannot guess what that may be. Main (1965) noted when searching for the Western Australian Nicholl's toadlet *P. nichollsi* amongst leaf litter, that the toadlets were often found upon their backs, exposing the under-surface which has markings resembling the fungal hyphae and their fruiting bodies common in the area in which this species is found. Obviously the coloration and behaviour assist camouflage, but it is difficult to imagine that the bright markings on the back could perform a comparable role. *Pseudophryne semimarmorata* is another toadlet with vividly marked under-surfaces. One is shown feigning death in Plate 3.

Pseudophryne often act as though defenceless, and the small size of these frogs and their apparent reluctance to flee when disturbed makes them rather endearing creatures. Oddly enough they seem to be unique amongst the frogs of Australia in being able to live in absolute harmony with other quite formidable animals. For example, on occasions *P. nichollsi* has been found within the nests of the bulldog ant *Myrmecia regularis*. Many naturalists can testify to the ferocity, apparent vindictiveness and severe pain that bull-dog ants can inflict. Just the slightest disturbance at the entrance to their nests results in a number of the largest and most agressive ants rushing out, spoiling to attack any intruder. Somehow, the Nicholl's toadlets are allowed to enter the ants' domain and live in the shelter of the cool, humid galleries. Why they are tolerated there and whether they perform any service for the ants in return for their presence is just not known.

In the Mount Lofty Ranges of South Australia there is a

parallel to the strange habits of *P. nichollsi*. During the dry summer months *Pseudophryne bibroni* is often to be found sheltering in burrows just beneath the surface of large flat boulders on the hill slopes. It is by no means uncommon to find the toadlet squatting side by side with a scorpion in a chamber at the end of the burrow. The association of these two creatures is particularly perplexing because each would favour eating the same kind of food. Seeing them sitting together, often in actual bodily contact, it is hard to visualize them as competitors.

Irrespective of the nature of its habitat, bedfellows and colour, a *Pseudophryne* remains distinctive by its body form, stance, alertness and so many other tangible and intangible features that are difficult to express. Unfortunately few of the other small species of leptodactylids form such distinctive groups, and few genera can be recognized with such ease. Part of the problem is simply the small size which makes it so very difficult to spot the ways in which they do differ. Added to this are the complicating factors of there being some species which vary considerably from frog to frog in colour and skin texture, and other species which look identical to one another but which in reality are quite different in their biology. When it is realized that identification of some genera hinges solely upon details such as whether teeth are present or absent in the upper jaw, or whether particular bones in the skull fuse together or leave a permanent space in the centre, the magnitude of the difficulty can be appreciated.

A good example of the complex problems that have existed in distinguishing small frogs is the old concept of the common froglet *Crinia signifera*. At one time practically any small slender *Crinia* with a slender body and very long toes was called by this name. The species is said to be polymorphic because at any locality there are likely to be several quite different 'morphs': some individuals with smooth skins, others that are slightly warty and yet others that bear ridges on their backs. With the added variation of colour from orange to brown or grey, with or lacking other markings, it is understandable that there was initially considerable confusion, and zoologists in several countries examining collections of Australian frogs named new species on what were really the variable morphs of one. H. W. Parker of the British Museum gathered together specimens in the collections of seven museums, and in 1940 concluded that there was just one species of froglet extending throughout the entire moister parts of Australia and also existing in New Guinea. His view held good until 1954 when J. A. Moore, a visiting American scientist, tried to apply biological procedures to put his concept to the test. Moore reasoned that the isolated population of *C. signifera* in the southern part of Western Australia should be capable of breeding freely with southeastern Australian *C. signifera*, if the two populations were really one species. The whole concept of species as populations able to breed together hinged upon this. The frogs certainly were not different in their appearance, but Moore showed that they could not produce normal offspring. They were in fact so 'incompatible' in their genetic make-up that he realized that they were really distinct species. As a result of this he proposed that the Western Australian frogs be regarded a separate species that he called *C. insignifera*.

Moore's studies turned out to have uncovered only the very tip of the iceberg, for subsequently several more species have been discovered and named, and the former '*C. signifera*' has been shown to be a 'complex' of species, sometimes called a 'species-group'.

Computers have been harnessed to try and unravel the problems of deciding just how some of the small frogs are related to one another. Blake (1973) was the first to attempt this sort of study in Australia, and it is partly as a result of his work that the large number of species of *Crinia* became split up into a number of more major different groups that are recognized as genera.

One of the most successful groups of Australian leptodactylids are members of the genus *Limnodynastes*, a word meaning literally 'lord of the marshes'. They do indeed dominate many marshes and areas of swampy ground, but some of the species inhabit dry areas and others extend into the tropics. Most of the species are chunky frogs with broad heads, smooth bodies and a rather drab coloration. All of them lay their eggs in nests of foam and they all have well-developed vomerine teeth extending in a long straight row across the palate. Several species have a strange, prominent, oval skin gland on the upper surface of the calf (Fig. 28).

Limnodynastes never really fall into the naturalists' 'rare' category. If they occur anywhere they seem to dominate the scene and are quite abundant. Species occur throughout Australia and there are from two to five in each State. Because the spawn of the *Limnodynastes* species is laid on and above the surface of the water, children searching for spawn are inclined to home in on the sloppy clumps but soon find that they are extremely difficult to transfer to a jar or plastic bag. The trouble is that some of the clumps are almost as big as dinner plates and, because of the large amount of water embodied in the jelly, they are so heavy and slippery that they simply cannot be lifted out of the water and maintained in anything resembling their original form. The liquid nature and strong cohesive strength of the spawn can be well demonstrated by the frustrating task of trying to 'pour' a clump into a small jar.

The concept of a marsh frog is best demonstrated by the south-eastern Australian species *L. tasmaniensis* (Pl. 4). It isn't as its specific name might imply, confined to Tasmania. It just happened that the first specimens were found there, and demonstrates how names based on this sort of criterion can ultimately prove rather misleading. *Limnodynastes tasmaniensis* actually extends from the Eyre Peninsula in South Australia to the northernmost tip of the Cape York Peninsula in Queensland, a geographic range of several thousand kilometres. No matter what man does to the environment, it seems that *L. tasmaniensis* does not just survive and persist, but virtually takes advantage of the situation. For example, in dry creek-beds littered with rubbish I have found it living in the moist refuges beneath sheets of rusty, corrugated iron. I don't habitually frequent rubbish dumps but I have noticed amongst the flotsam and jetsam in a disused and flooded quarry, spawn clumps attached to the handles of a partly sub-merged doll's pram. *Limnodynastes tasmaniensis* seems to be capable of exploiting any man-made situation. Its presence at a dam at a dry, remote area such as Iron Knob testifies to this fact.

There are several curious geographic trends in the colora-tion, size and call structure of the species. In some areas specimens have a perfectly straight, yellow line down the middle of the back (usually called a 'mid-vertebral line'). In others the line is reddish, or else there is a red line in the centre of a yellow line. In the Flinders Ranges of northern South Australia the frogs are larger than elsewhere, and almost inevitably lack a mid-vertebral line.

The corroboree toadlet *Pseudophryne corroboree*

3 TOADLETS

The marbled toadlet *Pseudophryne semimarmorata*

Limnodynastes tasmaniensis of southeast Australia

4 FROGS OF THE CREEKS

Rana papua of northern Queensland

Two types of call are known: one a single note, and the other a call composed of two to five notes. One day we may well find that there is evidence to recognize more than one species in what we now call *L. tasmaniensis*. However, this will not diminish a sense of admiration for frogs which have persisted to occupy areas influenced so drastically by man.

The sort of features that are used for distinguishing the various species of *Limnodynastes* are obviously tools of convenience. They give little indication of the magnitude of difference in the natural history of the animals concerned. An exception is the presence or absence of the shovel-shape of the outer metatarsal tubercle of the foot: an adaptation evolved only for digging.

Marsh frogs have little need to dig to avoid exposure to dry conditions. If creeks dry out and there is no other cover they seem to simply crawl down cracks in the ground or congregate together to minimize water loss. For the species of the arid zones the ability to dig below the surface makes the difference between surviving or perishing. *Limnodynastes spenceri* is a good example of the burrower, named after Professor Baldwin Spencer who first reported its habits in Central Australia. We have to assume that this sort of structural adaptation to burrowing has evolved on several occasions in Australian frogs because the modified tubercle turns up time and again in different genera. It is a sort of tool possessed by any frog adapted for burrowing in sand or clay soils, and it may well have evolved more than once in the various *Limnodynastes* species. In its burrowing habits, *Limnodynastes dorsalis* of Western Australia and its close relatives in the eastern States seem to be at a sort of halfway house. These frogs create burrows but pop out at the first opportunity to forage for food at night. They leave the impression of a reluctance to lose their independence and option of daily activity.

In many areas of Australia the various representatives of the *L. dorsalis* complex are called bullfrogs. Most of them are not attractive to look at, but their habits and patterns of activity are extremely interesting. Dr A. A. Martin of the University of Melbourne made a detailed study of these animals over a period of many years, and amongst his findings was the fact that in the Great Dividing Range, north of Melbourne, the frogs lived in burrows beneath the ground during the winter months. They were clearly not hibernating because from time to time they would call from their subterranean sites, indicating that they were quite awake. Martin tried to find out why they all seemed to emerge in the spring at the same time. He found that if the moisture content of the soil was high enough they emerge as soon as the soil temperature reached 12.5°C. (Martin 1969).

His observations highlight a rather odd feature of bullfrogs. On the one hand there is the evidence of their being loners, living quite solitary lives. And yet on occasions they act in unison in a quite predictable fashion, as though they are really puppets. Their migration to the creeks where they breed is a very good example of this phenomenon. One warm afternoon in October I watched hundreds of adult males descending the steep slopes of the Morialta Falls near Adelaide to the creek below. They hopped along, falling, performing unintentional somersaults and often rolling for several metres down precipitous sections of rock faces. The whole area was dotted with these creatures moving with a sense of urgency to reach their destination just as soon as they possibly could. Within a matter of hours they had all congregated in the creek and were calling vociferously a dignified bass 'top' to attract the females from the surrounding areas. There were no stragglers and it was almost a science fiction situation of members of a clan obeying a directive, acting in complete unison to orders unknown to man. Anyone can explain it away in terms of the frogs having reached reproductive capability and migrating when conditions for migration were ideal, but the passage of ten years has not dulled the sense of utter amazement I experienced at watching the migration taking place.

Mass movements of frogs are always impressive, and there are occasions when they are so startling that they are reported (usually misreported) in newspapers. The subjects are often juvenile water-holding frogs which have burrowed in their millions at the edge of rapidly evaporating pools. The heavy rains penetrate the soil, releasing them and enabling them to disperse far and wide from their birthplace in what is really their first genuine attempt at independent life.

The various water-holding frogs of Australia are all members of the Leptodactylidae. Their exotic habit of spending the summer months below the surface of the ground has led to a lot of interest and often elaboration in the popular literature. I recollect a story in a European natural history book that the emergence of these frogs in the spring interfered with the services of the transcontinental railway in Central Australia. It was stated that so many frogs were crushed on the rails that the wheels of trains were unable to gain traction on the slippery surface.

Certainly it is true that the *Cyclorana* species are rarely seen in just ones and twos. If you ever see any at all there are likely to be hundreds or thousands around, simply because there are not many occasions in the arid zones, where they most commonly occur, when conditions are suitable for them to roam. However, the limited number of specimens in museums in Australia indicates that few naturalists have been at just the right place at the right time.

Cyclorana is a curious genus for reasons other than its habit of massing. Until fairly recently it was considered to be a rather diverse group of animals. There were a couple of species that looked remarkably like the ground-dwelling members of the hylid 'tree-frog', genus *Litoria*, and we were led to believe that this was a classic example of convergence. That is to say that some of the *Cyclorana* had in an evolutionary sense gone off on a limb to occupy habitats and acquire habits and body form that were really the domain and prerogative of *Litoria*. We now know that the similarity to *Litoria* was not surprising for the species involved are wrongly classified species of *Litoria*. Happily *Cyclorana* is now a more uniform group of rather squat animals (Pl. 5).

The skulls of some of the *Cyclorana* species are as interesting to anatomists as the habits of the possessors are to naturalists. As a result of a process of depositing bone in an apparently unnecessary and elaborate fashion, a criss-cross pattern is created on the surface resembling the sculpturing of a waffle.

There are other leptodactylids with bones that are of interest because of the presence of a rich purple pigment. They occur only in eastern Australia and in fact only on the eastern side of the Great Dividing Range. Obviously the first thought that springs to mind is that pigmentation arises from an environmental influence of some kind. However, like an unsuccessful attempt to solve a rather baffling crossword puzzle, we have to wait for someone to show us the answers before we can really understand the meaning and significance of the clues.

Perhaps the most bizarre of all Australian leptodactylids is the turtle frog of Western Australia. The suitability of its common name is well demonstrated by the experiences of Dr Glen Storr at the Western Australian Museum. He tells me that he often receives telephone calls from members of the general public seeking information on young turtles that they have found. That this frog is the subject of their enquiries becomes apparent when they say that the turtles are so young that 'they have not even got shells on their backs'. This mistake is not as ludicrous as it may sound. If you can imagine a baby turtle with its shell removed, you will have an almost perfect picture of the turtle frog, *Myobatrachus gouldi*: a tiny little head and dimunitive legs jutting out from a fat body. The frogs feed only on termites, living in their galleries beneath logs. Happily the turtle frog is not a rarity. In fact it is abundant in the southwest of Western Australia, and even occurs in Kings Park adjacent to the heart of Perth.

Western Australia is famous for the profusion of wild flowers but a less widely known fact, no doubt of little importance to the tourist industry, is that it is the home of a wide variety of leptodactylid frogs. In the southwestern corner of the State where the climate is moist and described as 'Mediterranean' live a number of species of the toad-like *Heleioporus* and *Neobatrachus*. Lee (1967) made an extensive study of the *Heleioporus* species and reported that they differ from one another in ways that are unique amongst Australian frogs. For example, most of them have a strange growth of skin at the front corner of the eye (Fig. 6). Fry (1914) thought that the growths served as little valves to prevent sand from getting beneath the front edge of the eyelids when the frogs burrow in sand. It is still uncertain whether they can and do perform this function, but the shape, size and form of the flaps vary from species to species in a way that assists the identification of these animals.

Amongst the mass of data accumulated by Lee were interesting facts about the nocturnal activity of species. For example, at the Lighthouse Swamp on Rottnest Island he took hourly censuses throughout the night of the numbers of *H. eyrei* active in his study area. The figures that he obtained on the night of 12 December

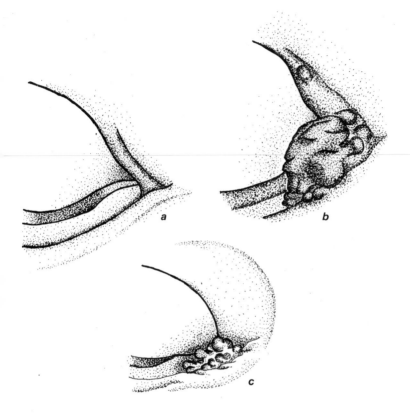

FIG. 6 How frogs differ in small details. The corner of the eye showing
skin flaps in *Heleioporus* species: *a. H. albopunctatus b. H. australiacus
c. H. barycragus* (after Lee 1967).

1956 are particularly noteworthy because they suggested that the
frogs did not all emerge at dusk and retreat into their burrows at
dawn. I have prepared Figure 7 from his observations to show that
the midnight hour was the absolute peak at which the greatest
number of frogs was abroad. Of course it does not really matter
whether more frogs were active at that particular hour than at
any other. What is important is the finding that a definite peak
existed at all. It becomes obvious that frogs don't just start
wandering in unison from dusk to dawn.

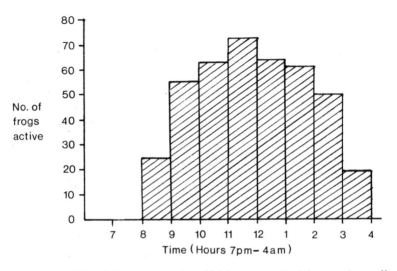

FIG. 7 Activity of the moaning frog *Heleioporus evrei* in Western Australia. Number of frogs active at each hour throughout the night (data from Lee 1967).

Some of the six *Heleioporus* species are quite distinctive. *Heleioporus albopunctatus* is greyish with distinct, large, white or cream spots on its body. *Heleioporus barycragus* which can be up to 80 mm long is a rich chocolate brown with yellow spots on the flanks. In contrast, most of the *Neobatrachus* species are fairly dowdy, nondescript animals which are much more difficult to identify. Most are moderately sized with a maximum length of around 60 mm. They have a rather rotund form and are mostly very drab brown, grey or dull greenish in colour. Their seeming tendency to obesity, varied pattern of vein-like markings on their eyes, and general clumsiness is reminiscent of rather portly old gentlemen suffering the after-effects of an alcoholic indulgence.

Appearances can be deceiving, and in reality *Neobatrachus* is a highly successful genus extending from the moist zones of the southern part of the Australian continent into the most arid parts of the interior. *Neobatrachus* extends far into otherwise entirely frog-less areas such as the Simpson Desert, and it is quite obvious that the genus deserves admiration rather than pity. By far the most widespread 'species' is *N. centralis*, for any individual from central Western Australia to western New South Wales is given this name. In reality we are likely to find that there are really two or more true species lumped together under this name – frog species which look alike but in fact behave quite differently. *Neobatrachus* of the arid zones has been neglected for a number of reasons. Obviously there has not been a deliberate effort to ignore the genus there; it is simply that when the frogs are active in the rainy seasons it is virtually impossible to travel on the unmade roads that lead to them.

Logically any approach to try and discover whether *N. centralis* comprises more than one species would involve visiting what is called the 'type locality'. This place is simply the locality where the original specimens (examined by the person who described and named the species for the first time) came from. In the case of *N. centralis* this isn't a straightforward task. The author (Parker 1940) stated that they were collected in 1905 by Mr H. J. Hillier '100 miles [160 km] east of Lake Eyre' in South Australia. Such a locality is far from the few navigable tracks and in extremely remote country. In addition '100 miles' sounds an approximation and, to the Librarian at the South Australian Museum, Mrs V. Ledo, and myself, possibly far from any place where a collector of frogs would be likely to roam. For this reason we sought the help of the Librarian at the British Museum to obtain copies of any correspondence from Mr Hillier. From the librarian's efforts we learned that Mr Hillier was an Englishman employed as a teacher at the Bethesda Mission at Lake Killalpaninna east of Lake Eyre, and that he collected a variety of animals for Dr G. A. Boulenger of the British Museum. From his correspondence, and entries in zoological catalogues of his specimens in London, we worked out that the type locality was probably on the Birdsville Track about 50 km west of where it was stated to be.

Pinpointing a type locality in this way is usually extremely helpful when biological studies become possible. Unfortunately the *N. centralis* problem may be unique because there is a distinct possibility that the breeding population sampled by Hillier has been displaced even further west. During catastrophic flooding, such as that witnessed in early 1974, creeks flood their banks and become virtually moving seas of water many kilometres wide.

Thus there is every chance that the population once inhabiting that portion of the Birdsville Track has been swept further west, possibly to oblivion, and replaced by frogs washed in from the east. Whether the problem I envisage is real or imagined only time will tell, but it serves to show that the concept of a type locality, as a fixed spot on the map, is potentially misleading as an absolute reference to populations that are not static.

To describe some of the leptodactylids as aquatic can be misleading. Actually there are very few frogs in the world that really spend the greater part of their time in water. Most of the Australian species are perhaps fairly typical of the fringe dwellers which are really streamside or marsh inhabitants, needing to swim only a few metres at a time from one vantage point to another. Certainly it would be wrong to think of aquatic frogs as legged goldfish content to constantly swim and feed. It means that for the most part the adaptations of their bodies to an aquatic life are minimal. Provided that their body form is reasonably streamlined to permit them to pass through water efficiently, it may in fact be undesirable to become further adapted, simply because this could potentially diminish their proficiency on land.

The large and muscular *Mixophyes* species of eastern Australia (Pl. 9) and *Cyclorana dahli* of the far north have extensive webbing between their toes. For life in water this is extremely useful because it provides a vast surface area for propulsion. In another family (the Ranidae) streamside frogs employ the same sort of principle, and in fact sometimes progress a stage further in the process of producing a fan-like effect by separating the bones of the base of the foot. However, these frogs are exceptional, for the majority of frogs living in or near water seem better adapted to life on land. For most of them the water is largely a daytime refuge which they vacate at dusk in their wanderings to find and locate food.

A leptodactylid which genuinely lives in water is *Rheobatrachus silus*, a most unusual creature found only in creeks not far from Brisbane. At first sight there is nothing really streamlined about its body and if anything this dull slate-coloured frog may appear to have a rather dumpy form. However there are two features that provide clues to its way of life. The first is the smooth shape of the head so that it presents no major obstruction to water, and the second the deeply webbed feet. From its movements in water *Rheobatrachus* can be seen to be a most highly skilful swimmer whose movements are quite unlike those of a terrestrial frog taking a dip.

The swimming ability of *Rheobatrachus*, which seems to surpass that of other frogs, can be judged through watching the way in which it propels itself upwards, downwards, forwards and even sometimes backwards. Changes in direction can be achieved with the slightest alteration to the position of the limbs, and the overall level of control of movement is superb, reaching a finesse that is rare in frogs.

A *Rheobatrachus silus* which I kept in an aquarium for several months spent almost its entire time in the water, and during the daylight hours would hide away in a hollow beneath a submerged rock. It had created this underwater cave by scraping a depression in the gravel floor beneath the rock, and it would swim there and crawl inside if disturbed during its nocturnal wanderings. *Rheobatrachus* can spend hours on end below the surface of the water without coming up to change the air in its lungs. The implications of this habit are quite profound because terrestrial frogs obtain oxygen and release waste carbon dioxide via the skin, pharynx and lungs. Underwater life requires oxygen just as much as on land so it would appear that *Rheobatrachus* possibly relies more heavily upon its skin as a gas exchange surface than non-aquatic frogs do.

For reasons that are unclear many frogs throughout the world have developed raised ridges of skin upon their backs. In Australia these ornamentations are the almost exclusive province of leptodactylids, and they reach their most striking development in the genus *Lechriodus* whose members have from one to three pairs extending the complete length of their bodies. It may well be that these ridges aid the process of camouflage in some way. Certainly the general colorations of their bodies – sandy brown; greenish; grey or dark brown – and the markings upon them, demonstrate fairly elaborate attempts to be quite inconspicuous. However to a naturalist's eye there seem to be a couple of contradictions. Firstly there is a patch on the side of the head which is so dark as to stand out, and secondly (in two species) extremely extensive areas of black on the sides of the limbs and even on the chest. It is quite possible that because leptodactylids are quite adept at changing their general coloration they lack similar control over these black patches, and that these patches have a protective role to play only when the animal is in its dark phase.

Males of *Lechriodus platyceps* have three separate areas of formidably sharp, black spines on their hands: one at the base of the thumb, another on the back of the thumb, and the third on the back of the adjacent finger. Drawings of them are in the publications of Noble (1931, Fig. 38) and Zweifel (1972, Fig. 11). Each separate spike brings to mind the ghastly form of a medieval mace and it is hard to appreciate that these patches are not weapons, but are used only in the process of mating to enable the male to hold the female securely. Zweifel noticed that a new species he was describing had less prominent spines and certainly by no means as sharp. This led him to credit the new species with the name *aganoposis* which means quite literally, 'gentle husband'.

In Australia there are several leptodactylids which are secretive creatures confined to quite high altitudes in mountain ranges. For example, *Philoria frosti* has been found only at Mt Baw Baw in the central highland region of Victoria. This and the various species of *Kyarranus* in New South Wales, Victoria and Queensland live at an altitude of about 1000 to 1500 metres, a zone which can become particularly cold in winter.

It may well be the need to avoid extremely cold conditions which has led these animals to hide away beneath the surface. Moore (1958) reported finding one species as much as 15 cm below the surface of a saturated sphagnum bog. At the same depth he found clumps of approximately 50 eggs in small masses about 25 mm in diameter. The tadpoles of *Philoria* and *Kyarranus* can swim but lack teeth, for they do not actively feed but live on the generous yolk mass which forms an inner food store (Littlejohn 1963).

Quite recently Chris Corben and Glen Ingram of Brisbane found an unknown species of *Kyarranus* in leaf litter. With its rich crimson upper surfaces and yellow belly this is a splendid addition to the Australian fauna. It is quite possible that there are several more species yet to come to our notice, and it looks as though naturalists may find the need to include a trowel amongst their array of field equipment.

4 Conquerors of the Mountains
MICROHYLIDAE

WHEN TRANSLATED quite literally the family name Microhylidae suggests that it is composed of a group of small hylid-like frogs and so, by inference, could be assumed to be a group of diminutive tree frogs. Quite a few of the species of microhylids certainly are small tree frogs, but the family also includes some species that are aquatic and many others that are ground-dwellers or burrowers. Some are incredibly tiny creatures which are less than 10 mm long when fully grown and whose young will sit comfortably on the end of a pencil, but other species are great, squat and obese.

There are very few naturalists who have seen microhylids, simply because the majority of these frogs are to be found only in tropical and subtropical rainforests, often at quite high altitudes, and the family has completely mastered the mountain terrain. In Australia we currently know of only six species, and five of them are restricted to the remnants of rainforest situated on the eastern coastline of northern Queensland. The sixth occurs there too, but curiously it is also found 1200 km to the west on the Coburg Peninsula in the Northern Territory. These two populations may be the remnants of a once widely dispersed species, or else it may simply be that no one has searched thoroughly in the intermediate area.

It is in New Guinea that the microhylids have run riot, with about eighty-five species now known to science. A host of others have been discovered which just reside in museum collections where they await the detailed study that is needed before they can be given scientific names, and their existence made known. Undoubtedly many more species have yet to be discovered, and I am sure that we will eventually find that microhylid species far outnumber any other family in Australia and New Guinea.

The apparent ease with which unknown species are found was demonstrated recently in the vicinity of Port Moresby. One would imagine that the chances of finding anything new near such a well-known locality is fairly remote, but on the steeply sloping lawn in the grounds of the Iarowari School at Sogeri, Mr J. I. Menzies found a species of a previously unknown genus which Zweifel (1972) named *Pherohapsis menziesi* in his honour. One evening in 1972 Jim Menzies took me to the school to show me living specimens of his prize find. Unfortunately the frogs behaved as though they were aware of our presence for, although we tramped up and down the lawn none of the *P. menziesi* called, so preventing us from locating the entrances to their burrows in the soil, and we returned to Port Moresby without seeing one.

As is the case with frogs of other families the form and shape of microhylids reflect adaptations to their differing life-styles. For example, the tree-dwellers have the end segments of their fingers expanded into discs to assist climbing whilst most of the burrowers have very short legs in proportion to the size of their bodies.

Identification of microhylid frogs is an extremely difficult task often requiring skilful and most meticulous dissection of preserved specimens. For example, it is usually necessary to examine the very tip of the upper jaw to see whether the major bones there (the maxillae) are separated from one another at the front of the jaws, or whether they make contact. In addition the bones of the shoulder girdle have to be examined to see whether the clavicles (collar-bones), and other bones are present or absent. It can take an expert hours to come to any decision about identification and, because of the existence of so many unnamed forms, the slightest variation between published descriptions and what he actually sees will leave nagging doubts about the accuracy of his work. The net result is that very few herpetologists are inspired to work on microhylids.

Working out the identification of microhylids is made doubly difficult because of the wide variety of appearance amongst frogs currently grouped together in genera. For example there is the genus *Cophixalus* which is largely composed of species having expanded discs on the tips of their fingers and toes, and which mostly lives in rock clefts and in trees, shrubs and other vegetation. However, a few species live on the ground or actually in burrows. These species lack finger discs and are more squat creatures with short limbs. In the genus *Sphenophryne* there is the same sort of variation except that the tree-dwellers are in the minority and most species live on or below the surface of the ground.

There are two ways of looking at this sort of similarity between members of different genera. On the one hand we can take our hats off and comment that it demonstrates the wonders of evolutionary convergence. That is to say that on different occasions the same sort of animal has evolved, but on this occasion from ancestors that were clearly heavily committed to a different way of life. However, we always have to be on guard against looking for explanations that are too complicated. Could it be that some of the odd-ball tree-dwellers and burrowers are wrongly classified? It certainly bears thinking about, and I don't consider that we yet know enough about microhylids to dismiss the idea.

In locating microhylid frogs half of the battle is recognizing that the calls that they make are the product of frogs, and not made by insects or birds. This is well demonstrated by a profound mistake that I made in New Britain. I visited the island in 1966 to try to find out just how many species of frogs occur there, and particularly to look for the small microhylid tree frog *Oreophryne brachypus*. At that time the only known specimens of that species were three collected at Ralum on the Gazelle Peninsula, at the eastern end of the island, by a German anthropologist in 1897 and which are now held at Humboldt University in East Berlin. I travelled to Ralum but found that the settlement and surrounding area was totally under cultivation; I could not find any microhylids amongst the coconut palms, and I concluded that the original habitat had been so destroyed that it was no longer suitable for tree-dwelling, microhylid frogs. Searches for a couple of weeks of the fringes of other coastal towns and the mountains in the interior failed to produce a single microhylid. Then one evening in a village in the foothills behind Kandrian on the south coast I wondered about a loud, high-pitched piping noise coming from a bush behind my camp. I had heard exactly the same sound before at other localities but had always assumed an insect to be responsible. Needless to say I found that the 'insect' was really *Oreophryne brachypus*, and, by tracing other calling frogs in the surrounding forests, I collected twenty-one more of them within the space of a few days.

Microhylid tree frogs have one thing in common which prevents any possibility of their being confused with their hylid counterparts. This feature is the shape of the discs at the tips of their fingers and toes. Whereas the discs of hylids are virtually circular, or at least evenly rounded, the microhylids have discs that are described as truncated, because it is as though the tips have been neatly cut off with a pair of curve-bladed nail-scissors (Fig. 8).

The internal structure of the microhylid finger discs is so different from those of hylids that it is possible that they function in a different way as well. The end bone of the hylid finger comes to a slender point and is slightly curved downwards, so that in profile it resembles a claw. This means that the tissue at the edges of the disc is in no way supported by bone, and the entire disc can be likened to a very thick pancake with a rod through the middle. In contrast the end bone of the microhylid finger is forked to form a Y-or a T-shape. The ends of this bone project out into the disc and

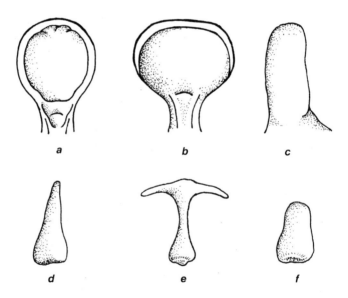

FIG. 8 Finger discs and their internal structure. *a*, *b* and *c* are the end joints of the fingers of a hylid, a microhylid and a ground-dwelling leptodactylid respectively; *d*, *e* and *f* are the bones inside them.

provide it with a very firm support (Fig. 8), but the disc itself is comparatively thinner.

Microhylids and hylids are often to be found together in the same trees, and there is no evidence to suggest that the climbing ability of the members of one family is superior to that of the other. However, it is a curious fact that there is no really large species of microhylid tree frog, and actually the vast majority of species are less than 40 mm long when fully grown. I don't think anyone has asked just why this should be, but there are several quite reasonable explanations. The simplest might be one of lack of opportunity for large species of microhylids to evolve. If the hylids arrived in New Guinea before the microhylids and exploited the tree zone fairly thoroughly, it could be that the only zone that microhylids could occupy was suitable solely for creatures of small size. However, there remains the more fundamental explanation that discs with more elaborate supporting bones are ideal for small tree frogs but quite unsatisfactory for large ones.

On the whole the microhylid climbers are a fairly drab group as far as colour is concerned. They tend to be brownish or very dull green, and there is none that can hold a candle to any of the extremely beautiful hylids. Markings on their bodies rarely contrast conspicuously with the background coloration, but some of them do have one or two strange features. For example, a few have a W-shaped mark on the shoulders, sometimes emphasized by being raised in the form of a fold of skin. Unlike members of the Hylidae the under-surface of their bodies is very rarely just a uniform white or cream. Instead, they are usually faint green, grey-brown or pinkish, and sometimes the skin is so incredibly thin and transparent that the internal organs such as the dark, greenish liver can be seen quite clearly.

In common with most other microhylids the majority of the tree frogs that have been found so far have been collected in the daytime by searching vegetation. The reason is simply that at many localities night collecting is difficult and often extremely hazardous. No one in their right mind is going to venture in darkness very far on steep mountain slopes that are hard to negotiate in daylight. It means that we have more information about where some species of tree frogs hide away during the daytime than about the more important aspect of their activities when they are abroad at night.

In the absence of any suicidally inclined herpetologists it is reasonable to predict that there is really very little likelihood that the secrets of the activities of many species will be uncovered for a long time to come. However, even the daytime hiding places are of interest because they show an ability by the members of this family to take advantage of any secluded refuge. A popular one is the egg-plant which grows on the trunks of forest trees. The base of the plant is so arranged that there are series of galleries and spaces communicating with one another. In them have been found *Oreophryne anthonyi* and *O. idenburgensis*, whilst a third species, *O. inornata*, sometimes hides inside the water-filled cut stems of climbing bamboo (Zweifel 1956).

There are at least some microhylids that hide amongst leaf litter or beneath rotting logs, and at night climb low shrubs. Not all of these could be predicted to be climbers from examination of the form of their hands. *Cophixalus ateles* falls into this category, because the discs of the fingers are fairly small and, in fact, the first finger is virtually vestigial, being just a tiny stump without a recognizable disc at the end. Several species of frogs in other families exhibit the same trend towards loss of this digit. It implies a fairly drastic change in habits, for the first finger is of vital importance in grasping, and any reduction infers that the possessors have no need to grasp. In certain special cases such as that of the leptodactylid *Assa darlingtoni* of the Queensland/New South Wales border, life on the ground amongst a dense mat of rotting vegetation is conceivably one in which this finger could be truly superfluous. However, the first finger must also assist in balancing and in distributing the weight of the body through the hand. How any frog that needs to be reasonably agile can afford to dispense with the service of a rather important digit is unknown, but it clearly has proved quite superfluous in the paths of evolution that have led to strikingly different frogs of equally varied habits.

So far all of the microhylids from Australia and New Guinea about which we have any information at all lay their eggs on land in moist situations, and none of them has a free-swimming tadpole. By passing their development entirely inside the egg membrane they have succeeded in becoming independent of free bodies of

The streamlined rocket frog *Litoria nasuta* of Australia and New Guinea

5 DIFFERENCES IN FORM

Cyclorana australis – a water-holding frog of northern Australia

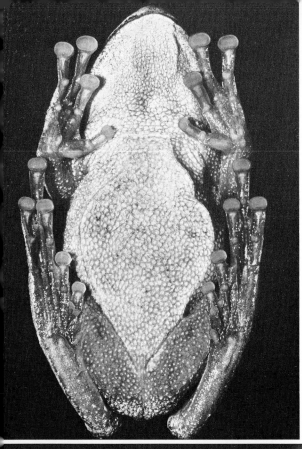

6 A COMMON TREE FROG

Ewing's tree frog at rest on a
window pane

The same frog on my finger

water for reproduction. Most of the adults that do live near to water are simply taking advantage of the cover provided by dense vegetation and heaps of boulders. Having managed to lose the customary dependence on water for breeding purposes, an adult life in water appears to be virtually a retrograde step and hence a reversal of all that frogs have strived for for millions of years. However, *Sphenophryne palmipes* of southeast New Guinea is evidently unaware of the ethics of the situation, for it is a genuinely aquatic frog. It is up to about 40 mm long, usually a dull slate colour and gains its specific name from the extensive webbing between its toes, a feature which is quite exceptional in microhylids. *Sphenophryne palmipes* has fairly large discs on the tips of its fingers and toes, and they probably help it to climb out of the water and on to rocks in the fast flowing streams and creeks where it is to be found. When Zweifel first reported this frog in 1956 he noted that unfertilized eggs inside the females were up to 4.5 mm in diameter. Large eggs like these are quite characteristic of microhylids from Australia and New Guinea suggesting that the breeding habits and breeding site of *S. palmipes* are in no ways different to those of the other microhylids. Hence it may be one of the few aquatic frogs in the world that leaves the water to breed.

Sphenophryne species seem to have an inclination towards exhibiting unusual features or habits. For example *Sphenophryne cornuta* is noteworthy in bearing a prominent cone-shaped wart on each upper eyelid, and in sometimes having the under-surface of the body and limbs a vivid red. *Sphenophryne mehelyi* of New Britain is also unusual because it indulges in a sort of communal sex-life, with literally hundreds of frogs congregating together to lay and fertilize their eggs at one spot.

Three of the six Australian microhylid frogs are species of *Sphenophryne* and, although the first became known to the scientific world in 1912, there is absolutely no published information on their lives. The squat form of these frogs and their stubby limbs suggest that they live on the ground and quite possibly in burrows beneath the leaf litter. The forest floor and particularly the mountain slopes is the home of many microhylid species and in New Guinea *Sphenophryne* is only one of several genera that have been found in these sorts of situations.

Amongst the most extraordinary of the forest floor dwellers are the *Barygenys* species, which resemble Easter eggs with legs. Their heads merge into their bodies and the tiny eyes look as though they were stuck on as an afterthought. It is easy to look upon these rather ludicrous creatures as ill-fitted to the rigours of the New Guinea terrain, but in reality they have been incredibly successful in adapting to a wide variety of situations, and their almost comical appearance is totally misleading. For example, one of the six species so far known occurs at sea level, and another on a mountain peak 3500 metres above sea level. They are obviously poorly equipped for navigating their way over obstacles and a sedentary life would seem to be called for. One species, *B. cheesmanae* was found by the intrepid explorer Miss Evelyn Cheesman of the British Museum in holes in the ground on the slopes of Mt Tafa, but all of the other species have been found in the open or beneath logs.

Burrowing techniques may well vary quite considerably amongst different species of microhylids. Whether any of them burrow using the 'back-foot shuffle' technique of Australian leptodactylids remains uncertain. None has developed the spade-like form of outer metatarsal tubercle, and there is evidence to suggest that at least some excavate holes with their snouts. For example there is *Cophixalus oxyrhinus* which has a most peculiar-looking snout which projects out from the head and is quite colourless at the tip where it is reinforced (Fig. 9). Just what goes on underground is a mystery, but the nature of the snout is well suited to digging and is not a delicate structure likely to be damaged by abrasion.

Barygenys is another genus that could conceivably use its snout for burrowing. The end is not reinforced in any way, but there are three vertical ridges at the tip which must surely perform some function. That they could act as cutting faces is suggested by the fact that they are most highly developed in *B. cheesmanae* (Fig. 9), the one species for which there is proof that it does live in burrows.

It is quite plausible that *Xenobatrachus* bridges the gap between the habit of burrowing into soft soil to create burrows, and burrowing beneath logs, stones or moss to hide away as effectively but perhaps with less effort. Viewed from above the body is roughly conical with a broad base tapering to a small triangular head. Most of the eight species are within the range of about

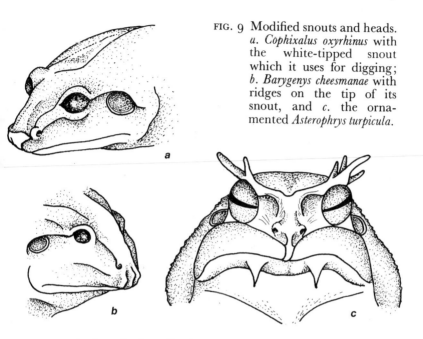

FIG. 9 Modified snouts and heads. *a*. *Cophixalus oxyrhinus* with the white-tipped snout which it uses for digging; *b*. *Barygenys cheesmanae* with ridges on the tip of its snout, and *c*. the ornamented *Asterophrys turpicula*.

30–50 mm in length, but *X. giganteus* can reach 90 mm, which is exceptionally large for a microhylid.

Xenobatrachus rostratus is a particularly spectacular species often having the upper surfaces of its body and limbs rich red or orange in colour. The pattern of markings on the under-surface is equally variable and Zweifel (1972) has provided a figure of six specimens from the Kaironk Valley to demonstrate just how much they can differ from one another. *Xenobatrachus obesus* is another striking species: tan above, yellow beneath and with one chocolate brown band along the side of the body, and another stripe, with a white centre, down the middle of the back. Living on the dimly lit, forested mountain slopes, where the sunlight rarely penetrates the dense screening canopy, the almost riotous use of colour is quite perplexing.

Xenorhina, a genus with, perhaps appropriately, a rather similar name to *Xenobatrachus*, demonstrates amongst its members a progression from the conical body plan to extreme obesity. At the absolute limit is *X. doriae*, which is up to 100 mm long and, as

Zweifel points out, is only 2 mm short of the largest species of microhylid frog in the world (*Platyhyla grandis* of the island of Madagascar). Although 90 years have elapsed since this giant New Guinea frog was first discovered, we still know absolutely nothing about its habits.

Ornamentation of the body in terms of skin folds, flaps projecting from the body etc. is rare amongst microhylids, but in New Guinea there is one particularly extraordinary frog called *Asterophrys turpicula* which is the exception to the rule. On various parts of the head, and in particular on the upper eyelids and on the chin, are pointed flaps of skin projecting outwards (Fig. 9). Its habits seem to be quite consistent with its fierce appearance, for this is an aggressive frog noted by Fred Parker to attack the hand of anyone who tries to pick one up. *Asterophrys turpicula* has a particular claim to fame in that it was the first frog from New Guinea to reach zoologists in Europe. Schlegel described and named it in 1837 in the course of his work on a large animal collection. The exotic nature of the frog and the remoteness of the locality were both noteworthy even at that time when collections arrived from many distant lands, with the result that other zoologists commented on it or otherwise referred to the species in works published in Holland, Germany, Austria, France, England, Belgium and America. Although by this sort of yardstick *A. turpicula* might rank as a well-known species, it remains a relatively rare one.

5 The Island Colonists RANIDAE

IN AUSTRALIA there is only one species of ranid frog, and the geographic distribution of the family Ranidae in Australia, New Guinea and adjacent islands is quite unlike that of any other in this area. What makes it so unusual is that the largest number of different species is to be found on Bougainville in the Solomon Islands and progressively fewer species westwards. This sort of pattern of distribution is a source of surprise because the family is a worldwide one, and there is every reason to suppose that it entered New Guinea from Indonesia and then radiated out into Australia and to the Solomon Islands via New Britain. If this assumption is correct it means that the family has fared best in the area where it has existed for the shortest time.

Without doubt the ranids are versatile animals, for in Africa and the Solomon Islands they have occupied a wide variety of different niches, evolving to form tree frogs and burrowers as well as streamside dwellers. The reason the family failed to evolve in this way in New Guinea may be likened to the approach of an experienced salesman. On arriving in a new territory and finding the market already exploited to the full by competitors who arrived there before him, he leaves a few samples, cuts his losses and moves on in search of greener pastures. Hence I believe that the Ranidae was the last family to enter New Guinea, and that it did so at the point in time when all of the most obvious niches for frogs had already been occupied. The hylids, leptodactylids and micro-hylids were entrenched in the trees, on the ground and even below the surface of the ground. All that was really left was the creek-beds and marshes and it was these that ranids monopolized.

When the ranids eventually reached the Solomon Islands it is quite possible that the only frogs that had arrived there before them were the two species of hylid tree frogs that live there today. Faced with almost boundless opportunities for exploitation in terms of available dwelling places, there was virtually an evolutionary explosion among the colonists. The ranids diverged rapidly acquiring various different characteristics and becoming masters of their new domain.

To naturalists in many countries on several continents it is a ranid frog, usually a *Rana* species, that typifies their idea of a frog. In Europe, Asia and America the spawn that graces jam-jars, aquariums and washbowls in school biology laboratories is ranid spawn. The adult frogs are dissected by students and the hind legs eaten at restaurants by the children's parents who would recoil at the idea of dissection.

In New Guinea there are altogether seven species of *Rana*, and they occupy the lowland swamps and the highland creeks. Several are similar in appearance to their counterparts in Europe, having elongate, triangular-shaped heads, with broad dark stripes on the sides like bandits' masks. The eyes are large, the bodies broad, and the hind limbs very muscular. They include some of the largest species of frogs found in the whole of Australia and New Guinea, four exceeding 100 mm in length and at least one of these approaching 200 mm.

Rana papua is by far the most widespread of the species, reaching New Britain, the Solomon Islands and northeastern Australia. Until quite recently the actual existence of the Australian population was known only because there happened to be a few specimens in several museums. However recent collecting has revealed that it is fairly common on parts of the Cape York Peninsula. *Rana papua* is really a lowland dweller growing to a length of about 75 mm (Pl. 4). In the highlands of New Guinea it is replaced by another species called *R. grisea* which lives besides streams and in the deep drainage ditches by coffee plantations and village gardens. It lays about 800 eggs and the juveniles are quite striking, for at the stage of their transformation from tadpoles they have completely uniform yellow under-surfaces. As the young get progressively larger they gradually lose this bright colour and become dull cream with brown markings on their throats.

The largest and one of the best known of the New Guinea species is *Rana arfaki*, first collected in the Arfak Mountains of Irian Barat. Nowhere does it appear to be particularly abundant and, because of its value as food, its existence may well be endangered by the predatory activities of man. This may apply equally well to the most recent addition to the known *Rana* species (*Rana jimiensis* shown in Plate 20), which so far has been found only in the dense mountainous area between Goroka and Telefomin. Whereas most *Rana* species have a conspicuous, taut tympanum behind the eye, *R. jimiensis* has this structure partly covered by its rough and distinctly toad-like skin.

Despite the variation in external appearance of *Rana* species, our limited knowledge of their habits suggests that they comprise a fairly uniform group of animals. Most live in, or at least very close to water and, when disturbed, dive into it in classic style. They swim well, and when pursued inevitably press their arms flat against their sides and kick vigorously with their feet to propel themselves through the water at high speed. Females lay up to about 1000 eggs and all species can be assumed to have a tadpole stage. This conclusion can be reached from an examination of the eggs in gravid females, because the small size of the eggs and the presence of pigment on them is indicative of an aquatic egg-laying site.

The *Rana* species have served as subjects for many studies that have led to a finer understanding of the ways of frogs in general. For example, how frogs breathe, how their blood circulates through the heart, and details of their powers of vision. Amongst the most interesting topics of relevance to naturalists is the mechanics of movement, which have clarified the roles of various groups of muscles in the process of jumping. Figure 10 is a modified version from a series prepared by Gans (1961) who used a movie

FIG. 10 The way in which a frog unfolds during jumping (after Gans 1961).

camera to record the sequence of events, as a series of separate stages. The selected stages are of the initial launching movement showing how the arms are lifted off the ground and tucked against the sides, whilst the legs progressively extend, throwing the body forwards and upwards on its ascent path. The arms are brought into play only during the latter stages of the descent to the ground, when they are quickly brought forward to take the initial impact on landing.

Irrespective of the extent of one's experience with frogs, to meet a giant frog of the genus *Discodeles* is an experience long remembered. It is simply that these are such large animals that sudden confrontation is a shock. *Discodeles* species can be likened to muscle-bound weight lifters. The recently discovered *D. malukuna* of Guadalcanal is perhaps an exception, being only up to 60 mm in length and evidently not robust, but the other three species found in the last century are extremely well covered. Their thighs are massive and they leap with a low trajectory but considerable velocity. To catch one by hand is an activity for the most athletic herpetologists, for it involves virtually outrunning the creature and grabbing it with both hands. In practice this is even more difficult than it sounds, particularly if the pursuit takes place at night and the forest floor is a maze of slightly exposed tree roots. During the daytime these frogs hide amongst boulders and grass near streams, but at night they wander far away in search of food. Their call is like the quacking of a duck, but on occasions they emit an unearthly groan.

Discodeles are so large that they have been the source of a great deal of interest to zoologists. It is certainly unfortunate that they are confined to New Britain and other islands off the beaten track for most workers interested in observing frog behaviour. However the first specimens collected were sent to Dr G. A. Boulenger of the British Museum with a good deal more than just the name of the place where they were found. The collector was Dr H. B. Guppy, an experienced naturalist who served as Surgeon aboard the British exploring vessel H.M.S. *Lark*. Dr Guppy gave Dr Boulenger detailed notes of his observations of young *Discodeles* hatching from their eggs. It appeared that he found the eggs in the foothills and carried them back to his ship in an open container. Glancing in at one stage during his walk he found that some of the frogs were breaking loose and jumping out. Many folk would have simply placed a lid on the container and continued walking, but Guppy was intrigued by the manner in which they escaped. He provides a description in a book written on his return to England (1887). Boulenger (1884), in his report of Guppy's finds, includes the same account and also superb illustrations of the adults, juveniles and eggs, and of the other species of frogs collected by Guppy. Plate 12 shows the giant eggs of a *Discodeles* species collected by Fred Parker on Bougainville.

Long before Guppy explored the Solomon Islands they were visited by vessels from several European countries, and the French were particularly sensitive about the failure of the English to acknowledge earlier voyages there. Fleurieu (1791) demonstrates the extent of this concern by entitling an account of previous explorations, 'Discoveries of the French in 1768 and 1769, to the southeast of New Guinea with the subsequent visits to the same lands by the English navigators who gave them new names'. Most of the extracts from the journals which Fleurieu cites are concerned with contact with natives but one section from the observations in 1769 of a crew member of the vessel *St John the Baptist*, commanded by Monsieur de Surville, includes a description of a frog. There is little doubt that it refers to *Ceratobatrachus guentheri*.

The extract is as follows: 'He saw also a toad, which he thought singular enough to deserve a particular attention: its back along the whole length of the body, is sharp and sloped on each side, like a penthouse, at a small distance from the shoulders, the head, or snout takes the form of a lance, equally sloped off like the back; and near the angle are placed the eyes, on a kind of scale, or cartilage; the feet have nothing in them uncommon, and the animal moves by bounds like the toads of Europe'.

Ceratobatrachus guentheri may have assumed a special role in the lives of the early inhabitants of the Solomon Islands. The evidence is probably not particularly convincing, but when the Spanish explorer Gallego visited St Isabel Island in 1567, his crew burnt down several shrines devoted to the worship of particular local animals, one of which was a frog. No details of the creature are provided in his manuscript, but it is safe to assume that the subjects would be of unusual appearance to merit elevating to such status.

Because *C. guentheri* stands apart from all other frogs in this respect, it seems the most likely subject.

Searching for frogs in an area not previously visited by herpetologists is an exciting venture because there is always the chance of finding species new to science. Three times in New Britain I collected new species of the ranid genus *Platymantis* solely through tracing calls that I had not heard previously. On one evening a guide and I visited a creek with steep rocky sides where we could hear the calls of several different species of frogs. Simultaneously we heard 'pink-pink-pink-pink' from the slope above us. We had collected frogs throughout the district and recognized that this was a species new to us. Words were unnecessary, and we quietly and very carefully climbed towards the spot where the call appeared to have come from. After climbing a distance of about ten metres it began to rain. A few large drops at first, but soon a steady downpour cascading down the slopes and soaking our clothes. The frog continued to call, and gradually we homed in on it until we were sure that we had reached the exact spot. Turning on our miner's headlamps we were disappointed to find that there was nothing to be seen but a sheet of water flowing over the rock. For several minutes we carefully scraped away the moss, and were rewarded with the sight of a tiny warty frog with red flashes on its legs. About 20 mm long, it was actually in the process of calling from its vantage point of a cleft in the rock face. The species now known as *Platymantis akarithymus* had been discovered.

Published information on the life-histories and biology of *Platymantis* species are unfortunately devoted to species occurring outside our area. I don't think that there is any reason to suppose that the New Guinea, Solomon Island and New Britain ones behave differently, and so for the present these papers provide our only reference sources. Readers wishing to learn more about these fascinating frogs should consult Alcala (1962) for observations on the development of species found in the Philippine Islands, and Gorham (1968) for field data on the two in Fiji.

Palmatorappia solomonis is another frog unique to the Solomon Islands. It is a small and quite exquisite, pale green tree frog with large eyes (Pl. 13). The first specimens I examined were sent by Fred Parker who had collected them on Bougainville. An odd feature was the presence of obscure purplish patches and irregular lines on their backs that did not resemble natural markings. When I wrote to Parker about them, he explained that the species has an incredibly delicate skin which bruises very easily despite even the most gentle handling. It can hardly afford to be particularly boisterous, and it would be most interesting to learn how it avoids injury.

No account of the ranid frogs would be complete without reference to a species which may not be a ranid and, to add to the confusion, may not even have come from New Guinea. In the natural history museum at Basel in Switzerland are two frogs which were supposedly collected at Lake Sentani, a vast freshwater lake near the north coast of New Guinea and inhabited by giant swordfish. Labels with the frogs declare that they were collected by Dr P. Wirz, an anthropologist who conducted research in that area. In 1927 J. Roux examined them and, thinking that they were hylid tree frogs, named the species *Hyla wirzi*. However it was later found that they were really members of the ranid tree frog genus *Rhacophorus*, widely distributed in Borneo, Indonesia and the Orient, but not previously known to occur in New Guinea. Whether *Rhacophorus* is a ranid or, as some zoologists maintain, a member of a separate family called the Rhacophoridae does not cloud the issue. What does matter is that no further specimens of *Rhacophorus* have been collected in New Guinea, and until someone returns to Lake Sentani to search for it, the authenticity of the locality labels will remain in doubt.

6 The Cane Toad *Bufo marinus*

THE TOAD *Bufo marinus* was introduced into Queensland in 1935 in an elaborate and quite ingenious attempt to control two species of beetles that were major pests of sugar cane. The introduction was made in the first place because it was hoped that the toads would eat sufficient numbers of beetles to ease, or hopefully eliminate, a potentially serious threat to the Queensland sugar industry. Why this step was taken, how it was justified by those involved and the subsequent spread and effect of the toad is one of the most interesting examples of man's attempts to harness animals for his own purposes.

Bufo marinus (Pl. 13) is a strongly built toad growing up to 230 mm in length and which feeds on a wide variety of animal and plant material. Its natural distribution extends from Argentine through the temperate, subtropical and tropical areas of South and Central America into Mexico. It is known by a great variety of common names and, since its introduction into Australia, has been called the American toad, giant toad, giant American toad, great Mexican toad, Queensland toad and cane toad.

The decision to import it into Australia followed introductions in a number of other countries and was really a consequence of these experiences. The first extension of the toad's natural range was probably the introduction into certain islands in the West Indies before 1850, in the hope that it would consume small rodents. Whether it ever fulfilled the importers' expectations was not known, but its prolific insect-eating tendencies raised the possibility that it might provide a simple means of controlling insect pests of crops, and in particular those attacking sugar cane. Thus in 1920 and 1924 a number of toads were shipped to Puerto Rico, and by 1930 they were well established there. Dexter (1932) examined the stomach contents of 301 Puerto Rican toads and found that 51 per cent of the items that had been eaten consisted of insects considered to be injurious to agriculture. She was particularly pleased at the large number of sugar cane pests called *Phyllophaga* or 'white grubs' that had been eaten, and concluded an address to an international conference with the words: 'All other methods of control of this pest have so far failed, and we strongly advocate the effective use, under favourable conditions, of this amphibian immigrant which is doing its full share of benefit to our sugar industry, and to which this International Congress should pay a tribute of gratitude'.

Raquel Dexter's words impressed delegates from many countries, including Mr Arthur F. Bell who attended the conference as the official representative of the Queensland Government. Travelling around Puerto Rico he saw for himself the extent to which the toad had become so well established. When he returned to Australia his colleagues were obviously highly impressed with the news of this interesting venture into biological control by which one animal is used to control another.

Australian agriculturalists awaited the results of further introductions into Hawaii in 1932 and then into the Philippines in 1934. The Hawaiian introduction was dramatic, for such was the rate of growth of the population at a site where half of the original immigrants were set free, that from the surplus 103,517 young toads were removed in the next two years for release in other parts of the island (Pemberton 1934).

Eventually the decision was taken to introduce the toad into selected sugar-growing areas of Queensland, with the object of controlling the 'Frenchi' beetle but more particularly the greyback beetle *Lepidoderma albohirtum*. As a result Mr R. W. Mungomery of the Sugar Experiment Station at Meringa travelled to Hawaii and collected 102 toads on 1 June 1935. The toads left Honolulu two days later and, upon their arrival at Gordonvale in north Queensland on 22 June, it was found that only one had died on the journey to Australia. With cold and dry winter months ahead it was decided not to release them immediately, but to keep them in a specially constructed, enclosed pond.

The importation had aroused considerable interest, but the enthusiasm with which the cane growers awaited the release of the toads for distribution in batches to the plantations was not shared by some other sections of the community. Misgivings were expressed by apiarists about the way in which the toads might eat their bees; other people were worried about the effect on poultry and on the native fauna. The prospect of toads croaking at night was not relished, and it was even suggested that toads crushed by vehicles upon the roads might create a traffic hazard. Some of these fears were undoubtedly justified whilst others were certainly far-fetched. However basically there was antagonism within a sector of the community, and the cane industry appears to have been irritated that the denials that they issued in the public media in no way satisfied or silenced the critics. Certainly in some instances the fears of the public were not treated as they should have been at a time when reassurance was needed.

At Gordonvale the captive toads surprised their keepers by taking advantage of a warm spell and breeding in July 1935, so that in the following month the first liberation was made in districts north of Cardwell somewhat ahead of schedule.

It happened that the Commonwealth Department of Health had taken note of cautionary views, and towards the end of 1935 imposed a ban on further releases, pending a more detailed study of the toads' feeding habits. It is relevant to point out that the difference in opinions had waged almost entirely between the canegrowers and the general public. At that time there were very few professional herpetologists, and an opinion from such experts would have been valuable.

One herpetologist, Mr J. R. Kinghorn, then Curator of Reptiles at the Australian Museum, did express his views in an article (1938) and emphasized the need for caution. The President of the Naturalists' Society of New South Wales, Mr W. W. Froggatt was more openly critical, stating (1936): 'This great toad, immune from enemies and breeding all the year round, may soon become as much a pest as the rabbit or the cactus'. However in the same year, data on food eaten by the toads was submitted to the Department of Health, and, because they were satisfied from those data that the toads had no undesirable feeding habits, the ban was lifted. Following the removal of the ban the distribution and liberation of toads started on a very large scale. The original imported stock had laid 1,560,000 eggs in captivity and in the

same period 62,000 young toads were released ('J.H.B.' –
probably Bell – 1936).

J. Covacevich and M. Archer of the Queensland Museum have
prepared a detailed account of the chronological sequence of the
liberations of the toad in Queensland and its present distribution.
I have incorporated data that they generously made available to
me in Fig. 11 which shows current distribution in Australia and
the southwest Pacific area.

Whilst the liberations were being made throughout Queensland
at the request of cane farmers, the controversy about the overall
merits of these actions continued to rage. Optimistic reports of the
feeding habits of the toads and assurance that the toads had
minimal undesirable effects failed to convince the local populace.
In fact because there were people taking matters into their own
hands and deliberately destroying toads, the possibility of taking
the step of seeking protection for *Bufo marinus* by State Government decree was contemplated in 1938.

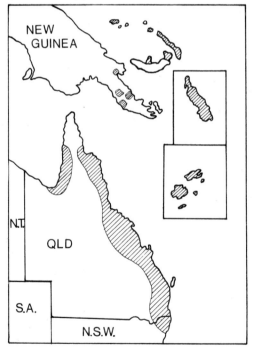

FIG 11 Geographic
distribution of
the cane toad
in Australia
and the South
Pacific.
Bougainville
and Fiji to the
east are shown
as insets.

During the same period the geographic range of *Bufo marinus* was being extended outside Australia. It was introduced into Fiji in 1936; New Guinea, New Ireland and New Britain in 1938–39; the Ellice Islands in 1939, and the British Solomon Islands in 1940.

In almost every case the introduction of *Bufo marinus* into a new area was followed fairly rapidly by enthusiastic reports of the success of the control ventures. Most of these reports were written by entomologists or agriculturalists directly involved in the introduction. The situation in Australia was perhaps unique to the extent that the initial reports were somewhat restrained. The writers seemed to realize that there was an element of risk in prophesying complete control of the pests that the toads were intended to destroy.

To assess the wisdom of the decision to introduce the toads it must be recognized that the entomologists and agriculturalists responsible for the initial recommendations were under tremendous pressure to control pests that threatened various industries. Their actions have to be viewed in the light of just what was happening in the early 1930's when only a limited array of chemical and other control methods were available to them. They were faced with potential crises and the toad seemed to offer a new, simple and economically feasible solution. Today such a proposal to introduce a foreign animal would undoubtedly be viewed with extreme caution. The modern approach to assessing the likely effects of the toad would rely to a great extent upon the opinions of ecologists, and particularly those with a wide experience in herpetology. Specialized expertise of this calibre simply wasn't available in Australia at the time that it was needed.

Only someone who has visited those parts of Queensland or New Guinea where the toad is most abundant can have any real concept of just how numerous the toads can become. Imagine walking on a garden lawn at night and having one toad to every two square metres. Thus with every step that you take toads are roving in front and on each side of you: a slowly moving sea of dark, shuffling, hopping creatures falling as they attempt to escape and jostling one another. Imagine walking along a path for a mile and you'll soon become extremely conscious of toads. There they will be almost every month of the year. On the verandah and on the stairs to the ground. Every morning the roads are littered

Bibron's Toadlet *Pseudophryne bibroni* with its eggs

7 THE TOADLET AND ITS EGGS

Breeding site of Bibron's toadlet. Each of the squares of white paper marks a separate egg clump in the depressions made by the hooves of a horse

Bullfrog spawn clumps near
Mt Disappointment,
Victoria

Tadpole and young frogl‹
of *Rheobatrachus silus*

with the crushed bodies of toads run down by vehicles the previous night.

Whereas most Australian frogs breed only once each year and lay no more than about 4,000 eggs, the toads may breed twice a year and lay 10,000 to 21,000 eggs at one time. It is therefore possible for a female to lay as many as 40,000 eggs per annum. Bell (1936) notes that on one morning nine females laid a total of 125,000 eggs.

The eggs are laid in elongate chains resembling lengths of transparent spaghetti with a continuous row of black dots zig-zagging down the centre. They are laid in either static or slowly moving water. Provided that there are adequate supplies of food, which needs to be plant material and other organic matter, the tadpoles grow rapidly and complete development into tiny toads in anything from 25 days to two months.

In much the same fashion as fishes, the tadpoles tend to form schools which can often be seen congregating together motionless on the floors of ditches. Quite what they are doing is uncertain, but I have watched a group of about 2,000 remain together in formation in this way for over an hour. *Bufo marinus* tadpoles are unusual in many ways: for example whereas most species seem to have a strong preference for feeding in a particular sort of place, on the floor of ponds, in mid-water or at the surface, *B. marinus* takes food anywhere. However this may be because their numbers may create a food scarcity so that they are forced to forage and take food where they can find it.

Nothing is known of the mortality rate either in the tadpole or adult stages, but I believe that the greatest number of deaths are likely to occur at metamorphosis into toads and in the first couple of months on land. Tadpoles in drainage ditches undoubtedly face the risk of being swept away during flash flooding caused by torrential rains. At metamorphosis other species are known to be at high risk of death by drowning if they are unable to climb from the water. This must often happen to the young of *B. marinus* in ditches with steep sides.

On leaving the water the small toads are usually only about 10 mm long and at that size they face the constant risk of being eaten by larger toads. Whilst they travel abroad at dusk seeking food, cannibalism is likely to be very high, and every time they pass beneath the shelter of fallen vegetation at dawn to hide away for the daylight hours, a larger toad may be there to welcome them. This risk of cannibalism obviously diminishes as the toads grow larger.

The life span of *B. marinus* in the wild state is not known, but there are several records for other species of *Bufo* living in captivity for ten to sixteen years. The ultimate record of longevity is of a toad befriended by the eighteenth-century English naturalist Tennant for thirty-six years, and which was thought to be about forty years old when it died. However in other animals the length of life in the wild is inevitably shorter than that in captivity where they are provided with a constant supply of food, and are not faced with the stresses of competing with other members of the population and other animals.

Assessments of the benefits of the various introductions varied from country to country. In Fiji, Hinckley (1962) found that plant-eating insects and other prey that were potentially harmful from an agricultural, and hence economic, viewpoint were included in the diet of 62 per cent of the toads that he examined. However on the debit side of the scale 65 per cent of the toads included in their diet insects that he regarded as potentially beneficial. He compared the diet of toads collected on lawns and gardens, banana groves and other different situations (Table 1), and concluded that because of the range of prey consumed *Bufo marinus* was neither extremely beneficial nor positively detrimental, but 'economically neutral'.

By 1952 experiences in the Philippines led Rabor to view the toad in an unfavourable light. It was not so much that they had failed to achieve the original objective, but rather that they had created an ecological imbalance in much the fashion that Froggatt (1936) had predicted could take place in Australia. In Manilla many cats died from eating toads, so permitting the rat population previously held in check by the cats to reach pest proportions. Two species of native frogs previously found in Manilla were said to have been displaced by the toads.

The Hawaiian introduction resulted in the control of a number of insect pests but not necessarily those that the toad was introduced to eat. Illingworth (1941) and Fullway and Krauss (1945) provide the data and so I won't repeat them here. Oliver and

A. Percentage of toads from different locations found to have eaten various kinds of prey.

LOCATION	Important pests	Millipedes	Ants	Beneficial predators
Lawns and gardens	40%	13%	80%	20%
Coconut plantations	20%	45%	65%	35%
Banana groves	65%	65%	65%	15%
Cane roads	40%	87%	7%	33%
Rice field	67%	0%	27%	7%

B. Summary of prey eaten by 114 toads in terms of economic importance.

CLASSIFICATION OF PREY	Total number eaten	Percentage of toads with such prey
Harmful plant pests	314	62%
Useful scavengers	287	66%
Beneficial predators	710	65%

(Data derived from Tables IV and V of Hinckley 1962)

TABLE I   Diet of *Bufo marinus*

Shaw (1953) believed that the benefits of the introduction there far outweighed the minor objections raised against it.

The situation in Australia is more difficult to assess. Unpublished reports by agriculturalists indicate very clearly that the toad failed to live up to expectations in controlling greyback beetles. One cause of the failure was that canefields simply did not provide the necessary form of ground cover for the toads to hide beneath during the daytime. Hence the toads moved to areas at the edge of the canefields where there was adequate cover, and fed in those areas after dusk.

The basic lesson learned from this experience just wasn't given adequate publicity, or else the information was ignored. Hence in 1962 owners of vegetable plots at Wau in New Guinea introduced at least 1,000 toads from the coastal town of Lae. It was hoped that the toads would feed upon caterpillars infesting cabbages. When news of the proposal reached government officers the owners were advised that the step was unlikely to be successful because the daytime shade available in the plots was clearly inadequate for the toads. However school children in Lae were offered payment 'in kind' in the form of one chocolate frog per live toad, the toads were crated up, flown to Wau and released amongst the cabbages. True to expectations the toads promptly migrated out of the cabbage plots and into the surrounding countryside where they found conditions more to their liking. An observer claimed that the majority had left the plots within two days.

This example is by no means an isolated instance. In 1964 Dr J. F. Simmonds, Director of the Commonwealth Institute of Biological Control, visited the Pacific and in the report of his visit stated: 'Whilst I was in New Guinea an attempt was being made on "general grounds" to introduce the toad *Bufo marinus* into Popondetta from elsewhere in New Guinea, since it was said that they virtually would jump to seize army worms dropping from foliage prior to pupation. However, it would seem logical before such an introduction was made to undertake a study of exactly what the toads were feeding on in other parts of New Guinea, since they may, under certain conditions, eliminate more of the natural enemies (predators, parasitized and diseased larvae) than of the pest itself. Moreover they do certainly represent a hazard to dogs which may be poisoned if they attack *Bufo*'.

Dr Simmonds' misgivings were shared by entomologists, but local plantation owners were under no obligation to accept the advice being offered to them. It would appear that they reasoned that anything was worth trying, and so they undertook the collection of toads at Lae and then released them at three sites. The toads failed to make any impression on the severity of the army worm infestations, but *Bufo marinus* is now well established at Popondetta.

Cane farmers would be hardly likely to regard the introduction of *B. marinus* into Australia as a failure. The presence of anything that can and does eat pests of cane will be welcomed by them. However the toad did not remain in the cane-growing district but extended far south, eventually reaching northern New South Wales. Any judgment of the merit of the introduction obviously has to reach beyond the opinion of the industry initially involved. However it has undoubtedly been of tremendous value in

Australia in a way not envisaged by those responsible for the importation. In fact it may well be that the principal benefit of its presence in Australia has been as an experimental animal for use in secondary schools, universities and in a wide variety of fields of medical science.

The toad is regarded as an ideal laboratory animal. It is amenable to being handled, has minimal food requirements in captivity and so is an economical proposition, does not require expensive accommodation and is readily available.

Toad collecting is now a very big business. It started around 1950 when universities in the southern States found that they simply were unable to catch enough local frogs, of adequate size, suitable for teaching and experimental purposes. Toad collecting became a part-time occupation for a few enterprising Queenslanders, and the orders increased as the student intake at universities and schools steadily rose.

In the early 1960's the Apex Clubs at Ingham, Cairns and Innisfail realized that the sale of toads would provide a unique fund-raising source for their various charitable ventures. The Ingham group operated in a most business-like fashion and soon built up a reputation as an efficient supply service. In 1962 they sold 1,300 toads, but by 1969 sales topped 11,600 and total sales had involved the air freighting of 65,000 toads. The revenue from these sales and Australian and State Government subsidies enabled a home for elderly citizens to be built and fully equipped. It is too tempting to avoid calling the residence 'Toad Hall'.

During the initial stages of toad collection many were sent to clinical laboratories for use in a diagnostic pregnancy test. Within recent years this method has been replaced by simpler and more rapid tests developed by drug companies, and toads are no longer used for this purpose. However the vast increase in the number of high schools teaching biology, and the establishment of many new universities and colleges of advanced education, means that the toads are still in very great demand. I would estimate that about 100,000 toads are now used in Australia each year for teaching and experimental purposes. Bearing in mind that toads are now being exported even to France and to New Zealand, it is clear that toad collecting is a substantial business enterprise.

Without the presence of *B. marinus* in Australia it is certain that some aspects of teaching and scientific research in this country would have been curtailed. It is this, the fringe benefit of the introduction, that has to be taken into account in deciding whether the presence of this species is the disaster that some people maintain.

The impact of *B. marinus* upon the environment and particularly its influence on other animals is difficult to assess. At the time of the introduction the rich frog fauna of Queensland was very poorly known (only two-thirds of those species now known to occur in Queensland had been discovered). There is no proof that competition or predation eliminated or even reduced the populations of frogs from any area. Despite this, the initial claims that the toad does not eat frogs were quite wrong. Dexter's (1932) inability to find frogs in the diet of Puerto Rican toads after the toads had rampaged around for ten years eating everything that they could find, could well mean that very few native frogs were left in the area. My experiences are that *B. marinus* does eat native frogs, but it is possible to witness this happening only near the fringes of the distribution of the toads.

What complicates the issue is the fact that the toads abound in the cleared areas created by man, and the main feature inhibiting their dispersal is dense vegetation. Gardens, paths, roads etc. provide the toads with a perfect hunting ground. At night it is a common sight to see a couple of dozen toads congregating in a broad circle around the base of lamp-posts, patiently waiting for flying insects attracted to the light to fall to the ground. There simply are no native species of frogs that behave similarly. In fact there seems to be a parallel with the introduced common house sparrow which may not have displaced native birds from towns, but is simply one of the few birds capable of living in such close proximity to man. This argument may not be upheld in the outskirts of the suburbs. The sheer dominance of the numbers of toads and their voracious feeding habits undoubtedly poses a threat to the more timid native frog species.

Sifting fact from fallacy in the numerous reports of the effect of the toad on man and other animals is extremely difficult. There are well-authenticated reports of cats, dogs and pigs dying after eating toads, and to attempt to minimize the likely frequency of these events does little to placate the owners. The oval-shaped parotoid glands situated on the toads' shoulders (Fig. 12) do contain sufficient toxic substances to kill most animals that eat a toad, including some species of snakes. The primary function of these toxins is certainly to deter an animal from devouring toads, for under duress the toad can squirt the creamy yellow secretions out through many tiny pores in a spray for a distance of about one metre. If these secretions come into contact with the eyes I can personally testify that they cause pain and local irritation. Dogs that hold a toad in their mouths experience great distress, and owners of pets may rightly express indignation about the presence of a hazard that would not have existed in Australia if *B. marinus* had not been introduced.

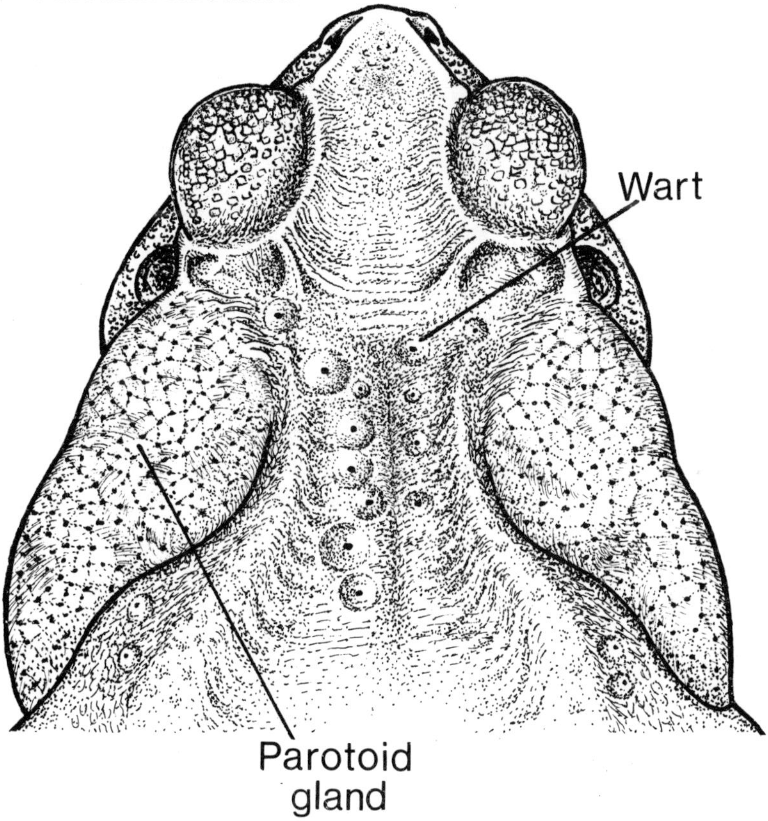

FIG. 12 Parotoid glands on the back of the head of the cane toad.

The effects of toads on poultry was investigated by J. H. Buzacott. He demonstrated that poultry seem to be immune to the toxins because a fowl that had eaten 142 young toads did not exhibit any apparent harmful effects.

Contrary to popular opinion, there is no danger to man from simply handling toads. Human fatalities in the Philippines and in Fiji occurred following consumption of them by people who habitually ate frogs and were not adequately forewarned of the dangers of eating *B. marinus*. Quite recently two members of a Peruvian peasant family died just from eating a soup prepared from toad eggs.

As the geographic range of *B. marinus* continues to extend from the many sites of introduction (with and without the willing assistance of man), our main concern should be just what the effects on the native fauna are likely to be. The breeding potential is such that it is likely to displace or at least diminish some of the populations of the native species with which it comes into contact. Just how far it is likely to extend geographically is uncertain. As early as 1936 Mungomery predicted that the range 'could probably extend far into New South Wales coastal districts, until continued severe frosts and cold weather become limiting factors.' The presence of *B. marinus* in New South Wales is now a fact and the range in Queensland is extending further west. From the Natural History Museum at Vienna in Austria I received a toad collected at Mt Isa in 1963, with the cryptic note that they were unaware that toads had been recorded there. It proved to be the first record of that species so far west.

I would anticipate that *B. marinus* will slowly and progressively increase its geographic range in Queensland, but the real danger lies in toads entering the high rainfall areas of the Northern Territory and northern Western Australia.

In June 1974 twenty toads imported into Darwin for dissection at a high School escaped in an outer suburb. In the following months there was a similar mishap at Perth Airport when fifty escaped from a smashed crate. Intensive searches led to the recovery of all but one of the toads but at considerable cost. These well-publicized events were followed by the introduction or tightening of legislation controlling their importation into the Northern Territory, Western Australia and Victoria. South

Australia introduced legislation a few months previously.

Those who feel that the toad is unlikely to be able to survive in low rainfall areas should note the studies of Warburg (1965), who found that the rate of water loss through the skin was no greater than in any of the native species adapted to arid conditions. Ormsby (1957) predicted that this would prove to be the case, and considered that there was no reason why *Bufo marinus* should not become established in and around Sydney where he considered conditions are quite suitable.

A possible method of reducing the 'nuisance' of large numbers in at least some of the townships might well be achieved by a cleanup programme. The point is that the toads are unable to withstand prolonged direct sunlight. Hence they tend to hide beneath fallen banana fronds, large leaves and other piles of vegetation on the ground. Crates and general junk stored beneath houses provide the sort of places that enables them to live close to human habitation. If as much of this material as possible could be removed, the toads would be forced to live further from homes.

As yet there are very few natural predators of toads, and those that do feed on them are either far from abundant or not particularly desirable. Several of the creatures observed feeding upon toads have been reported by members of the North Queensland Naturalists' Club. Cassels and St Cloud (1966) reported two instances of finding partly disembowelled toads near water, and believe the predator to be the white-tailed water rat. In 1967 Adams found the remains of toads eaten by the common rat, whilst Cassels (1970) observed a bird called the koel feeding on the toad.

Perhaps the most extraordinary predator of all is the aquatic, insectivorous bladderwort plant (*Utricularia* species) which normally feeds upon water fleas and minute insect larvae. The bladders are triggered by small sensory hairs which, when touched by small creatures, cause the bladder to open rapidly and suck in the prey. Mungomery (1936) observed that small *B. marinus* tadpoles suffered this fate, particularly in watercourses when the water level was low and the tadpoles had to swim through dense mats of *Utricularia*.

Fishes and turtles are suspected to eat *Bufo marinus* tadpoles but I know of no confirmation of these suspicions, and the list of known predators in Australia is a short one. In Hawaii Baldwin, Schwartz and Schwartz (1952) quoted observations demonstrating that the introduced mongoose ate toads. In fact five captive mongooses which ate twenty were said to be 'alive, saucy, active and in excellent health' following their meal. The only known occurrence of fatality of toads in epidemic proportions also occurred in Hawaii. In the Botanical Gardens there toads gobbled up petals falling from trees, probably in mistake for food. Unfortunately for them the trees were examples of *Strychnos nuxvomica*, better known as the strychnine tree. The toads died in convulsions and analysis of the petals showed that they contained 1.023 per cent of pure strychnine (Arnold 1944).

In 1966 I visited New Britain to study the native frog fauna, and I was asked by the Department of Agriculture Stock and Fisheries to undertake a brief survey of the impact of *Bufo marinus* there. One of the interesting findings that came out of that study was the fact that in the centres of the populations toads were exceptionally emaciated. In fact many died each day from starvation. In the space of thirty years at Kerevat, near Rabaul, ground-dwelling insects have become so scarce that there are just not enough to provide food for all of the toads that live there. Such is the scarcity of food that the Principal Entomologist reported that toads were even eating the introduced snail, *Achatina fulica*. The shells must be fairly indigestible because large shells have been known to puncture car tyres.

At night the emaciated toads at Kerevat wandered far out on the lawns and roads and, as dawn approached, they were simply too weak to reach shade and so died in the early morning sun. I brought some of these emaciated toads back to Adelaide for examination. Dissection showed that their muscles had wasted away to such an extent that they were scarcely more than living skin and bone. Such animals were so common around Kerevat that the local people have an appropriate pidgin English expression for them, 'bone nothing'. Certainly little more remained.

The sort of situation that exists at Kerevat can only result in a serious depletion of certain components of the insect fauna. It raises the hope that other populations in Australia and elsewhere will eventually reach a more tolerable equilibrium. Professor Brongersma (1958) has predicted that *B. marinus* will greatly harm the New Guinea fauna, and has urged that attempts be made to destroy it.

I hope that the available evidence will be interpreted in such a way that, at least in Australia, total destruction of *Bufo marinus* will be considered unwarranted, because of the indirect benefits it is providing. Nevertheless ways must be found of inhibiting its dispersal into new areas, and of reducing population densities in the areas where it occurs already.

7 Reproduction

FROGS VARY IN just about every detail of their reproductive behaviour and the subsequent pattern of development of the young. It isn't just a question of species choosing to be different for the sake of it. Rather the variation is a mirror of the environmental difficulties that have been overcome, and demonstrates a wide variety of success stories.

One of the most widespread of the species likely to be collected in the ponds of southeastern Australia is the tree frog *Litoria ewingi*. A substantial fall of rain in the late summer or early autumn induces the male frogs to call in what can become a deafening chorus. Surprisingly enough the females are attracted to the ponds by this noise, and upon their arrival they are suddenly grasped by the males in a characteristic clasp around the armpits. In this, the axillary embrace, the fortunate male effortlessly rides pick-a-back. To maintain his grasp the male is equipped with special holders located on the inner surfaces of each thumb and termed nuptial pads. The pads are brown or black, and so easy to see that a glimpse at a frog's thumb helps to tell whether it is a male or a female. Nuptial pads vary in shape and structure from species to species; a range of them is shown in Figure 13.

Carrying the male on her back, the female swims out into the water and lays her eggs whilst grasping an aquatic plant or perhaps the downturned tip of a reed. As the eggs leave her body, so the male sheds his sperm upon them. It sound a most primitive method of fertilization with the odds heavily weighted against success. The only test is to have a look at clumps of spawn to see how many eggs have failed to commence development. As it happens, unfertilized eggs seem to be exceptional, so this technique of fertilization is evidently very good.

The emerging eggs are coated with a material which swells up on contact with water to form the jelly-like mass. The jelly

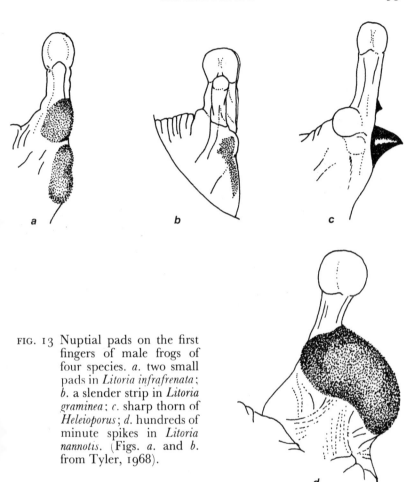

FIG. 13 Nuptial pads on the first fingers of male frogs of four species. *a*. two small pads in *Litoria infrafrenata*; *b*. a slender strip in *Litoria graminea*; *c*. sharp thorn of *Heleioporus*; *d*. hundreds of minute spikes in *Litoria nannotis*. (Figs. *a*. and *b*. from Tyler, 1968).

surrounds the egg in a series of complex layers so that each egg and its jelly are separate units. The female lays a short string of these jelly-coated eggs around a submerged plant stem, then moves on to lay more elsewhere. The life in water of delicate, soft balls of jelly is extremely limited. Particles of mud carried in the water stick to the spawn, and the clump of spawn is about to disintegrate from wear and tear by the time the young tadpoles are ready to emerge.

In the early period of their life outside the egg capsules the tadpoles are not able to fend for themselves. They can swim only with difficulty, arching their bodies and tails from side to side. The first few days seem to be an apprenticeship for the rigours of life ahead, and it is only after this initiation that they appear at ease in water.

The tadpoles spend their lives feeding, and their rate of growth is really rapid. The first hint of their terrestrial destiny is shown by the development of a little knob lying against the tail at the end of the body. This is the hind limb bud, and from it the entire limb grows.

The front legs develop in partnership with the back ones, but the front ones are hidden from view. It is only in the final stages of limb development, when the front legs press against the skin hiding them from view that there is any indication at all that they exist. At the completion of their development the limbs bulge against the body wall, spoiling the otherwise perfect symmetry of the rounded body. When the tadpole decides to bring its front legs into use it thrusts one through the spiracle or aperture from the gills, and the other through a specially weakened area of skin on the opposite side of the body.

Rapidly the tadpole shrinks in size: the tail is absorbed into the body. The head and body become smaller as the soft tissues collapse and tighten around the bones beneath (Fig. 14).

Amongst the more unusual forms that spawn can take is that of the marsh frogs or *Limnodynastes* species so well known to naturalists. It forms vast, white, foamy blobs on the surface of the water, and it may be necessary to look closely to be convinced that there has not been a disastrous discharge from a detergent factory (Pl. 8). In the breeding season the females of the *Limnodynastes* species develop special structures needed to enable them to produce this well-known but, in world terms, bizarre spawn. From the edges of their fingers the females develop broad flanges which increase the surface area of each finger (and therefore of the hand as a whole) and produce a paddle-like effect.

These special flanges are of use to the frog only during the actual process of laying of the spawn. The male grasps the female around the lower waist (an inguinal embrace) so that the female has both arms and hands quite free. She is therefore able to paddle the

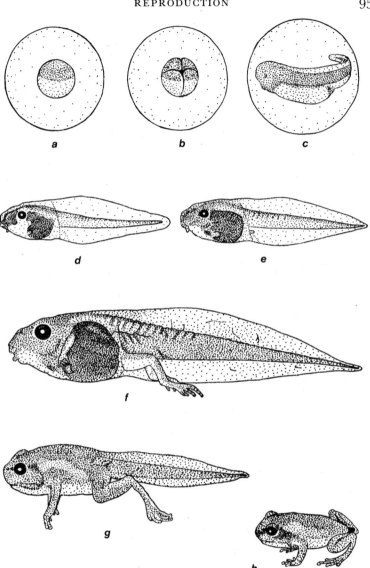

FIG. 14 Development of the tree frog *Litoria verreauxi*. The eggs are drawn on a slightly larger scale than the tadpoles, and the juvenile on a small scale.

water in front of her. This paddling directs a current of water and trapped air bubbles backwards beneath the emerging eggs and, as a result the jelly surrounding the eggs is gradually whipped up into a buoyant foam (Pl. 12).

Even the most casual observer will spot that the bulky, black *Limnodynastes* tadpoles are different from the pale, slender, and much more lively *Litoria ewingi* tadpoles. Where tadpoles differ most conspicuously is in the structure of their mouthparts, features that can only be observed properly with a good hand lens or else a microscope. Figure 15 shows a variety of tadpole mouthparts, including some with several rows of teeth and others with none at all. However, it is in the early stages of development that frogs differ from one another to the greatest extent.

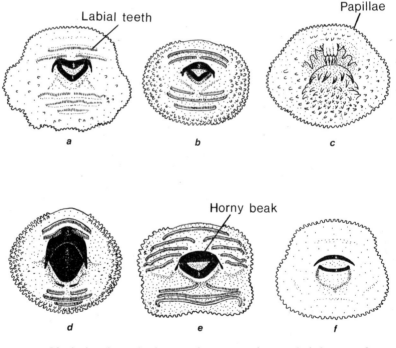

FIG. 15 Variation in tadpole mouthparts: *a, b, c* and *d* the tree frogs *Litoria citropa, L. verreauxi, L. glandulosa* and *L. peroni* respectively; *e. Heleioporus australiacus*; *f. Taudactylus diurnus.*

Adult frog

9 THE GREAT BARRED FROG AND ITS SPAWN

Portion of spawn clump

An artificial lake in the highlands

Rainforest at 2500 metr
where tree frogs abound

There are many frogs whose life-cycles seem to be designed to delay the emergence of their young from the eggs, so shortening the span of life spent in the tadpole stage. The most abundant of the examples that have taken a step in this direction are some of the *Pseudophryne* toadlets.

What the toadlets do is to lay their eggs on land which may be moist for only a short time. In the Mount Lofty Ranges, near Adelaide, there is a place where each year *Pseudophryne bibroni* lay them in depressions made by horses' hooves. The sites of fourteen clumps of eggs are marked in Plate 7. The first of the spring rains provides the stimulus to mate and deposit eggs; usually there is moisture enough to allow the eggs to develop until each egg contains a tadpole that is ready to emerge. There may be quite a delay before there is another deluge heavy enough to release the tadpoles from the outer envelope of the capsule. In the meantime the adult frogs often remain with the eggs in the depressions as though concerned lest any misfortune should befall them.

When there are heavy rains the ground becomes flooded and the tadpoles leave their egg capsules and are washed into a pool or pond where they finish their development in the normal way.

There are very many species which have completely eliminated the free-swimming tadpole stage. Such a habit is practised by all of the microhylids and probably all of the New Guinea ranids except *Rana* species, and for them the 'tadpole' stage is spent entirely within the egg capsule. The capsules of most microhylid frogs are firm and round, much like those of the *Pseudophryne* species. The most obvious difference is that most microhylids have each capsule connected to the next by a transparent cord, so that each clump resembles a string of beads. As yet we know very little about the development of microhylids, and there is not a single published account of a complete life-history. It is unfortunately necessary to try to reconstruct the process of development from a few field observations and limited preserved material.

Developing microhylids never really resemble free-living tadpoles. For example the arms as well as the legs develop externally, and the appearance of the embryo is always dominated by a vast abdomen of yolk (Fig. 16). Most species of microhylids do possess a tail, although on first consideration there would appear no need for such an organ.

FIG. 16 Embryo of a microhylid taken from its capsule.

Microhylid embryos lie passively on their backs resembling a row of babies in adjacent cribs. It is absolutely fascinating to watch them through a microscope. A couple of taps of the microscope base heightens the similarity to babies; they become aroused quite rapidly from their passive state and they all wave their arms and legs about as though awakening from sleep.

To withstand the kicking of the embryos the outer capsule has to be durable, pliable and strong, and these characteristics raise the question of just how the juvenile frogs escape at the end of development. In the case of *Cophixalus darlingtoni* I was once fortunate enough to watch the process, having been attracted to extreme activity within capsules that I had collected a few days previously. With abrupt and rapid movements they fully extended their arms and legs to stretch the capsule wall as far as they could. One split the capsule with its arms and then, by extending its feet, forced its body through the hole and escaped within ten minutes. Another split the capsule with its feet and experienced much greater difficulty, spending an hour emerging backwards.

The capsule of some of the largest frogs in the Australian Region (the ranid *Discodeles* species of the Solomon Islands) is enormous (Pl. 12) very tough, and presents an obstacle that cannot be overcome by kicking alone. As an escape-kit the young frog is equipped with a spike on the tip of its snout, enabling it to pierce its capsule in much the same way that some reptiles perforate their shell.

Judging from the viewpoint of our own standards of practice we may regard frogs as very poor parents. The idea of just depositing eggs and leaving them quite defenceless to fend for themselves and to survive or perish, appears the height of neglect. That many frogs can do this and yet see the perpetuation of their species is at least partly due to the production of such a large number of eggs that a few will survive to reach maturity. However, ignoring the ethics of this general habit, there remain a few species which lay very few eggs and do in fact play an extremely active role in assisting or even ensuring the survival of their young.

None of the examples of parental care exhibited by Australian and New Guinea frogs are sufficiently well known to have been included in any of the textbooks on animal biology. Parental care, by definition, implies care by one or both of the parents to assist the survival of the offspring. To some extent all frogs do this in placing spawn in a situation where there is a reasonable chance of survival. However we tend to look for something more, and particularly of activity by the parents after the eggs have been laid. Perhaps the simplest form of parental care, in terms of behaviour, is the appropriately named midwife toad of Europe (*Alytes obstetricans*), in which the male carries the strings of fertilized eggs entwined around his groin and hind legs until he finds a suitable pond in which to lay them. The arrow poison frogs of Central and South America progress a stage further in that the males carry tadpoles upon their backs.

The above examples are quite mundane in comparison with the parental care of some of the tree frogs of South America. Four genera there carry eggs on their backs, or within pouches on their backs. *Pipa* carries its young in deep pits in the skin and other soft tissues of the back, but perhaps the most bizarre example of all is the famous *Rhinoderma darwini* of Chile, named after Charles Darwin, where the male frog uses his tongue to introduce tadpoles into his mouth. These then pass through the vocal sac apertures into his extremely large vocal pouch. The tadpoles remain inside his vocal pouch until they have transformed into juvenile frogs.

The frog fauna of Australia, New Guinea and the adjacent islands has been so sadly neglected, that it is only within the last decade that examples of parental care have been reported in scientific journals. In fact the most extraordinary example of parental care in the world was discovered here only in 1973.

The first detailed report of parental care from Australia and New Guinea involved the microhylid frog (*Sphenophryne brevicrus*) sitting upon clumps of eggs in small hollows excavated beneath rotting vegetation. Subsequent observations by numerous herpetologists lead us to believe that most microhylid species behave similarly. The frogs all lay so few eggs that it is possible for each egg to be in contact with a portion of the skin of the adult.

It has been suggested that the role of the parent frog is to perform a defensive function. It has been thought that the adults are there to protect the eggs from marauders that may eat them. Certainly there is no possibility that the adults could provide warmth to incubate the eggs, and the presence of the adult has to be explained in some other way. I favour a different explanation because I have tried to rear microhylid eggs which have been removed from the care of the adults. The attempts always proved unsuccessful because the eggs rapidly became covered with fungal growths and then perished. To the best of my knowledge fungal growths have never been found on eggs beneath frogs, and the implication is that in some way the frogs prevent the fungi from gaining a hold. Observations on some North American salamanders seem highly relevant to this issue because it has been demonstrated that a salamander that 'sits' upon its eggs in much the same way has antibacterial and antifungal substances in its skin. Comparable studies have yet to be undertaken on Australian frogs and, until they are, my explanation of the function of the 'brooding' habit of microhylids must be regarded to be uncertain.

Cogger (1964) reported the first example of transport of young by a local adult frog. In the high mountains of New Guinea he found *Cophixalus pansus*, and provides just a tantalizingly brief glimpse of what must be an extraordinary habit: 'This frog, which is a member of the family Microhylidae, lays a number of large eggs joined together by a string of mucus; they are laid on land, and are tended by the female until they hatch, not as tadpoles, but as fully formed frogs; and for a short time they are carried about on the back of the parent'.

Assa darlingtoni (Pl. 11) lives beneath rocks and rotting wood on the border of Queensland and New South Wales and provides a more specialized form of parental care. I. R. Straughan and

A. R. Main discovered that males have pockets in the groin in which the developing tadpoles are carried (Fig. 17). They found that the females lay on an average about ten large eggs, up to 2.6 mm in diameter. Within the pockets of the males they found similar numbers of tadpoles. The male frogs, which reached 20 mm in body length carried young each of which was as long as 11 mm.

The pouches have to be very large to hold the young and they increase in size to such an extent that they extend for the entire length of the body. As a result the stomach and other vital organs are compressed so much that it probably becomes impossible for the adult frog to feed.

Glen Ingram of Brisbane has recently been lucky enough to witness the most vital event in the biology of *A. darlingtoni* – just how the tadpoles manage to get into the pouches. He found that the male enters the spawn mass and moves around until it is virtually enveloped in the middle of it. The tadpoles within the spawn clump move over the father's back until they locate the aperture to a sac. They then force their way inside, using their heads to push open the aperture in the skin.

Queensland provides another and certainly the oddest example of parental care. In streams not far from Brisbane there lives a rather unusual aquatic frog: *Rheobatrachus silus*. The existence of

FIG. 17 A hip pouch of the male marsupial frog *Assa darlingtoni*.

this frog became known only very recently through the work of Liem (1973). In its appearance this frog is quite unlike any other to be found in Australia, and in fact it resembles the African clawed toad *Xenopus* fairly closely. It is up to about 50 mm in length, has very long and rather pointed fingers, short and strongly muscular limbs and paddle-like feet. It looks very drab, being a dark slate colour, and is not the sort of creature that most naturalists would give a second glance to. What makes *R. silus* so interesting is the fact that the female carries developing tadpoles and fully formed juveniles in her stomach for the duration of their development!

This extraordinary habit first came to light as a result of chance observations by Chris Corben of Brisbane. He was in the process of transferring a frog from one vivarium to another and, to make his task easier, started by removing the rocks beneath which the frog spent much of its time. He noticed that the frog seemed exceptionally distressed, swimming quite frantically around the tank. Quite suddenly it rose to the surface of the water, opened its mouth and ejected six live tadpoles. One of them is shown in Plate 20.

When the frog was in its new home it usually hung suspended in the water, in an almost upright position, with its nose and eyes just above the surface and its body vertical. The presence of more tadpoles in the stomach prevented the frog from floating as most do, for the extra weight had transferred the centre of gravity of the frog further backwards. When the frog drifted to the glass wall of the tank, movements in its abdomen could be seen quite clearly. As the frog became more and more bloated over the following three weeks, the shapes of the tadpoles still inside the stomach could be seen quite clearly against the taut skin.

Seventeen days after the emergence of the tadpoles a juvenile frog 12 mm long was found swimming in the vivarium (Pl. 20). The following day two more juveniles made their first appearance and, rather reluctantly, the decision was taken to preserve the frog with the object of retaining as many as possible of the young remaining inside the parent for later study. However, as soon as the adult was grasped by the hind legs it arched its body upwards, opened its mouth to its full extent and, with a great heave of its body muscles, threw out eight perfectly formed young frogs in the space of just two seconds. Five more frogs were ejected in the same fashion over the following few minutes.

These observations and detailed study of the tadpoles enable us to predict some of the details of the likely habits and behaviour involved in this form of reproduction. As shown in Plate 20 the tadpole is unusual in having such a pale abdomen. The abdomen is actually cream in colour, and there is no trace of the long intestines which characterize tadpoles that enjoy an independent life. In fact the intestines are only just in the process of formation, and the entire abdomen is virtually a giant food reserve of yolk. From the fact that there is still so much of this initial food source (provided when the egg is laid) we can confidently predict that the tadpole does not need to obtain other food and is actually incapable of feeding.

The female probably swallows the eggs shortly after they have been laid and fertilized. If any other frog did this the eggs would be broken down in the stomach and digested rapidly. Clearly there has been some means of stopping the secretion of acid and digestive enzymes in the stomach before the eggs are swallowed, and preventing secretions for the entire period that the young are carried there. In any case feeding has to stop or there would not be adequate room for the tadpoles as they increase in size.

The breeding seasons of frogs vary from species to species just as much as the patterns of development of tadpoles and the habits of the parents. At many localities where there is permanent water, tadpoles of one species or another can be found in almost every month of the year. At other localities bodies of water occur only after unpredictable heavy rains, and it requires a specialized approach by the adults and their offspring for development to be completed.

The attainment of the mature reproductive state when the female is gravid with eggs and the male possesses the highest number of mature spermatozoa is obviously not directly influenced by rainfall. However the adults may have to attain such a state of reproductive maturity that they become able to reproduce at very short notice, and for many of them heavy rains constitute this 'serving of notice'. There is also an advantage that there are differences between the onset of reproductive maturity between species. If all of the pond-breeders at any one locality reproduced simultaneously there would be a period of great competition for food amongst tadpoles, followed by a longer period in which the food resources in that pond were not being used at all.

Most species tend to breed only once each year so that there are possibly only one or two nights in any year when the eggs of that species are laid. There remain however a number of species which can and do breed in almost any month and they seem to achieve perpetuation on the basis that some at least of their progeny will survive.

Good examples of the 'try and try again' breeding policy are *Litoria ewingi* and *Limnodynastes tasmaniensis*. When male frogs call from ponds formed by summer rains they are not making any assessment of the future persistence of the ponds. Conditions are right for mating and spawning and, to the frogs that happen to be in the vicinity, this is all that concerns them. They cannot predict that the rains may again be replaced by a period of extreme heat. Thus the ponds rapidly evaporate and thousands of tadpoles developing from eggs laid in the transient wet period die. The next time there are heavy rains the performance can be repeated with equally catastrophic results until, as summer passes into autumn, the ponds cease to evaporate and the progeny survive to complete their development.

Where there are these very long periods of breeding activity there has been uncertainty about whether the same individual frogs lay eggs on different occasions each year. Some observations by Bruce Walpole of Adelaide show that some individual frogs are quite capable of breeding on numerous occasions in any year. In his garden he constructed a finely meshed enclosure containing an area of vegetation and a pond in which he placed just one female and two male *Limnodynastes tasmaniensis*. In twelve months that female laid spawn on more than twenty separate occasions, spaced out at intervals of approximately one clump per fortnight. There were additional occasions when mating resulted in the laying of nothing but masses of jelly lacking any eggs at all. No doubt she lacked mature eggs to lay but it did not inhibit her breeding behaviour. The situation was certainly an artificial one, but the fact remains that sexual maturity and sexual activity were maintained throughout the entire year by the same individuals.

8 Diet and Feeding Habits

UNTIL A NATURALIST actually begins to search for frogs, the only ones that he is likely to come across are those that are moving about in search of food, or advertising their presence more conspicuously by calling. Of all the activities of frogs the drive to obtain food to survive is undoubtedly the most important one.

Because most frogs are active only at night and are mostly rather timid animals, it is a very great problem to be able to watch them feeding naturally in the wild. In any case it is virtually impossible to be able to identify at a distance with any degree of accuracy the items of food that they are eating. As a result of these difficulties most of our knowledge of what frogs normally eat has been obtained from examination of the contents of the stomachs and intestines dissected from specimens that have been killed and preserved. Faecal pellets voided by frogs shortly after their capture have also been examined, in much the same way as the regurgitated pellets of owls, but these remains are only the indigestible portions of food items such as snail shells and insect legs; of the soft-bodied prey there is no trace at all.

Frogs do not chew their food, nor in fact in any way break it up into portions before swallowing. This is certainly fortunate for the zoologist in terms of making it simpler for him to identify food items recovered from stomachs, but to the frog it means that the gape of the mouth poses a severe limitation on what can or cannot be eaten. Obviously small frogs are simply unable to consume the range of prey that is available to large ones because they just cannot swallow some of the bigger items. It therefore seems logical to consider diet in terms of what frogs of a similar size eat, rather than compare species which would involve embracing both small, young frogs and large, old ones whose mouth-gapes may vary considerably.

In all small frogs insects predominate in both number and

volume in the diet. However, mites, snails, earthworms, spiders and other small animals are eaten. By far the most comprehensive studies of the diet of small Australian frogs are those of Main (1957) who examined the stomach contents of seven different species found in the southwest of Western Australia, and Pengilley (1971) who made an equally detailed study of five species inhabiting southeastern Australia.

The larger the frog, the more food it needs. It can do one of two things: eat a larger number of small items, or concentrate upon obtaining more substantial prey. Certainly some frogs seem perfectly content to devote much of their time to eating, as is well demonstrated by the Western Australian turtle frog *Myobatractus gouldi* and Holy Cross toad *Notaden nichollsi*. Calaby (1956, 1960) of the Commonwealth Scientific and Industrial Research Organisation has demonstrated that these two species eat enormous numbers of termites. In the stomachs of two specimens of the 'turtle frog', he counted 474 and 463 termites respectively, and in one specimen of the Holy Cross toad over 300.

Bearing in mind that in most natural history books frogs are described as insect-eaters, just what else they can and do eat is really extraordinary: scorpions, centipedes, lizards and baby birds. Even creatures as indigestible as land crabs are eaten by the giant *Discodeles* frogs of the Solomon Islands (Boulenger 1884) whilst *Litoria aurea* in New South Wales is known to eat small tiger snakes. Fleay (1935), who made this observation, illustrates his article with a photograph of two frogs eating the same snake, one consuming the head end and the other the tail. When they met in the middle . . . 'they meditated over the problem for an hour or two, until the more energetic of them made up its mind and wrested the prize from the other.'

Anyone who has kept frogs in captivity for even a short space of time will be well aware that it is absolutely essential to separate large ones from small ones, simply because cannibalism is so rife. This habit is an equally common occurrence in the natural state. There really is no concept of kinship, and if its neighbour is small enough to be eaten, a frog will quickly regard it as food.

As indicated by the range of diet, frogs feed upon land, but there are at least a few species quite capable of capturing food under water. Fish have been recovered from the stomach of several species in other parts of the world, and I have watched water-holding frogs feeding upon aquatic worms foolish enough to expose themselves on the floor of an aquarium.

Quite frequently, grass, seeds, petals and other vegetable matter have been found in frogs' stomachs. It has usually been assumed that this sort of material either was eaten accidentally with an insect or some other food item which happened to be resting on vegetation, or that it was snapped up in mistake for food. However, on some occasions, the quantity of vegetable matter recovered from a stomach has been so considerable that it has seemed highly unlikely that it could have been consumed unintentionally.

The idea of frogs or toads being able to obtain nourishment from plant material seemed beyond belief until 1966 when an American, Alexander, reported some remarkable observations that he had made. In his garden in Miami, Florida, there lived a colony of *Bufo marinus* (introduced into that part of North America as it has been into Australia), and he noted that each day the toads visited a mulch pile to eat a wide variety of household scraps dumped there. He observed them eating lettuce leaves, portions of avocado pears, broccoli, carrot peelings, corn-on-the-cob, peas and rice. He noted that the toads were also extremely partial to any canned meat left in his dog's bowl. In New Britain, cats and dogs commonly have difficulty in preventing toads from actually joining them to share their evening meals. I have watched dogs eating frantically whilst holding their bowls with one front paw and pushing away toads with the other.

Bufo marinus is an unusual species, not primarily because of what it eats, but in the much more basic phenomenon that it recognizes as food, material which does not move. Throughout the world there are very few frogs or toads that will show the slightest interest in an object that is motionless. In fact experiments have been carried out in which frogs have died of starvation although surrounded by freshly killed insect food. The behaviour of *B. marinus* cannot be regarded to be evidence of possession of a higher intelligence, because they respond in exactly the same way as any other species will to a small moving object appearing within their range of vision. Thus they snap up smouldering cigarette stubs and stones thrown in front of them, and have even been known to attempt to capture and eat bouncing table-tennis balls.

Although the process of capturing food can be a virtually automatic response to sudden movement, the arrival of food in this way is quite fortuitous, and most animals need to travel far and wide and forage for their prey. Sometimes their sense of sight may be wholly involved in finding food but the sense of smell and hearing may play a more major role at other times. For example, it seems unlikely that sight would assist burrowing turtle frogs to locate subterranean termite galleries, or be of much use in capturing termites in total darkness.

Most frogs capture small prey with their tongues which they flick out and return to their mouths in just a fraction of a second. To follow just how the frog manages to perform this feat requires an understanding of the structure and position of the tongue, and particularly the position it occupies on the floor of the mouth.

In man the tongue is an extremely sensitive and mobile organ. We bring it forward to the centre of our lips when cautiously tasting, because it helps us to establish whether what we are about to eat or drink is palatable. We use the tongue to remove food particles from the teeth, gum margins and lips and to moisten the delicate outer lining of the lips. The tongue also plays a major role in speech. The functions that it performs are almost entirely carried out within the mouth and there is really no strictly functional role in protruding it other than as a rather crude expression of contempt.

In terms of the area of the floor of the mouth that a man's tongue occupies, it is proportionately about the same size as a frog's. Where the tongues differ is mainly in the way in which they are attached to the floor of the mouth and in their ability to stretch. Whereas in man the attachment is at the back, and the free portion of the tongue lies forward, the frog's tongue is attached at the front and the free portion lies backward (Fig. 18). Because of the difference in the position of attachment, the frog's tongue can be protruded out of the mouth for considerable distances, whereas the ultimate achievement in man is the ability of a few gifted individuals to touch the tip of the nose.

The progressive sequence in the movement of the frog's tongue that takes place during the capture of an insect is shown in Fig. 18. The procedure is little more than a rotating action, in which the tongue passes through an arc of 180°. It results in the top of the tongue firmly striking the prey and, because its entire upper surface is coated with a sticky secretion, the tongue acts rather like an old-fashioned fly-paper. A disadvantage is that the tongue may pick up small specks of dirt and other rubbish at the same time as the prey and, because there is no means of getting rid of the unwanted material, the whole lot has to be swallowed after the tongue has been withdrawn into the mouth.

Watching a captive frog feed it will be noticed that immediately after the tongue has been returned to the mouth and the jaws

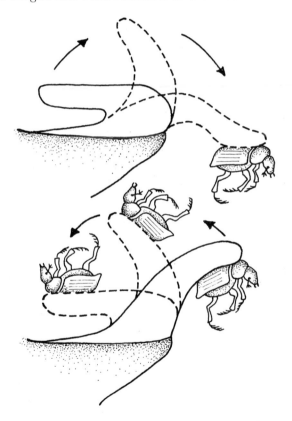

FIG. 18 The sequence of movements of the tongue during feeding. *Upper,* outward movement to capture a beetle; *lower,* reverse movement transferring beetle into mouth.

closed, the eyes frequently descend downwards and so disappear from view. Sometimes they will rise momentarily and then again descend. Exactly why the eyes should bob up and down in this way is uncertain, but it is my opinion that they assist in transferring the food item backwards towards the pharynx prior to swallowing.

The eyes of the frog are not located in a completely bony socket. There is only a thin but tough membrane separating the eyes from the roof of the mouth, and examination will show that they actually protrude into the mouth cavity and can be detected as two large bulges (Fig. 19). One of the striking features of the majority of species of frogs is the way in which the eyes are so prominent, and there are obviously situations when the ability to lower them is virtually essential to avoid injury.

When there is food actually in the mouth and the eyes are in the depressed position the under-surface of each eye is likely to come

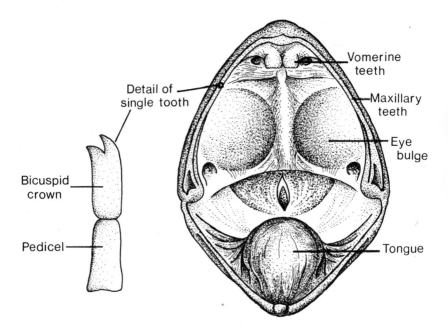

FIG. 19 Inside the mouth.

into contact with the tongue. There is no risk of the eye being damaged because its outer layer is very hard and unresilient, and the eyes could at least partially crush soft-bodied prey lying on the surface of the tongue. By then pushing the tongue forwards against the eyes the prey would be slid backwards to the very back portion of the mouth, and so to a position where it can be swallowed.

A few frogs do not use tongues in the process of capturing their prey. In Africa and South America there are frogs completely lacking tongues altogether, and this group of frogs is given the special name 'Aglossa' (tongueless) to describe this curious state. The Queensland leptodactylid *Rheobatrachus silus* is scarcely better off because its tongue is very thin and completely fused to the floor of the mouth, and so cannot be flicked out. Many other Australian leptodactylids and a few hylids too have tongues almost completely fused to the floor of the mouth. *Litoria aurea* is a good example and, being fairly large, is easy to watch in captivity. An individual in one of my vivaria demonstrates their technique of engulfing prey when I waggle my little finger a short distance from its nose. It leaps forward and grabs the finger in its jaws, usually fastening them at the end of the first joint. It then places both hands further back on the finger, lifts its feet off the ground on to my palm and tugs away with all its might. When it discovers that the end segment of my finger is quite firmly attached and simply will not come off, the frog releases its hold.

When food is captured with the tongue, withdrawn entirely into the mouth and subsequently swallowed, the teeth obviously play no part in the feeding process. In fact not all frogs possess teeth and it is tempting to suggest that their presence in some genera is a superfluous and entirely unnecessary feature. When frogs have any teeth at all they are confined to an upper set which surround the entire margins of the upper jaw. There are usually at least 100 teeth altogether and they are all similar in shape and size. Frog teeth are like those of other amphibians in their rather peculiar structure. They are said to be pedicellate because the crown sits upon a tall, stalk-like root termed a pedicel (Fig. 19). The crown is also unusual in having a forked (bicuspid) tip of two rather sharp prongs. Salamanders, newts and other amphibians have the same type of tooth structure and it is partly for this reason that all amphibians are assumed to have evolved from a common ancestor.

All of the Australian hylids and ranids possess teeth, but some leptodactylids and microhylids lack them. Some genera include species that possess teeth and others that lack them, but it does not appear to influence diet.

Although the lower jaw does not possess true teeth, there are a few frogs throughout the world that have developed 'tusks' (pseudoteeth but hardly 'false' teeth). Two examples are to be found only in New Guinea but there is also the well-known tusked frog of New South Wales, which has a pair of extremely prominent tusks fitting into special pits in the roof of the palate above them (Fig. 20). As yet the function of these tusks is unknown and the most unusual feature is that the male has very much longer and sharper tusks than female.

Pseudoteeth are more commonly found on the bony palate, in particular upon the vomerine bones which partly surround the internal nostrils. As a result they are called 'vomerine teeth'. They may consist of just a few rounded and weakly developed protuberances, but more often are a row of about ten sharply pointed spikes on the tip of raised portions of the vomerine bones.

FIG. 20 Male tusked frog *Adelotus brevis*. Females have shorter tusks.

Bullfrogs mating prior to laying spawn

11 CONFORMISTS AND NON-CONFORMISTS

A male marsupial frog which carries the young

Separate eggs and newly hatched young of *Discodeles* of Solomon Islands.
Scale in inches

Frothy spawn clump of Peron's marsh frog *Limnodynastes peroni*

Invariably the vomerine teeth lie very close to the internal openings of the nostrils (choanae). Vomerine teeth are very well developed in the various species of *Limnodynastes*, forming an exceptionally elongate row that may almost bridge the palate. In the obese *Xenobatrachus* of New Guinea the vomerine bones bear a pair of extremely long and very sharp spines termed odontoids, one behind each choana. Many frogs, especially smaller species, have no vomerine teeth at all.

It seems highly unlikely that vomerine teeth can be involved in killing prey. After a substantial meal the stomach of a frog can be seen to bulge and press against the body wall, indicating that the prey is still alive when it enters the stomach. The prey is probably killed only by the action of acid and enzymes in the stomach or perhaps through suffocation there. The role of the vomerine teeth may be to perforate the body of the prey by spiking it, so releasing some of its contents and assisting the taste buds to function.

'Palatability' is defined as something being agreeable or pleasant to taste, and any animal that chews its food thoroughly has plenty of time to decide whether it finds that food pleasant or not.

Frogs are perhaps less cautious in their initial selection than we are, and need a rapidly effective tasting procedure. Without it frogs could readily swallow material of a toxic or otherwise potentially harmful nature.

Vomerine teeth could be of extreme importance in assisting tasting because they are positioned so close to the ducts of glands which secrete amylase and protease enzymes (intermaxillary glands). Because food is retained in the mouth for such a short period there is simply insufficient time for much digestive breakdown of food to occur there, and it has been suggested by Francis and Eisa (1951) that the primary role of these enzymes is to enhance the liberation from food of material to which the tastebuds will respond.

The secretions of the glands on the palate can be carried from the openings of the gland ducts to the vomerine teeth, and from there to the taste buds on the palate. This mechanism involves the action of countless millions of microscopic hair-like structures called cilia which cover the entire surface of the palate. They also line the floor of the mouth on each side of the tongue. The action of the cilia is co-ordinated into a series of undulating waves, much like the movement of waves approaching the seashore, and upon their crests they constantly sweep a dense film of sticky mucus, secreted from cells at their base, backwards to the oesophagus.

At some point in this movement towards the oesophagus there is a very good chance that the food material will cross a taste bud which will perform a monitoring role to establish whether it is palatable or unpalatable. Thus, at this juncture, passage towards the oesophagus will be allowed to continue, or the frog will sense an error and attempt to get rid of the object. Many frogs simply open their mouths and allow the prey to escape of its own volition if it is still capable of doing so. Others will remove the prey by protruding the tongue or, rarely, by scraping it off with a hand. Once the prey has been swallowed, dietary indiscretions are far more difficult to remedy; the stomach has to be compressed and the abdominal muscles brought into play to expel the stomach contents. However the large *Cyclorana australis* is a species that can empty its stomach very rapidly in this way.

Tasting, the function of special enzymes and the role of the cilia interact together to provide a sort of quality control in diet, but there also must be some method of controlling the quantity of food intake. In the course of a substantial meal we become in-increasingly, and perhaps reluctantly, aware that contrary to our wishes the stomach can accept food only up to a certain limit. We recognize a sense of distension and possibly slight discomfort. This awareness results from the presence of a highly specialized sensory mechanism in the form of extremely sensitive stretch receptors within the muscular wall of the stomach. These receptors monitor the extent of distension of the stomach, and send impulses to the brain. By this means a mammal is made aware of what is termed the state of satiation, so that it voluntarily reduces intake according to the extent of distension of the stomach. Ultimately it stops eating.

Although no one has yet undertaken the elaborate experiments that would be needed to confirm that there are stretch receptors in the stomachs of frogs, there are other observations showing it is highly likely that they exist. Heatwole and Heatwole (1968), working on an American toad found that the size of the food items eaten by individuals was directly related to the amount of food already eaten. Thus, whilst they ate a meal of insects offered to them, they progressively selected items of smaller size, so indicating that they were aware of just how much they had already eaten. However, the vast quantities of food sometimes found in stomachs would indicate that frogs, like man, may on occasions, choose to ignore the warning signals received.

The ability of frogs to discriminate between items of food which are palatable, or at least harmless, and those which are unpalatable and perhaps potentially harmful, is of considerable interest. The reason is that it provides one of the few avenues open to us to demonstrate the ability of frogs to learn by means of their personal experience. A vast number of different factors is involved in establishing whether an animal is really selective, implying that it favours certain kinds of food and ignores and possibly genuinely avoids others. For example, from season to season there is variation in the presence, abundance, and therefore availability, of particular kinds of prey. The predominance of one kind of prey in the stomachs does not necessarily prove that a frog has deliberately gone out of its way to select it. It has to be shown that other kinds of prey which were just as readily available have been avoided; evidence of discrimination is needed. For example, there are observations of Calaby (1956) on the diet of turtle frogs living in termite nests. It is not surprising that this species feeds almost exclusively upon termites. The frogs are being selective in their choice of where they live which, in turn provides an abundant but inherently uniform, source of food. Whether or not the turtle frogs have selected that site because of the nature, or the abundance, of the food that is available there is immaterial. It is certainly true to describe a turtle frog as a termite-eater, but it would be premature to regard it as a selective feeder until there is evidence that it prefers termites when other food is equally available.

As far as avoidance of potentially harmful prey is concerned, much depends upon its ability to control and curb its natural impulse to capture it with its tongue. Cott (1936) found that toads will gradually learn to associate the eating of bees with the unpleasant experience of being stung. It was however a slow and undoubtedly painful process. Some recent studies on the effect of chemical substances known as phenols on the movement of cilia suggest another means of reinforcing the process of learning. Phenols and their derivatives occur in many plants and animals, and although some are the source (to man) of highly palatable flavourings such as vanillin, the active constituent of vanilla essence, other phenols are extremely obnoxious and utterly repulsive.

The relevance and importance of these findings is that the particular substance that gives its name to the phenols has the ability of completely paralysing cilia for longer periods of time than any other substance so far tested. This means that a frog eating a bug or other insect containing phenol would not only experience an exceptionally unpleasant taste but also would be absolutely unable to get rid of that taste. The cilia, on which it relies for cleaning material from the mouth, would not operate for several hours. It may well be that unpleasant experiences of this kind teach frogs to avoid particular kinds of prey.

Selection assumes that an animal really has a choice and is not faced with the pangs of hunger that make selection seem a luxury. Under such stress other creatures will eat virtually anything. For example, starving reindeer have been known to eat frogs, and men have attempted to eat shoe leather. Even if selection really does take place in frogs there exists an additional and totally unknown factor influencing the matter, namely the possibility that individual animals have their own preferences. All that can be concluded from what is known at present is that most frogs are to be considered 'opportunistic feeders' which simply eat quite indiscriminately what they happen to find.

The diet and feeding habits of tadpoles are quite unlike those of adult frogs. Unfortunately there is very little information at all on the range of diet of Australian and New Guinea species, and no detailed investigation has yet been undertaken here on the way in which any of them obtains its food. As a result references have to be made to work on foreign species.

A large number of New Guinea frogs (all the microhylids and most of the ranids) and a few Australian frogs too, do not really feed at all. These species are the ones which have 'direct development' within the egg membranes, so that they lack free-living tadpoles, or the tadpoles having been provided with adequate yolk reserves do not require food from other sources (Chapter 7).

The structure of tadpoles is completely dominated by those organs involved in obtaining and digesting food. Thus there are two striking features about them: firstly the mouth is often very large indeed, and secondly the body is virtually packed with coiled intestines. What is not apparent until the tadpole is dissected is that there is a vast chamber between the external mouthparts and the oesophagus leading to the stomach. This chamber is termed the bucco-pharyngeal cavity.

In its structure the bucco-pharyngeal cavity and the area around it is extremely complex and varies in detail from species to species. At the risk of simplifying the situation, it is best to visualize an ovoid-shaped cavity with an aperture at each end and a series of minute pores near the base. At the front of the cavity are the external mouthparts, consisting of varying numbers of rows of 'labial teeth' surrounding what is called the 'horny beak', and which really functions in much the same way as true toothed jaws.

The labial teeth consist of rows of hundreds of tiny black spikes upon ridges of dense, white, fibrous tissue. There may be two or three rows above and below the horny beak, or as many as five or six rows. The lower rows are usually more numerous than the upper ones. The horny beak is similarly black in colour, but is a stronger, larger and much more substantial structure, and takes the form of an upper and lower crescent-shaped structure with serrated edges.

A tadpole when feeding benefits from the fact that there is a constant current of water passing in through the mouth and out through the so-called spiracle or common exit of the gills. All that the tadpole has to do is to direct food particles into this current and then prevent them from being washed out through the spiracle. The way in which tadpoles do this is quite fascinating.

The labial teeth usually function as scrapers. They tend to rasp off very small portions of plant and animal material, and direct these particles into the path of water entering the bucco-pharyngeal cavity. At the same time the horny beak rhythmically chomps up and down. Sometimes it will chop these particles into smaller segments, but in some species the size of the horny beak is so large in proportion to the size of labial teeth, that it is possible that this beak can also rasp off food particles from a floating object.

The passage of water through the bucco-pharyngeal cavity is

very rapid and there is still cause for caution in stating just how the food particles are trapped. Savage (1952) in England, Severtsov (1969) in Russia and Kenny (1967) in Trinidad provide different interpretations for different species. In the case of the larger particles of food it seems reasonably well established that they become trapped in a sort of fish-net of strands of mucus, constantly secreted and passing chain-wise from the bucco-pharyngeal floor into the oesophagus. The smaller particles miss this chain and would escape but for the existence of a second chain within the filaments of the gills. What happens is that to exchange oxygen and carbon dioxide from the water effectively there has to be an extremely intimate contact between the gills and the water passing through them. Even the smallest food particle is an enormous object in terms of the contact of the hair-like filaments of the gills. As the particles enter this system of filaments they meet a second system of cords of mucus, and it is these which trap them and carry them away into the oesophagus.

Because Savage, Severtsov and Kenny differ so widely in their observations, it may well be that tadpoles differ from species to species in the manner in which food particles are extracted. The details of the method may remain a matter of some contention, but the remarkable efficiency certainly is not. For example Dodd (1950) reported that African *Xenopus* tadpoles could remove particles as small as 0.2μ and Kenny (1969) estimated 5μ as the lower limit of particle size retained by the gill filaments of the West Indian hylid *Phyllomedusa triniatis*. These observations are important for another reason because they clarify whether tadpoles do or do not feed upon bacteria. Certainly tadpoles are unlikely to actually see them, but there are some very common aquatic bacteria such as *Escherichia coli* which form chains several microns across – far too large to pass through the gill filaments – and so they probably are a part of tadpole diets.

My own studies on the gut contents of Australian tadpoles shows that not all species are particle feeders, no matter how well they may prove to be equipped for it. For example an unusually large tadpole of *Neobatrachus pictus*, which had a snout to vent length of 25 mm, a total length (measured from the tip of the snout to the end of the tail) of 90 mm, and no less than 620 mm of intestines had swallowed plant fibres up to 22 mm in length as well as the wings and portion of the body of several different species of insects.

Cannibalism is common amongst tadpoles; the weak individuals are invariably attacked, killed and eaten by a pack of their stronger brethren. The habit may be most prevalent when populations are dense and the competition for the little food that happens to be around is extremely high. Moore (1961) suggested that the tadpoles of *Lechriodus fletcheri* in New South Wales may be habitually carnivorous and cannibalistic, but Martin subsequently demonstrated that it appeared to be just the result of too many tadpoles and not enough food, and that it was not a normal habit.

9   Obtaining Water and Avoiding Heat

FROGS NEVER DRINK but instead obtain the water that they
need principally by absorbing it directly through the skin. The
skin has to be permeable to absorb water, and herein lies a great
disadvantage: water can pass outwards and so be lost just as
readily as it can be absorbed and gained. By experiments it has
been shown that in a totally dry atmosphere frogs lose water so
rapidly that they can survive for only a few hours. Even under
less extreme conditions the water lost over a period of 24 hours
can be equivalent to as much as 30 per cent of the initial body
weight.

Just how frogs survive and in fact can flourish away from areas
of free water is achieved by any combination of a multitude of
different methods. These adaptations can involve patterns of
behaviour by the frogs, various structural modifications of the
skin of the upper and lower parts of the head, body and limbs,
by efficient means of water intake and of water storage etc. All of
these factors will vary from species to species, often according to
the sort of place in which they live. For example the risk of serious
dehydration does not exist for creatures living in water whereas,
at the other extreme, survival in arid areas poses exceptional
problems.

The need to avoid or at least minimize water loss is of such
utmost importance that it influences their daily patterns of
activity. The vast majority of frogs are principally nocturnal
animals, but we rarely stop to question just why they are nocturnal
and not diurnal. The simplest explanation is that by emerging at
dusk, and being active at night, they are exposed to the elements
during the cooler part of the day. Certainly the rate of water loss,
by evaporation from the surface of their skins, will be lower at
night than if they moved around in exactly the same area during
the warmer hours of daylight.

The habit of diurnal activity appears only in those species which live either in water or where the air is absolutely saturated. *Taudactylus diurnus* of eastern Queensland acquired its name from this habit and Straughan and Lee (1966) noted that it was found 'out of water on rocks, debris or overhanging vegetation along mountain streams in rainforest'. They observed that the frogs 'readily entered flowing water, and lay on the bottom between or under rocks and debris, sometimes for considerable periods even when the water was flowing rapidly'.

Exposure to sunlight is a risk for some of the tree frogs, but the characteristic pose that they adopt when resting at least partly reduces water loss. They minimize the exposed surface area by neatly tucking their hands and feet beneath their limbs, and pressing their limbs hard up against the sides of their bodies. Those that have delicate webbing between their fingers and toes are protecting these structures, which are extremely thin and would be seriously damaged if exposed to the sun's rays for very long. The beautiful, green, dainty tree frog in Plate 14 has adopted this protective position. It may well be a universal habit, for in central France I have seen the common European tree frog in an absolutely identical pose on the leaves of blackberry bushes beside creeks.

The same basic principal of minimizing the exposed body surfaces is employed as a communal venture by some frogs during short periods of drought. By sharing a refuge such as a crack in a rock, and packing themselves in like sardines in a tin, they can greatly reduce the area of skin which is not in contact with a moist surface (in this case their neighbours' bodies) and so open to the air. It represents one of the few examples to be seen amongst frogs of individuals co-operating to enable them to achieve mutual benefit. This particular habit is termed 'aggregation' rather than 'congregation' because the individuals virtually unite to form one mass, rather than simply getting near to one another.

At the edge of a dried-up swamp not far from the River Murray I once found several aggregations of adult marsh frogs, crammed into cracks in dead tree-stumps. In one crack I found as many as thirty frogs. I convinced myself that it wasn't a case of there being just a few suitable cracks in tree-stumps in the vicinity, and that the frogs had occupied the only ones that were available. There were numerous other cracks that to my eyes appeared equally suitable, and yet those were not occupied, and I found no frogs hidden away on their own.

Whilst collecting frogs in southern New Guinea, Neill (1946) found some living in the cavities of egg-plants. He found as many as twenty-three in one plant, but these seem to have been congregations and it is possible that they simply shared a home during the daytime and emerged each night. Slevin (1955) found seventeen *Litoria caerulea* in the fireplace of a station homestead, and as many as twenty *L. rubella* together under the bark of a tree.

Johnson (1969a) noticed that the juveniles of three species of *Limnodynastes* aggregated when he exposed them to dry air in the laboratory. He was able to show that the average weight loss (simply water loss) of individuals in an aggregation reduced as more and more individuals became involved in the aggregation. In fact when five frogs aggregated together, the water loss for each frog was half the loss experienced by one frog on its own (Fig. 21).

In areas of moderate rainfall droughts are usually temporary

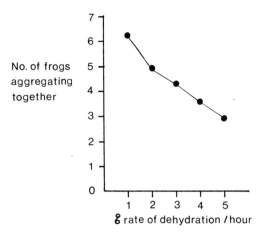

FIG. 21   Effect of aggregation on the rate of water loss. The loss per individual is reduced as more and more frogs aggregate together (data from Johnson 1969).

events of fairly short duration. It is in the deserts, where long rainless periods are the rule rather than the exception, that the more elaborate behavioural and other changes are to be found amongst frogs. The expression 'desert adaptation' can be mis-construed and it is perhaps desirable to state clearly that, unlike mad dogs and Englishmen, most desert frogs avoid exposure to the sun. In fact they live far below the surface of the hot ground in moist or water-filled cells at depths not penetrated by the drying heat.

The only visible structural adaptation to the strange habitats of the desert frogs is on the broad, fleshy sole of the foot. One of the two tubercles there is highly modified, projecting underneath as a shovel-shaped process. In two species of burrowing frogs the tubercle is jet black and has a very sharp cutting edge. The frog burrows by a complicated and most effective shuffling technique involving moving the feet outwards and so scraping the soil away from beneath its feet, and then pushing this soil sideways. As a result the frog digs a pit beneath its body and progressively deepens it to produce a vertical shaft which eventually collapses above it. In Plate 15 a *Notaden bennetti* from Queensland is shown digging and disappearing from view.

The life of these burrowing frogs remains an enigma. Walpole (1964) provided a few valuable clues when he constructed a narrow chamber with glass walls, filled it with sand, and placed a juvenile *Neobatrachus pictus* on the surface of the sand. The frog burrowed down and, after a period of sixteen hours, had formed a cell 25 mm below the surface. It was not hidden from view, because the glass walls of the tank were only 12 mm apart, and sub-terranean conditions were created by covering the entire tank with a neatly fitting envelope of black cardboard. From time to time Walpole gently removed the envelope to watch the frog. On no occasion did he observe any spontaneous activity, but he found that the frog was not dormant because, if he gently tilted the tank, the frog would adjust its position to compensate for the change in what was the floor of its cell.

Some of the most valuable information on the natural history of burrowing frogs has been obtained by the residents of remote areas. Fletcher (1891) reports the notes of one of his correspon-dents, Mr J. T. Rose, who had studied the water-holding frog at

Walgett in western New South Wales, at a time when it was known as *Chiroleptes platycephalus*. Rose stated: 'I have found it in a well-formed hollow just large enough to hold the animal completely, about one foot underground. I have dug up some scores of them, but I never found water in the cavities (i.e. as Mr Aitken says is to be found in the clay balls formed by certain frogs in tropical Australia in which they sojourn during droughts); neither is the surrounding earth particularly hard except just in the dry season; just now (May) the walls of the cells are about as hard as potter's clay after the turning-table period, and before being dried. I send you a portion of one of the cavities which contained a specimen of *Chiroleptes*, and from the knife marks you will see that it was not particularly hard when first found'.

Mr Rose packed some live specimens in tins of soil and sent them to J. J. Fletcher who found that they had formed small chambers in the course of their journey to Sydney. Fletcher examined them closely, and considered that the chambers might be made by the frogs 'puffing themselves out, and by turning themselves round and round' to compress the soil and produce the firm, smooth, inner wall.

Sir Baldwin Spencer (1928) described finding frogs in soil so hard that a hatchet was needed to cut it: 'About a foot below the surface we came upon a little spherical chamber, about two and a half inches in diameter, in which lay a dirty, yellow frog. Its body was puffed out into the shape of an orange, with its head and legs drawn up so as to occupy as little room as possible. The walls of its burrow were moist and slimy and the animal was fast asleep, with the eyelids drawn up so tightly over the eyes that the natives assured us that it was quite blind'.

Irrespective of where frogs hide away during the daytime, or during periods of short or prolonged drought, the fact remains than many must be exposed to drying conditions at some time or another. One of the most fundamental steps for life away from water is to at least reduce the rate of water loss through the skin. As far as the frogs of the arid zones are concerned Bentley (1966) puts the case rather well when he says that 'the most valuable evolutionary novelty which they could invent to assist their survival there would be a more impermeable integument'.

In aquatic frogs water content can be maintained within fairly precise limits. In most circumstances, water loss is most likely to take place from the exposed, upper surfaces, and it is quite possible for water intake to occur simultaneously through the skin of the abdomen. Frogs that have lost appreciable amounts of water adopt a characteristic posture when placed subsequently upon moist material. This habit has been documented by Johnson (1969b) who, repeating experiments first undertaken overseas, found that Australian frogs flatten their bodies hard down against the moist surface, and even spread their limbs out slightly to increase the surfaces of the limbs contacting the accessible moisture.

The skin of the abdomen is either entirely smooth or has a distinctly irregular and rather 'warty' surface (in which case it is said to be granular): there are no intermediate forms. I suspect that his clear-cut difference in the texture of the skin-surface is associated with the need to take up moisture. My reason for the assumption is because all of the frogs that have granular skins spend much of their time away from water, whereas totally aquatic frogs invariably have a smooth skin on their lower areas. The granularity (see the under-surface of the brown tree frog in Plate 2) has the effect of increasing the surface area and therefore of increasing the area through which water can be absorbed. In addition, the spaces between the individual granules are narrow and could well have a sort of capillary action by drawing water through the meshwork of channels in a continuous column across the surface of the skin. What is significant about these granular surfaces is that they are confined to the areas of skin pressed against the moist surfaces during the water absorption pose.

The skin of a frog is only loosely attached to its body, resembling a snugly fitting glove. This can be demonstrated by gently rubbing the skin of a frog's back with the tip of your finger. You will find that almost any area of skin can be moved forwards, backwards or sideways. Attachment of skin to the underlying muscles and bones occurs only at particular sites where there are sheets of fine, transparent membranes. Each of these membranes is the wall of a separate lymph sac, creating a series of moist compartments surrounding the body and limbs. Kampmeier (1969) visualized these sacs as maintaining an envelope of moisture, bathing the body. It means that the body is really surrounded by an aquatic medium, despite the fact that the frog may live on land.

The lymph sacs beneath the skin (subcutaneous) are normally little more than transit centres for water passing to or from the body tissues. However they can be used for water storage, becoming absolutely bloated in some of the burrowers just before they commence their subterranean spells. *Cyclorana platycephalus* of Central Australia is called the water-holding frog because of this habit. It becomes surrounded by loose, floppy bags of water.

Many of the burrowers of the arid regions face long periods of drought. Digging to depths often more than one metre below the surface, they create cylindrical cells, often in impervious clay, in which they remain even for two years or more. The habit of inactivity during the summer months is referred to as aestivation, which literally means 'summer sleep'.

The burrowing frogs have evolved a unique method of reducing the loss to the surrounding soil of the water which they have so elaborately stored. Several species of *Cyclorana* and *Neobatrachus*, and one *Limnodynastes* species, all inhabitants of arid areas, secrete a special outer skin layer which separates from the remainder in one piece so that it forms a cocoon. This phenomenon was discovered by Lee and Mercer (1967) who found that the cocoon surrounded the frog and was complete across the eyes and cloaca but that the nostrils were connected to the outside by small tubular inserts. In some of the frogs examined by them the cocoon sealed the mouth as well.

In frogs that had been beneath the ground for three to five months the cocoon was still soft and pliable and was barely separated from the skin. In two frogs that had been underground for seven and ten months respectively the cocoon was dry but flexible, and attached only at the head and the extremities of the limbs. In their experiments the investigators tested the rate of the passage of water vapour through the cocoon, as opposed to the rate of water loss in a series of motionless frogs lacking cocoons. They showed that a cocoon would have the effect of reducing water loss, but they pointed out that the experimental frogs also would have been losing water in the form of vapour in air expired from their lungs, so that the conditions for comparison were not ideal.

The absorption of water by frogs has been studied in numerous species. The method by which frogs accomplish it is usually described as osmosis (Bentley 1966), a process in which water passes from an area of low salt concentration to one of high concentration (the frog) through a membrane (the skin). In soil, the loss or gain of water has been shown to vary according to the moisture content of the soil and the size of its particles.

Osmosis is certainly taking place across the walls of the tiny capillary blood vessels, drawing fluid from the spaces between the cells surrounding them. However the whole concept of water intake was revolutionized by the studies of Scholander and his colleagues (1968, 1969). They had shown previously that in mangroves and trees in deserts there was an enormous negative pressure, or pull, being applied to the sap and equivalent to as much as –60 atmospheres. Professor Scholander thought that the puckering and folding of the skin of dehydrated frogs could be produced only by a similar sort of physical pull being applied from the inside. Through a tiny nick in the skin he pushed a minute wick of moist cotton-wool into the lymph sac beneath and connected the wick via a glass capillary tube to a water manometer capable of recording small pressures. He and his colleagues demonstrated that there was indeed a negative pressure being applied to the skin, and equivalent to as much as –10 cm of water. They believe that the spaces (interstices) between the cells in the tissues of the body are reduced as water is lost and so they describe the condition as 'negative interstitial fluid pressure'. This pressure builds up (that is to say, becomes more negative) as the animal loses more and more water.

Some observations by Warburg (1967) show just how this principle of the degree of negative pressure being associated with the extent of dehydration can be put to good advantage. He dehydrated representatives of three Western Australian species, weighed them and then placed them in water. After one hour in water, he reweighed them and found that they had absorbed from 11 to 17 milligrams of water per gram of body weight. At the end of the second hour the frogs were again weighed and it appeared that the increase had reduced to 2 to 6 mg/g. After eight hours of rehydration the hourly intake was consistently as low as 2 mg/g. Obviously a dehydrated frog has the means of rapidly correcting a major reduction of its water reserves.

Direct contact with water, with moist surfaces or a moist atmosphere are not the only sources of water available to frogs. For example, the water content of dietary items undoubtedly makes a small contribution for insects can be composed of as much as 90% water. There are also occasions when dew may form on frogs' bodies. Lasiewski and Bartholomew (1969) were able to show that under experimental conditions condensation could increase body weights by about 1 per cent. They thought that after a hot day, the pocket of air in a temporary, open-ended burrow, would remain more warm and humid at night than outside. Hence some of the nocturnal foragers could be cooler than the burrow temperatures on their return, so that condensation from the burrow atmosphere was at least a possibility.

The behaviour of frogs that enables them to avoid or at least minimize dehydration, and the ways in which they can efficiently absorb water are only parts of their evolutionary success story. The co-operation of the kidney and the bladder is required to ensure that these organs are capable of modifying their normal functions of extracting and eliminating the water within the body. In most vertebrate animals the bladder is simply a repository permitting concentrated urine to be collected over a period, and discharged at intervals. Most frogs suffer the disadvantage of being unable to produce a particularly concentrated urine, but fortunately the bladder can become a vast storage tank whose contents may be reabsorbed in time of need. In some frogs so much water is retained in the bladder that its content can weigh almost as much as the remainder of the entire animal.

The frog's bladder is not just a bag which can be blown up to any size. Actually when distended it has a bilobular (two-lobed) shape which can be appropriately, but not decently, likened to other vertebrate organs. The ability of a frog to hold any great quantity of water in the bladder seems to be related to its need to conserve water. Thus the aquatic species, which have ready access to fresh supplies, have small bladders capable of holding only low volumes. It is in the arid zones that bladder capacity reaches the ultimate pinnacle of perfection. At this upper limit the defect of being unable to produce urine in a concentrated form is no major handicap. For example, Ruibal (1972) has demonstrated urinary concentrations of as low as one per cent in an

American toad, and it is unlikely to be any higher where bladder contents approximate 50 per cent of the body weight. Thus reabsorption of water by such an animal could proceed for a considerable period before the inorganic salts in the urine approximated levels throughout the body.

The inability to produce concentrated urine is a consequence of the way in which adult frogs normally excrete nitrogenous waste material in solution, in the form of urea. Names seem to be coined for any habit and this one has resulted in frogs being described as ureotelic. In effect it means that, at the time of its greatest need, a frog is unable to exploit to the greatest extent the 'free' water existing in its body. In 1970 Loveridge upset this broad generalization about frogs, by revealing that there is an African tree frog which has overcome this evolutionary deficiency. It excretes water as a solid in the form of bags of crystals of uric acid (uricotelism). His discovery of a frog employing a method previously thought to lie within the domain of reptiles was quickly followed by a report from Shoemaker and his colleagues (1972) that there is also a South American tree frog which is uricotelic. Neither of the two uricotelic frogs avoids exposure to dry conditions, but just how they reduce evaporative water loss through the skin is not yet known.

Frogs not only vary in the rate at which they lose water, but also in their ability to tolerate water loss. From species to species the tolerance is not a matter of luck, for they don't seem to acquire abilities that are unlikely to be beneficial. Main and Bentley (1964) examined the ability of a variety of species to tolerate dehydration and found that *Litoria moorei*, an inhabitant of creeks and swamps, died after losing 30 per cent of its body weight, whereas the arboreal *L. caerulea* survived after losing as much as 45 per cent. There are obviously numerous situations in which body temperature, and particularly skin temperature, will influence loss of water by evaporation. In addition this evaporation has a sort of feed-back effect by causing a cooling of the skin surface in a manner similar to that of perspiration in man.

The terms 'warm-blooded' and 'cold-blooded' used to differentiate between different kinds of animals are unfortunate and inaccurate. The distinction is really being made on whether the animal has an inbuilt temperature control system, maintaining body temperature within precise limits, or lacks that refinement and so has a temperature fluctuating with changes in the temperature of the surrounding environment. On a hot day it is quite possible for there to be the ludicrous situation where a so-called warm-blooded animal has a cooler body temperature than a nearby cold-blooded one. These days it is becoming more common to hear frogs being called 'ectothermic' (a much more appropriate word indicating that temperature is controlled by external factors), contrasting with 'endothermic' for animals where the control is regulated internally.

In recent years a vast number of papers have been published reporting the minimum and the maximum temperatures that various species of frogs can tolerate, without causing their death. From the literature quoted by recent reviewers of this rather macabre field of thermobiology, it is easy to gain the impression that it is a new area of investigation. However the founder was probably the famous English surgeon and scientist, John Hunter. In 1778 he reported his observations to the Royal Society:

The frog being, in its structure, more similar to the viper than either to fowl or fish, I made the following experiments on that animal. Exp. XXX   I introduced the ball of the thermometer into its stomach, and the quicksilver stood at 44°. I then put it into a cold mixture, and the quicksilver sunk to 31°; the animal appeared almost dead, but recovered very soon; beyond this point it was not possible to lessen the heat, without destroying the animal. But its decrease of heat was quicker than in the viper, although the mixture was almost the same . . . .

Hunter had demonstrated the existence of a minimum temperature, below which the frog (probably European *Rana temporaria*) could not survive. This parameter is now known as the 'critical thermal minimum' and 'cold lethal'. However the greatest amount of work has focused on the other end of the range on the so-called 'critical thermal maximum'.

There is now a wealth of information on the range of temperatures that frogs can tolerate. From species to species, and even amongst different geographic populations of species, these tolerances differ. Brattstrom (1970) provides data on 42 species inhabiting eastern Australia and demonstrates that the rates and ranges of acclimatization also differ quite strikingly. Acclimatization involves an adjustment to a new 'standard' temperature. It isn't just a case of an animal becoming used to higher or lower temperatures, as we might when moving from one country to another, but it actually affects the critical thermal maximum.

It is not until data are tabulated from species inhabiting numerous different niches, habitats, altitudes and climatic zones, that any clear picture of their value emerges. Brattstrom was able to show that frogs from tropical northeastern Queensland could not survive when temperatures were dropped to around 10°C. In contrast he found that the frogs at cooler, high altitudes of south-eastern Australia, such as the Victorian Alps, could tolerate and in fact breed at temperatures approaching 0°C, whilst the geographic intermediates at mid-altitudes could survive at 5°C.

Brattstrom has suggested that the ability to acclimatize to new temperature ranges dictates whether or not species can colonize new geographic areas. He points out that in general, 'species with wide ranges of adaptability have the widest geographic ranges'.

Most of what is known about frogs and their temperature tolerances has been obtained under carefully controlled laboratory conditions. However Warburg (1972) showed just how the selection of different niches at any particular habitat influenced the range of temperatures experienced by the frogs. On a day at Alice Springs when the air temperature was 38°C, it was 35°C in the shade, 33°C beneath a rock, 32°C in a rock crevice and 29°C in a burrow.

Avoidance of very low temperatures in winter is obviously more difficult because the cold is so penetrating. Frogs cannot survive being frozen and so they need to hide away in positions where they are not exposed. Dead and decomposing vegetation probably provides the most suitable insulation, but I am unaware of any reports of frogs being found in Australia actually in a state of hibernation. There are several likely candidates, one of which is *Litoria ewingi* in the Victorian Alps for it extends above the area of the winter snowline. In northern New South Wales members of another species appear to congregate to share a hibernation site. Near Ebor, Marion Anstis found a group of sixteen *Litoria grandulosa* beneath a rotting log. All were lethargic and moved slowly (Tyler and Anstis 1975). This appears to be the only documented account in Australia of communal hibernation in a refuge which, because of its role, is termed a hibernaculum.

10 Breathing

FROGS OBTAIN OXYGEN from their surroundings and release waste carbon dioxide by a number of techniques at different sites (respiratory surfaces) in their bodies. They retain some of the methods probably used by ancestral amphibians and possess others characteristic of higher vertebrates. There are advantages and disadvantages in this diversity, but frogs could be viewed as being apparently reluctant to commit themselves entirely to lungs for breathing.

There is probably considerable benefit to be gained from not relying entirely upon one method or another. For example, the period that a frog can remain under water would be reduced if it relied entirely upon lung breathing, simply because there is the obvious drawback of requiring the air in the lungs to be changed periodically.

In frogs, gas exchange occurs at three sites: the skin, the roof of the mouth, and the lungs. The intake of oxygen and the release of carbon dioxide to and from the tiny capillary blood vessels close to the surface of the tissues, is a process of diffusion in each direction across a moist membrane. There is no uniformity in the extent to which frogs exploit any one of these respiratory surfaces. Species vary considerably, with the lungs being the most important site of gas exchange in some species and the skin of paramount importance in others. From season to season, and even from hour to hour, there are probably major changes in the dominance of each in an individual frog.

The skin of frogs has several specialized features to enable it to serve a respiratory function (termed cutaneous respiration). The most obvious is the development of a dense network of blood capillaries to provide efficient absorption and a transportation system to and from the surface. The specializations in the blood vessels extend deeper, for arterial blood travels from the heart to the skin through special arteries whose branches extend through-out the greater part of the surface of the body. Similarly there is an equally specialized network of major veins involved in returning the blood to the heart. Vessels of this kind are to be found only in frogs. Salamanders and other amphibians lack them and, in fact, there are no counterparts in other animals.

In water the process of gas exchange through the skin is virtually little more than a technique of extracting the oxygen held in solution by the water. The available oxygen varies according to the temperature of the water, and it has been suggested that the famous foreign, aquatic 'hairy frogs' evolved their fur-like coats to increase their body surface, and hence the surface area in contact with water. This sort of phenomenon is rare and has no real parallel amongst frogs in Australia and New Guinea. Noble (1931) and Porter (1973) reproduced the same illustration of the male *Astylosternus robustus* of Cameroons, with its extraordinary long hair-like growths which are really cylindrical outgrowths of skin. Parker (1936) examined a specimen of another species of hairy frog and calculated the total surface area of the thousands of 'hairs'. He found this was quite considerable, being equivalent to the surface area of the remainder of the body.

The hairy frogs focus attention upon the major limitation of cutaneous respiration. As frogs increase in size, so their outer surface area, which is the cutaneous respiratory surface, also in-creases. However, it is accompanied by a disproportionately greater increase in body volume. The principle can be demon-strated by bringing together two cubes of identical size. Doubling the volume by this means has clearly not doubled the external surface area, because one face of each cube has been effectively 'lost'. The maximum size that frogs attain is undoubtedly partly governed by this, the physical relationship between surface area and volume. There has to be a balance between the ability to obtain oxygen, and the oxygen consumption of the body.

All frogs adopt cutaneous respiration to a greater or lesser extent. However, when they are out of water there remains the fundamental requirement to maintain the skin in a moist con-dition if it is to continue to function as a respiratory surface. Certainly frogs possess the means of keeping the skin moist, for they lose water rapidly by evaporation from the surface. When they live away from water this evaporative loss must be reduced so that they do not die from dehydration, so there have been adaptive changes to the structure of the skin and in behaviour. Obviously this creates a conflict, for it is not in the best interests of the respiratory role of the skin. Thus in the face of this conflict modern frogs have succeeded in reaching a partial compromise. It has been achieved by placing the moistening requirement mainly within the domain of mucus glands, whose role in evaporative cooling has been discussed in Chapter 9. Lillywhite (1971) found outlets to sixteen of these glands in one square millimetre of skin on the upper surface of the thigh of an American specimen of *Rana*. The close proximity of the ducts of the glands to one another and the rate of discharge of their contents (up to seventeen times per minute) would have the effect of maintaining at all times an entire but scarcely detectable thin, moist film.

For many years it has been known that the visible pulsations of the mouth floor of frogs are involved in respiration. It is a separate process taking place within the confines of the mouth chamber, and termed 'buccal', 'buccopharyngeal', or sometimes 'oropharyngeal' respiration.

The movements of the floor of the mouth (buccal movements) involve the alternate raising and lowering of the entire structure. The actual rate of these movements varies quite considerably. There are periods when they are slow and separated by gaps of inactivity, but with the onset of any nearby disturbance or activity by the frog the rate speeds up dramatically. During these movements the nostrils are open and the mouth and the glottis leading to the larynx and lungs are closed (Fig. 22). Thus the effects of the buccal movements is to suck air into the chamber and then expel it out through the nostrils. This means that air is continually passing across the roof of the pharynx at the back of the mouth, where the lining is richly endowed with capillary vessels which are involved in gas exchange.

The role of the lungs (pulmonary respiration), and particularly the way in which they are filled with air, have aroused great interest because, before the research of Gans, de Jongh and Farber in 1969 there was considerable uncertainty about the sequence of events that took place and just how inflation of the lungs was accomplished.

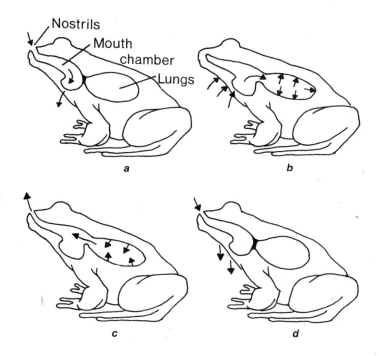

FIG. 22 Stages in air exchange. *a*. mouth chamber is filled as its floor is lowered; *b*. air is shunted into the lungs by raising the mouth floor; *c*. the lungs are emptied; *d*. the mouth chamber is refilled (modified from de Jongh *et al.* 1969).

The lungs of frogs are mostly very simple structures: nothing more than elongate, thin-walled bags. A few species have increased the inner surface of the lungs by the development of ingrowing ridges, and even pockets resembling the alveoli in the lungs of higher vertebrates. Most frogs lack a windpipe (trachea), and the tubes (bronchii) leading to each lung are extremely short, with the result that the lungs are hardly separated from the base of the larynx into which they open.

Before proceeding with their experiments, Gans and his colleagues made detailed observations of the outward signs of respiratory activity in the frogs that were to become their subjects. Nothing escaped their attention. They noticed that during buccal respiration the buccal movements were quite isolated and that neither the nostrils nor any other part of the head and body moved at all, even at times when the buccal floor was oscillating one hundred times per minute. However, they observed that there were occasions when movements of the buccal floor took slightly longer to complete and appeared to have greater amplitude. They noticed that on those occasions the nostrils closed, and that other movements could be detected in the muscles beneath the skin of the flanks. When those events occurred in the frog sitting in water they generated waves, whilst floating frogs bobbed up and down slightly.

It seemed highly likely that the stronger movements of the buccal floor were an outward indication of the lungs being filled. It looked as though the floor was acting as a simple pump to inflate them. Reasoning that there would be different pressures inside the various chambers of air inside the frog, a way had to be devised of recording them and so Gans and his colleagues anaesthetized the frogs and inserted, through tiny holes, short lengths of minute plastic tubes into the mouth cavity, 'arynx, lungs and body cavity. After the frogs had recovered from these minor surgical procedures, the tubes were attached to pressure transducers linked to electronic recorders in such a way that the changes in pressure taking place throughout the body could be recorded simultaneously. Slender wire electrodes were inserted into muscles to monitor their contractions; electrocardiograms were taken, and masks made to fit neatly over the frogs' nostrils so that emerging air could be collected and analysed.

The experiments confirmed that the lungs were being filled by the pumping action of the buccal floor. More important was the unexpected finding that the frog fills its mouth with air just before emptying the lungs, and that the expelled air from the lungs does not appreciably mix with the air held in the mouth (Fig. 22). They found that the expired air leaving the lungs emerges in the form of a fine jet-stream which probably squirts across the roof of the mouth chamber, leaving the fresh air in an undisturbed pocket at the base. Thus the lungs can be refilled with fresh air extremely promptly, but it seems a rather elaborate way of going about it.

De Jongh and Gans point out that the ancient lungfish refills its lungs in the same way as the frog, so suggesting that the technique is basically an old one common to many ancestral animals. It implies that modern frogs are employing the tactic that when you are on to a good thing there is little point in changing.

One of the most intriguing questions about the various methods of respiration employed by frogs has been to establish the relative importance of each of the different respiratory surfaces: for example, whether the skin is more important than the lungs. One method of investigation has involved the task of comparing the number of blood capillary networks in each square millimetre of these surfaces. Much of this work has been undertaken by anatomists in Poland with the result that European frogs have been the subjects of their investigations.

The actual total length of the capillary vessels in the skin, mouth cavity and lungs is incredible. The common European tree frog was examined by Czopek (1955), who calculated that for each gram of body weight there were more than 45 metres of capillaries in the respiratory surfaces. On the basis of the body weight of adult frogs the total length of respiratory capillaries in that species must be between 200 and 300 metres. The figures may appear ridiculous and it is easy to assume that an enormous error has been made. The total surface area of the human lungs has been described as equivalent to the surface area of a tennis court, and it is only when comparisons like this are made that it becomes possible to appreciate the extent of branching of structures at a microscopic level.

Foxon (1964) expressed the capillaries in each of the respiratory· surfaces as percentages of the total. Of fourteen species, the vessels in the mouth cavity accounted for no more than three per cent, and almost all species had a greater length of capillary vessels in the lungs than in the skin.

The mouth cavity accounts for such a small proportion of the capillaries, where gases are exchanged, that it is tempting to assume that its role in respiration is a very minor one. If the blood transporting the gases passes through all of the capillary vessels at a similar rate and, on leaving the respiratory sites is equally saturated with oxygen, the assumption may be reasonable. Nevertheless the importance of each site changes from season to season, and there are periods in the lives of many frogs when each method of respiration will assume the greatest importance. For example, during prolonged periods of inactivity, such as occur in aestivation or hibernation the frogs are relying entirely upon their inner food reserves, principally stored as fat in yellowish, finger-like streamers near their kidneys. In the case of the burrowing frogs in summer, the inactivity of the animals is essential to minimize the demands being placed upon their food reserves. From recent studies on American frogs it is now known that in this passive state the oxygen consumption falls by about 80 per cent. It is obviously desirable that the frogs obtain any oxygen required with the minimum of physical effort. Hence, ideally, pulmonary and buccal movements should cease because they involve considerable work by muscles, and the skin be left to cope with the reduced gas exchange requirements of the animal. However, when slight extra demands are placed upon the frog, perhaps when it is disturbed by sounds and vibrations transmitted through the soil, the buccal respiration is adequate to cope with the additional demand for oxygen (Seymour 1973a, 1973b).

Hibernating frogs with body temperatures only slightly above freezing point have little scope as far as choice of respiratory surfaces is concerned. Subjected to very low temperatures frogs at first become slow and lethargic, and eventually quite motionless. They may ultimately lack the ability to use their muscles; pulmonary and buccal respiration may be beyond their scope of physical movement, and cutaneous respiration is the only means by which they can obtain oxygen.

Respiratory requirements probably demonstrate more than any other natural function that frogs as a group have gained considerable benefit from failing to specialize unduly. But for cutaneous respiration they could not survive cold winters and simply would not exist today in vast areas of the northern hemisphere. Similarly, at the other extreme, cutaneous respiration is probably vital to permit survival underground in desert regions during prolonged droughts. Hence although there are considerable disadvantages in having a relatively delicate and permeable skin, this feature, above all others, has permitted their almost world-wide distribution.

Eggs and tadpoles obtain oxygen by a variety of means. Some of these methods are the forerunners of those employed by adult frogs, but others are specialized adaptations suitable only for an aquatic life.

During the early stages of their free life many tadpoles develop external gills, extending out from the sides of the head and which, as the tadpoles move through the water, extract the oxygen in solution. The gills vary in shape from a forked structure with three or four prongs projecting out from a bar, to elaborate, branched structures bearing numerous twigs and twiglets of progressively smaller diameter. Sometimes the external gills resemble wings bearing a row of feathers. In Australia and New Guinea external gills are present in some species but absent in others.

In comparison with tadpoles found in other parts of the world none of the Australian and New Guinea species have particularly well-developed external gills. It has been suggested by Noble (1927) that the extent of the external gill development in any species reflects the ease, or relative difficulty, of obtaining oxygen experienced by the tadpoles. For example, in situations where spawn is laid in small pockets of water, and it is customary for there to be habitual overcrowding by vast numbers of tadpoles, the oxygen content of the water is likely to be low. This may result in a demand for an increase in the respiratory surface to improve oxygen extraction if the tadpoles are to have the slightest chance of surviving.

No matter how elaborate the form of the external gills may be, they usually persist only for a few days. Whilst the gills are present, rapid internal changes are taking place, resulting in the development of internal gills, functionally resembling those of fishes to the extent that water enters through the mouth and passes across the internal gills before leaving the body.

A simplified diagram of the internal structure of the head of a tadpole at the internal gill stage is shown in Figure 23. From species to species there is considerable variation, but it would appear that the general principles involved in irrigating the gills is substantially the same. The mouth opening leads into a vast chamber termed the buccal cavity, which is separated from the pharynx behind it by a movable valve arising from the mouth floor and termed the ventral velum. Another and much smaller valve, the dorsal velum, is positioned at the back of the pharynx

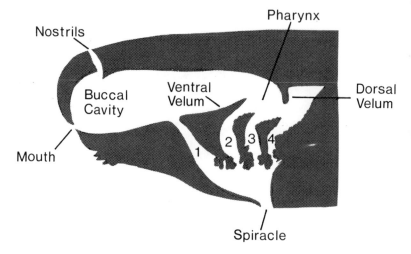

FIG. 23 A section through the head of a tadpole drawn diagrammatically to show each of the apertures. The numbers identify the gill clefts (after Gradwell 1970).

and projects downwards from the roof. At the base of the pharynx lie the gill arches, which are separated from one another by narrow clefts leading to the gill cavity, and thence to the outside via a single aperture called the spiracle.

The internal gills are far more elaborate than the form of external ones, having rows of thousands of minute, hair-like processes projecting out into the gill clefts. The density of these 'hairs' is such that they create a definite obstruction to the passage of water through the clefts. Thus if a tadpole simply swam around with its mouth open it is unlikely that there would be any flow of water through the gill clefts, so a pumping mechanism is needed to drive the water down.

Water is sucked through the mouth into the buccal cavity by the constriction of muscles which lower the floor. The mouth is then closed and the floor is raised. This increase in pressure quickly closes off tiny valves beneath the nostrils sealing them off and preventing water from escaping through them. Most of the water is forced into the pharynx, but some passes out through the first gill cleft. Muscles controlling the pharynx are then brought into play. Their contraction increases the pressure there, pushing back the ventral velum and so preventing backflow into the buccal cavity. Hence, because the only means of escape is via the spiracle, the water is forced down through the gill clefts and gill cavity beneath (Gradwell 1968, 1970).

Close to the gills is another respiratory surface termed the operculum. Gradwell (1969) examined this structure, which is little more than a soft sheet of tissue forming the wall of the gill chamber. He found that the meshes of capillary blood vessels were as high as 650 per square millimetre, which is a higher density than occurs in the skin of any adult frog. The subjects of his study were unusually large tadpoles with high oxygen demands, and such extreme development of the operculum as a respiratory surface may be characteristic only of such large tadpoles where other respiratory surfaces are unable to cope.

From time to time tadpoles swimming about in a pond or stream rise rapidly to the surface, roll over and give the impression of feeding for a few seconds. A closer view in an aquarium will show that the mouth is opening and closing in a steady fashion as though chewing, even though no food can be seen. These events are an indication of the use of the lungs, which, in most species, develop progressively during their tadpole life. *Bufo* species survive without possessing lungs at all, developing these only at the conclusion of their aquatic life.

Strawinski (1956) undertook a comparative study of the respiratory surfaces of tadpoles and concluded that of all of these surfaces the skin was probably the major site of gas exchange for the greater portion of their life. However, conclusions about tadpoles in general would be very risky, and the more interesting issue is just why individuals possess so many different techniques. Savage (1961) regards the variety as a sort of safeguard to their survival. He points out: 'If the conditions in their pond turn out to be dangerous they cannot go in search of better ones, as animals that live on dry land or in the sea can do, but must possess reserve mechanisms that can be brought into play to deal with the often violent fluctuations in their habitats'.

11   Communication by Sound

STUDY OF THE NATURE and purposes of the various sounds produced by frogs provides details of just how frogs interact with one
another and communicate amongst themselves for various
purposes. In addition it yields information providing an insight
into the more intimate details of their daily lives.

By far the best known type of frog sound is the mating call
which is emitted only by the male frog. In general it serves as an
attractant because males tend to precede females to the breeding
sites where they call vociferously to the females to come to them.
The males can congregate in phenomenal numbers and, during
the breeding season, call both by day and by night. It is at these
periods that the general public tend to approach museums seeking
ways of destroying or at least silencing the frogs, and explanations
of the reason for the sudden increase in noise does little to placate
the more indignant enquirer.

It is not always clear just why male frogs call at times other than
the mating season when the sexual drive is lacking. This sort of
calling activity between the breeding periods tends to be classified
as territorial calling. There are some species which do have
territories or areas over which they assert a proprietary right and
sometimes it can be demonstrated in large vivaria. In their
natural state it really means that they are advertising their
presence to other frogs but the habit is a risky one because they
may also inform their predators of their whereabouts.

In my garden at Belair in the Adelaide foothills there live about
half a dozen Ewing's tree frogs, *Litoria ewingi*, which I have
observed closely for a number of years. Certainly I am convinced
that there is some form of interplay between them and a very clear
social hierarchy, but whether the sense of dominance and
sequence with which they call to one another is an expression of
advertisement of their respective territories is unclear. A solitary

male who lives in an open water tank is inevitably the first, and frequently the only frog to call. As I write tonight he has been calling on his own for over an hour, producing calls of short duration, possibly lasting for only about one second and repeated at intervals of thirty to forty-five seconds. If and when he is joined by a fellow *L. ewingi* inhabiting a clump of dense vegetation ten metres away, his pattern of calling changes dramatically. The duration of the call trebles in length, whilst the periods of silence between the bursts of notes may shorten to around fifteen or ten seconds. Frogs in other parts of the garden that up to this stage have been mute begin to join the chorus. Until it reaches the ultimate point that it becomes impossible for an observer to record their actions with any certainty, there is no doubt that a strict sequence of calling is being followed. Nevertheless the 'leader' in the water tank continues to dominate the chorus by having more turns than anyone else. Eventually one or two of the frogs fall silent and gradually the chorus peters out altogether.

The onset of light falls of rain, particularly in the summer after long dry spells, frequently causes frogs to call. A well-directed garden sprinkler aimed at vegetation sheltering frogs can produce the same result. This sort of calling is referred to as 'rain calls', but it may be that the rain or artificial shower is just a stimulus to jog the frog into activity and so produce territorial calling. I find that I can induce the *L. ewingi* to call at almost any time of the day simply by putting my tongue against the roof of my palate and imitating the sort of rapid, repetitive clicks of their calls. However they recognize that my efforts are a poor imitation, for they will rarely respond more than once or twice.

Whereas the mating and territorial calls produced by any one species are similar to the human ear, distress calls are quite different and in fact recognized for what they are. When grasped by a snake, frogs often emit a high-pitched scream. One desert frog, *Cyclorana cultripes*, seems to exhibit a rather nervous disposition for it screams in anticipation. When you reach to pick one up it commonly opens its mouth wide, screams piercingly and simultaneously jumps absolutely vertically high into the air to fall in a heap on the ground where it had been sitting. Distress calls of a less dramatic kind can be produced almost to order in male frogs just by gently holding them by their back legs. It causes them to inflate their vocal sacs and produce a series of chirrups.

I know of no better example of the unusual nature of distress calls than to describe the characteristic distress behaviour of *L. infrafrenata*, which is the biggest of our tree frogs and is particularly common in New Guinea. This great animal has a mating call like the deep-throated barking of a large and particularly angry dog, but the distress call is quite different. Dr L. B. Holthius, of the Rijksmuseum at Leiden, was the first person to draw my attention to the difference when he described in a letter his experience with this species in a remote part of the northern lowlands of New Guinea.

It was in the evening and already rather dark. We saw a Papuan coming in to our camp but could not at first discern what he was carrying. The animal which he held by the hind legs made a very loud, penetrating miaowing sound. It so closely resembled the miaowing of a cat that at first we wondered how it was possible that cats were found in this area far away from any town, and our conclusion was that it was some marsupial making this sound. When the Papuan came close and we could see that he carried just a frog we were very surprised. This observation, made by three zoologists (Professor Brongersma, Dr Boeseman and myself) and two forestry officers, got into the local press and met with much disbelief. However on two occasions I heard of similar observations. The most striking was obtained from Mr D. Smits on Japen Island off the New Guinea coast. He told me that one evening when his cat was outside he heard a very strange miaowing in his garden and, thinking that his cat was in trouble, he went outside. In the grass he found his cat staring fascinated at a big tree frog. To his enormous surprise the miaowing was coming from the frog and not from the cat.

Whilst collecting frogs and reptiles in swamps in the far north of Arnhem Land, Harold Cogger of the Australian Museum heard frog sounds that may have been expressions of their indignation. Relating his experiences in 1973 he says: 'Suddenly the air would be rent by a piercing and fearful scream, which, the first time I heard it, gave me a terrific fright. On each occasion the screaming was found to emanate from the limb of a nearby tree, where, after some effort with an axe, the culprits were always found to be a tree monitor or goanna, *Varanus timorensis*, and one or more green tree frogs *(Litoria caerulea)*. The goanna, on entering the hollow limb, would find its way blocked by one or more

The cane toad *Bufo marinus*

A Solomon Islands tree frog *Palmatorappia solomonis*

The dainty tree frog
Litoria gracilenta at rest

Notaden melanoscaphus at
Darwin deliberately exposin
its limbs to the sun

sleeping frogs. Unwilling or sometimes unable to reverse in the confined hollow, the goanna would try to force its way past the loudly protesting frogs. This was so common that by the end of a month I regarded it as an almost daily event. We never found any evidence that the goannas might be feeding on the frogs'.

From time to time 'warning calls' have been described, being the grunts or squawks emitted when frogs are disturbed and leap away. It seems to be an extremely common trait amongst the streamside dwellers before they plunge into the water. It has been suggested that these noises serve to warn the other frogs in the vicinity of the existence of danger. I've heard various *Rana* species do this in New Guinea but on no occasion did the noise ever result in any mass exodus of the frogs that happened to be near by. I believe that all that the noise indicates is that one frog has had a surprise, and is expressing it, or possibly expelling air prior to diving into water.

The last type of call that has been classified is termed the 'release call'. It is uttered only at the mating site as the adults are in the process of finding partners, and is produced either by a male clasped in mistake for a female by another male, or by a female clasped after she has already mated and laid her eggs. In each instance the release call serves to notify the ardent captor that he is wasting his time, and should direct his attention elsewhere.

The structures involved in call production fall rather conveniently into two separate categories. The first of these organs are the 'primary vocal structures' which are simply the larynx and vocal cords, whilst the 'secondary vocal structures' are the pharynx, mouth cavity, the vocal sac and the modified jaw muscles that surround the vocal sac. The mouth chamber and pharynx are considered part of the 'secondary' vocal structures because they function as a resonance chamber, virtually reinforcing the sounds produced by the primary vocal structures. However most male frogs have progressed a stage further in evolving additional resonance chambers beneath the floor of the mouth. These chambers are called vocal sacs and are of a form unique in the animal kingdom.

The most common type of vocal sac lies in the throat region to which it communicates by slits on each side of the tongue situated in the floor of the mouth (Fig. 24). This sort of vocal sac can be inflated much like a balloon and is often almost spherical in shape (Fig. 21). The only major exception to the general form of vocal sacs is to be seen in the *Notaden* species of Australia's arid regions. Instead of having a single balloon beneath the throat, the vocal sac extends up on to each side of the head. No one has yet seen the shape of the inflated vocal sac in *Notaden*, but frogs in other parts of the world with such two-lobed sacs have the appearance of wearing a pair of water wings when they inflate them. This is unlikely to be so obvious in *Notaden* because the skin above the sacs is very thick and not so elastic.

There are a number of species of male frogs which resemble females in that they do not develop vocal sacs. In the case of *Heleioporus* and *Neobatrachus*, which are animals with large rounded heads, the mouth chamber is high and domed. They can further increase its volume by depressing the floor of the mouth downwards. Hence it looks as though the volume of the mouth chamber is large enough to meet the requirements for sound resonance; vocal sacs in these genera are unnecessary because their calls can be heard at a considerable distance.

It is likely that *Heleioporus* and *Neobatrachus* never evolved vocal

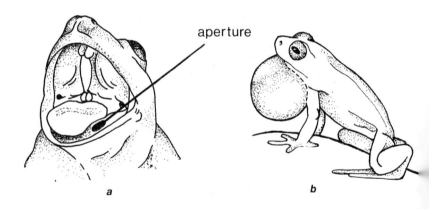

FIG. 24 Vocal structures of the male frog. *a.* open mouth showing the aperture to the vocal sac; *b.* a vocal sac when inflated causes the throat to swell.

sacs because they found a different means of achieving resonance, but the same argument cannot be applied to the few species of other genera that lack vocal sacs. Several species of *Litoria* and *Nyctimystes* and one species of *Taudactylus* (*T. diurnus*) lack vocal sacs but are probably unable to enlarge the mouth chambers. They still possess voices but their calls are soft and muted. For example, there is *Litoria lesueuri* of the eastern States which is a large frog but its call can be heard only a few metres away. A frog of its size possessing a vocal sac could well be detected at a distance of about 100 metres. A sacless frog can be compared to someone trying to play a violin with the sound box removed.

In other countries many of the species lacking vocal sacs breed near waterfalls or boulder-strewn creeks where the noise of the torrent would probably make it impossible for croaking to be heard. *Taudactylus diurnus* often lives in this sort of situation, and its ancestors may have reached the stage where even a loud voice was of little value to them. The other species lacking vocal sacs do not face this sort of problem of background noise and finding a solution to this strange happening remains an intriguing area for future research.

The stages of call production are demonstrated by the sketches shown in Figure 25. The first step in the sequence involves inflation of the lungs with the mouth sealed and air entering through the nostrils. The nostrils are then sealed as well and air is expelled

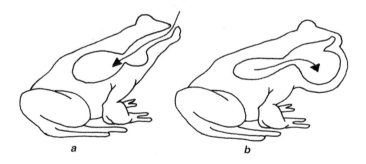

a   b

FIG. 25 Process of inflation of the vocal sac. *a*. with the nostrils opened the lungs are inflated; *b*. the nostrils are then sealed and air is shunted from the lungs into the vocal sac via the mouth cavity.

in a series of short puffs through the larynx, so vibrating the vocal cords. Because there is no other way in which the air can escape from the body, it passes through the apertures of the vocal sac and the vocal sac becomes inflated. Some species certainly inflate the vocal sac without producing any sound, probably resulting from control of the vocal cords by the muscles of the larynx. You may notice the vocal sac very gradually increasing in size as the frog calls, indicating that the air is only being expelled from the lungs and is not being shunted back and forth between the resonance chambers and the lungs. Suddenly the calling stops and the vocal sac may partly or entirely deflate before the next burst of vocal activity. Air may be released through the nostrils or transferred back to the lungs.

The study of frog mating calls has been one of the most rewarding areas of research for about twenty years. It resulted from the realization of zoologists such as Blair (1958) that each species of frog has a call that differs from that of every other species. There is inevitably something about it that makes it as specific as the different songs of birds. This alone provided a new and extremely useful means of distinguishing species, but it was followed by the finding that any female is attracted only to the characteristic call produced by the male of her own species. In fact it was eventually demonstrated that the females genuinely ignored other calls, so mating call data assumed even greater importance in the eyes of zoologists. Here was a vital and yet so simple means of 'isolating' the species; of minimizing accidental interbreeding of species in situations where this might prove possible. Thus the mating call became known as a 'pre-mating isolating mechanism', and a new tool for exploring the basis of evolution was placed in enthusiastic hands.

With the aid of a portable tape recorder any field naturalist can record the calls of individual species and learn to recognize the ways in which the calls differ. In many cases one can so readily distinguish them by ear that a tape recording need serve as nothing more than a reminder. However there are obvious difficulties when writing about calls if you have to liken them to other known or unknown noises, or describe them by some other means. For example, I might describe the call of *Limnodynastes tasmaniensis* in the vicinity of Adelaide, as being like the noise made by a small boy trying to imitate machine-gun fire. Lee (1967) wrote that the call of Western Australian *Heleroporus eyrei* took the form of a 'long low moan'. Conveying accurately what is meant assumes that we all have the same ideas of machine-gun fire and moans.

Sometimes calls are described in a way which is really a faithful attempt to convert the sounds heard into the words they resemble. This means creating new phonetic words in the hope that correct pronunciation will convey the sound to the reader. For example Moore (1961) describes the call of *Kyarranus loveridgei* as 'a slow guttural "oric" ',and the equally small *Uperoleia marmorata* as 'a short, sharp, rather high-pitched "akh", explosive in character'.

The more complex and drawn out calls become more difficult to describe. Hence Harrison (1922) thought the call of *Litoria aurea* best described as 'craw-awk, crawk, crok, crok, whilst Moore (1961) considered that it resembled 'wr-a-a-a-ack, wr-a-a-a-ck'.

Often we don't do justice to our powers of sound perception, for by ear we can gain more than just a general impression of the call. For example, it is possible to count the number of notes if they are not too closely spaced together and, if the call lasts for long enough, measure its total duration with a stopwatch. Littlejohn and Martin (1969) devised an identification key to the twelve species of frogs found around Melbourne based solely on descriptions of the mating calls of the frogs, the places that they chose to call from and the season of the year when they were likely to be heard calling. However, describing calls in a way that enables them to be recognized is virtually impossible when the calls really are very similar to one another. It may remain possible to be able to detect differences but this is of little help without means of comparison and description.

The standard recording procedure is to locate a frog that is calling and, with the minimum disturbance, place a microphone as close as possible to it. The observer then moves back to a tape recorder some distance away and patiently waits for the frog to start calling again. It is not as easy as it may appear: background noises of other frogs, insects, birds, vehicles etc. are all going to be recorded when the recorder is operating, and for each 'perfect' recording there will be many unsatisfactory ones. Finally it is important that the frog whose voice has been recorded should be captured and preserved for reference purposes.

In the laboratory, analysis can be performed with the aid of a cathode-ray oscilloscope or a sound spectrograph (audiospectrograph): instruments which enable the sounds to be transformed into a visual image that can be studied in detail. Anyone interested in details of this sort of analysis will find splendid accounts in the paper of Littlejohn (1965) and the introductory section to a recent book by Duellman (1970).

The actual magnitude of differences between the calls of species can be incredible. Selecting call duration as an example, there are several Australian and New Guinea frogs with calls that have a total duration of only 10 milliseconds or so. At the other end of the scale is the microhylid *Sphenophryne dentata*, found only at the extreme southeast end of New Guinea, whose call persists non-stop for 90 seconds – 9 000 times longer. Bearing in mind that the frequency, the number of pulses, the pulse repetition rates etc. are all independently variable, the possible combinations are almost infinite so that each species can have a different distinct call.

Under artificial conditions in the laboratory it has been shown that the female does show interest and will actively approach the call of her own kind. This has been established by ingenious experiments known as call discrimination tests. Littlejohn (1968) provided a description of the experiment and a photograph of the experimental chamber (discrimination chamber) in use. The discrimination chamber consists of an elongate box with a window at the top and a miniature loudspeaker mounted at each end. From recordings obtained in the field special tapes are prepared repeating the same call over and over again. Considerable attention is paid to every detail; the box is cooled to the exact temperature that existed in the field when the original recordings were made, and the sound volume is as nearly as possible the same as that uttered by the frog.

Several females of a species are then introduced into the chamber and when they have settled down and become used to their new surroundings, the speakers are switched on. Through one speaker comes the call made by the male of their own kind, and through the other the call of a different, but possibly closely related species. The normal pattern of behaviour is that each female approaches the speaker producing the call of the male of the same species. She moves progressively towards it and may in fact end up actually sitting on the speaker.

In repeated trials Littlejohn and his colleagues found that even when they sometimes switched the tapes over, so causing the 'right' call to come from the opposite end of the discrimination box, the females were not fooled. The frogs soon realized that a switch had been made, and changed the direction of their movements, homing in on the call that they found so attractive

It is particularly intriguing to find out just how females find the right mates when as many as six species are calling simultaneously from the same pond, producing a complex cacophony of sound. The female is assisted in her task in a number of different ways. The most apparent is that males of the different species involved are not distributed haphazardly throughout the area but tend to form minor congregations. For example, some species call when they are actually floating on the surface of the water, possibly touching a plant for support. Others call from the edge of the pond, whilst others call from the land surrounding it, in burrows on the bank or from low vegetation. This sort of separation is termed spatial isolation and it probably improves the chances of the female finding the male of her own kind.

Until fairly recently many zoologists were dubious about the ability of frogs to distinguish the call of their own species from others when the differences between the calls seemed to be of a minor nature. It was thought that frogs did not possess ears that were sufficiently refined to permit them to differentiate to such an acute degree.

We now find that the ears of the frog function as frequency filters, rather like radio receivers tuned only to one station. The male calls are broadcast at specific frequencies that are picked up by the female 'receiver', and choice of individual transmission wavelengths by different species calling together prevents the radio hams' problem of 'jamming'. Loftus-Hills and Johnstone (1970) showed that the responses of the brain to sound differed in each of nine Australian species that they studied.

The distances at which frogs are capable of hearing mating calls is another new area of research. In the past there have been major problems in getting any accurate measurements of the intensity or volume of sound. However Loftus-Hill and Littlejohn (1971) overcame them and recorded a range of 88 to 105 decibels in five species. From what had just been learned about hearing, they calculated that the small species *Ranidella parinsignifera* could probably not detect its own call at a distance greater than about four metres, whereas *Litoria ewingi* probably hears males of its own species at distances of up to one hundred metres.

12 In the Face of the Enemy

THERE ARE VIRTUALLY MILLIONS of animals seeking out frogs and feeding upon them, so that frogs are the cannon fodder of the animal kingdom. Each stage of development from egg to adult faces its own particular dangers, and at no time of day or night are frogs and their offspring free from attack. Species of frogs survive principally because, despite the carnage, there remain sufficient numbers to breed each year and so perpetuate their kind.

There are relatively few creatures that feed upon aquatic frog spawn, and fishes probably constitute the major predator. I have watched small fishes, introduced into lakes in New Guinea to control mosquito larvae, actually devouring the entire spawn clumps of the tree frog *Litoria darlingtoni*. This sort of habit may be fairly common but it is a matter of luck observing it happening and we know little about what happens beneath the surface of the water where there may be other enemies.

The only other creatures that I have seen eating frogs' eggs are insects. The foam nests of Australian *Limnodynastes* species, often anchored at the sides of ponds, are accessible to hungry ground-dwelling insects and are occasionally eaten by ants. A more specialized egg-feeder is a fly occurring in the New Guinea high-lands. Its larvae attack only a particular sort of spawn clump, characterized by a very firm, gelatinous, outer coat, which is laid by many montane, hylid tree frogs. The fly larvae bore their way through the jelly mass and, as they progress from egg to egg, leave a network of tunnels behind them. There is a similar predator of frogs' eggs in Brazil for which life in jelly-like or viscous sur-roundings presents no problem. In Texas some of the close relatives of these flies breed in pools of crude petroleum.

Tadpoles are almost constantly on the move and no doubt they attract the attention of a greater variety of predators. There are several different kinds of large aquatic insects which have been reported to feed on them. For example, some of the giant water bugs can grow to a size of 70 mm and include small fish as well as tadpoles in their diet. Equally formidable enemies are the great, glossy black, water beetles of the family Dytiscidae, and their equally ferocious larvae. In other parts of the world the members of this family eat tadpoles, and there is no question that they do so in Australia and New Guinea.

At the sides of ponds *Dolomedes* is sometimes to be found, a particular kind of spider which is an expert at capturing small animals under water. McKeown (1943) states that tadpoles and even goldfish 90 mm long have been devoured. He says that the spider can remain absolutely motionless on the surface of the water for hours on end, its legs spread out to buoy it up. However, immediately suitable prey passes beneath, it dives, wraps its long legs around the prey and plunges in its fangs. As soon as the animal succumbs to the injected venom the spider drags it out of the water and eats it immediately.

Worrell (1970) lists tadpoles as common food items in the diet of most species of freshwater turtles occurring in Australia, and several species of water snakes are also said to consume them. It is likely that those birds that normally feed upon small fishes and frogs will eat tadpoles as well. In fact when tadpoles are in dense congregations, such as when pools are rapidly drying up, they are particularly prone to attack and a common rat will take enormous numbers. A good example occurred some years ago at the edge of coastal sandhills at West Beach near Adelaide, where shallow pools containing thousands of large tadpoles of *Neobatrachus pictus* were visited each night by the common rat. The rats carried the tadpoles to discrete spots on the adjacent land, sensibly discarding the silt-filled intestines. These they dropped into neat piles which, over the space of a few days, reached the size of upturned saucers.

Snakes constitute the most serious menace to adult frogs and to judge from what Worrell (1970) writes, there seem to be very few which don't habitually eat them. It is a pity that we just do not know whether all frogs are eaten indiscriminately or whether there are some species of frogs that are absent amongst snake diets, so raising questions whether they are rejected or ignored through possession of effective defence mechanisms.

Amongst the snakes the common keelback *Amphiesma mairii* of Australia and New Guinea is particularly renowned for its frog-eating habits. Tyler and Parker (1974) found seven specimens of an undescribed species of the leptodactylid *Ranidella* in the stomach of one of them. Barbour (1910) has also described a species of frog new to science as a result of finding one in a snake's stomach.

Birds are much more selective in their feeding habits than most snakes and lizards, and a few species definitely feed upon frogs. Cleland (1918) found only a single frog in one of 224 bird species killed for the preparation of museum specimens. However Lea and Gray (1935) included in their survey more of the birds that inhabit or feed near water. They found that frogs are eaten by herons, snipes, water-rails, cormorants, egrets, whipbirds, curra-wongs, kookaburras and kingfishers. In New Guinea a sacred kingfisher removed from a table in the open air specimens of the microhylid *Cophixalus parkeri* that I had gone to much trouble to collect on the nearby mountain slopes.

There do not appear to be many published records of mammals eating frogs in Australia other than those reported to feed upon *Bufo marinus* and discussed in Chapter 6. I have seen cats, dogs, and pigs eating frogs to supplement their diet, and there are several records of the bat *Macroderma gigas* eating frogs in the Northern Territory. The knowledge of fish as predators is equally poor although many undoubtedly eat native frogs. The cruel habit of some anglers of using live frogs as bait and the availability of rubber frog lures indicates how we must regard fish as frog eaters.

There remain a few creatures which would not be expected to harm adult frogs in any way, but do in fact capture and eat them. The first group of these are diverse types of spiders, and particularly funnel-web spiders and trapdoor spiders.

The idea of an insect eating frogs is little short of remarkable, and certainly poetic justice. The insect involved is the praying mantis and in South America, where some mantises are particularly large, these creatures are known to be capable of eating many small vertebrate animals. The only published record that I have been able to trace of such an event occurring in Australia is reported in the form of a letter to the editor of the Victorian Naturalist appearing in Volume 79. Apparently Mr K. M. Nash heard the distress cry of a frog and investigated the cause. In the grass he found a young golden bell frog (*L. aurea*) about 30 mm long, held upside down by a large brown mantis. The mantis was on a thick grass stem, clutching the frog around the hind legs, and was in the process of actually eating the frog alive. In the Northern Territory the mantis is a common predator of frogs (M. J. Ridpath, pers. comm.).

The list of enemies of frogs would not be complete without mentioning man. Whether he collects frogs as a source of food or for other purposes, or simply destroys them, he is genuinely a major enemy. However the topic is such a vast one that a separate chapter has been devoted to it.

To avoid detection by their enemies the majority of frogs employ some form of camouflage which renders them indistinguishable from their background. This objective is achieved in a number of ways by use of colours or other more elaborate methods of deception.

By far the simplest example of camouflage is the uniform leaf-green coloration of some of our tree frogs. To the untrained eye these frogs are difficult to distinguish from green foliage, even at very short distances. Although it is common to associate tree frogs with green body-colour, only five out of forty Australian species are uniformly green. Some other species bear green patches, but the vast majority are grey or brown with lighter and darker markings upon them. Probably what matters most is the background colour of the areas where they sit and rest.

When we are searching for frogs that happen to be motionless and silent, we retain a mental image of the typical shape of a frog: its head, body and limbs. Searching becomes a process of trying to detect just a portion of a frog outline, but deception is often achieved in remarkable ways.

For example the characteristically contoured lines of the hind limbs can be deliberately confused by the presence of contrasting bars of colour which cross from one portion of one limb to the adjacent position on the next, giving the impression of fusing those portions together (Fig. 26). Broad contrasting lines running along the length of the back probably achieve a different effect by virtually splitting the image into sections.

There are more complex ways in which frogs interrupt the

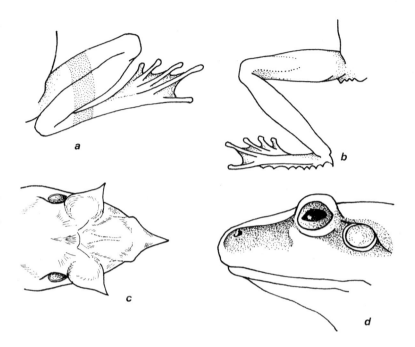

FIG. 26 Camouflage techniques. *a.* band across hind legs; *b.* skin lappets; *c.* skin flaps on snout and eyelids of *Litoria prora*; *d.* dark head stripe on *Litoria nigrofrenata*.

image of the outlines of the body, sometimes by physically changing their contours. *Litoria eucnemis* and *L. prora* have developed rows of pointed skin flaps, termed lappets, along the outer edges of the forearm and the hind leg to the heel (Fig. 26). When these frogs are sitting at rest the flaps form an irregular outer border to the body shape, and the natural contours are much less obvious. *Litoria prora* has proceeded a step further in developing a long pointed flap of skin projecting from the tip of the snout, and other flaps on the eyelids (Fig. 26).

One of the most difficult structures for frogs to conceal are their eyes which tend to be extremely prominent. Time and again frogs have overcome this problem by having the lower portion of the eye darker than the upper portion and by developing broad bands of dark colour on the sides of the heads. As seen in Figure

26d the band typically extends from the nostril to a position behind the head and, because the upper limit of the band is just on a level with the middle of the eye, the eye is split into two. From a quick glance the concept of the true spherical shape of the eye is lost, for only the upper half is readily visible. When viewed from above the eyes are still prominent and there remains the characteristic roundish shape. However the true shape is often masked by creating a gently curving band of darker or lighter tone. Separating off the front of the head in this way, and dividing the eyelids into front and back halves, destroys the symmetry of the eyelids which would reveal the presence of the animal.

One of the best examples of mimicry amongst Australian frogs is practised by *Nyctimystes hosmeri* which occurs at Tully Falls near Cairns. This tree frog is predominantly a drab reddish-brown colour, but against this background there are striking spots of white. When small the spots tend to be circular but they have irregular borders and black centres when they are larger. In fact these areas of white, and white and black, are very much like mould growths. I have never had the opportunity to observe this frog in its natural state but I can only assume that there are genuine mould growths on the trees in which they live, and against which they harmonize. There are other frogs with irregular white, cream or lemon yellow patches on their backs identical in shape and form to the lichens found on the trunks of dead logs and living trees in the montane forests of the New Guinea highlands.

All of the examples of colour and patterns mentioned so far provide means of avoiding the attention of other animals. However many of these same frogs, and numerous others, have developed absolutely vivid coloration on those areas of their limbs and bodies which are hidden from view when they sit at rest. For example, a frog may be predominantly dull grey or brown above but the hidden surfaces of the back of the thighs and groin can be bright orange, crimson, black and yellow, or even violet (Plate 17). It now seems to be generally agreed that these 'flash markings' have been developed to surprise and possibly momentarily confuse an enemy. Hence if a frog became aware of a predator approaching from behind and made a leap for cover, the predator about to grasp the drab frog would suddenly see a flash of bright colours. The flash markings could quite possibly startle the enemy and, for the victim, anything that interrupts or confuses the predator could provide just that little extra time, creating the difference between survival and capture.

In Australia and New Guinea flash markings are particularly common amongst tree frogs, the most predominant colour combination being black on a yellow or pale orange background. This choice of colours suggests that they do function in an attempt to draw attention away from the predator's previous conception of the drab animal, for black and yellow in combination are the height of advertisement. It is awareness of this fact that has caused highways departments in some Australian States to paint the upright posts of traffic signals in horizontal bands of these colours because they are more conspicuous and more readily noticed than when painted black and white.

Throughout the animal kingdom there are harmful animals that rely upon a black and yellow coloration to warn off creatures likely to interfere with them, but there are confidence tricksters which bluff their way through life by being black and yellow and yet quite harmless. The corroboree frog in Plate 3 bears spectacular black and yellow stripes along its body. No one has yet studied the skin secretions of this frog to establish whether it might be harmful for animals to eat it. Spending much of its life hidden away beneath sphagnum moss, it is difficult to comprehend the purpose of such brilliance. A glance at *Notaden bennetti* in Plate 2 demonstrates another way in which a frog can be distinctive using just black against yellow. As is mentioned below, *N. bennetti* is not bluffing in its attempts to warn away other animals.

Whether frogs have the ability to blend into their background, or whether they deliberately advertise their presence, a new dimension is added to their survival repertoire if they can change their colour. There seem to be definite limitations to the actual range of colour changes that can be displayed by most species; this may be in some way related to the various ways in which frogs produce the colours that we see. For example none of the species of green tree frogs actually possess any green pigment at all.

The green colour of frogs can be explained by considering the way in which the sky appears blue. There is no blue pigment in the sky, but it attains this appearance through the scattering of light rays by millions upon millions of tiny particles in the earth's atmosphere. The deeper layer of the frogs' skin provides a similar sort of situation, for there the light rays are scattered in just the same way, but by contact with tiny crystals in special pigment cells. These crystals reflect the light upwards but, in passing back through the skin they penetrate a different group of cells containing yellow pigment. Hence the blue light passes through a yellow filter and so appears green.

The yellow pigments are rather unstable and in dead frogs placed in alcohol the pigment rapidly passes out into solution. Thus with the yellow filter lost the frog changes from green to blue. This explains the rather ridiculous name of the lovely green tree frog *Litoria caerulea* arising from a word which means 'blue'. All that happened was that the first specimens to reach England in the eighteenth century were pickled ones. Reports of live blue frogs do occur in the popular press from time to time and it would seem likely that the cause of these abnormal frogs is simply that they lack the yellow carotenoid filter.

Most frogs seem to possess the ability to lighten or darken their skin. It is not uncommon when reading descriptions of frogs to find zoologists describing the colour of a frog in its 'dark phase' and its 'light phase', because the two extremes differ so widely. The substance involved in these colour or tone changes is usually the black pigment, melanin. The pigment cells containing melanin granules or particles are called melanophores and are rather strange in shape, having many irregular radiating arms (Fig. 27). The melanin granules can be moved about within the body of the cell. Thus when the granules are rather evenly distributed throughout the cell and so quite widely dispersed from one another, the cell assumes a rather dark colour. However when they all congregate together the area of pigment is confined to a smaller area and appears paler.

Occasionally there are frogs that completely lack melanin and are termed albinos, which are popularly but quite wrongly thought to be white. In the course of the last fifteen years I have seen two albino juvenile *Limnodynastes tasmaniensis* and one albino tadpole of *Neobatrachus pictus*. One of the juveniles is shown in

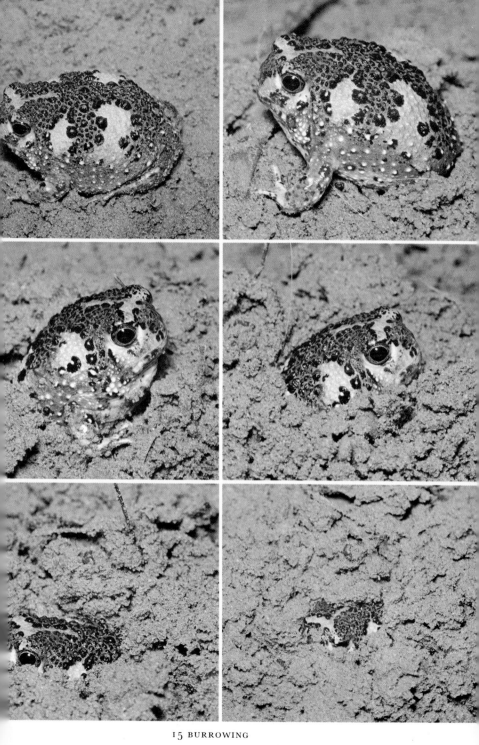

15 BURROWING

This sequence shows (*l. to r. from top*) how a burrowing frog, *Notaden bennetti*, buries himself in the desert soil by digging a vertical shaft with his feet

Disrupted outline in *Ceratobatrachus guentheri*

16 CAMOUFLAGE

The dark eye-bar in *Litoria brevipalmata*

a   b

FIG. 27 Movement of granules of pigment in skin cell. *a*. the cell is dilated and the granules are dispersed; *b*. the edge of the cell is constricted, and the granules are concentrated together.

Plate 19; it is not white, but basically pink in colour, probably caused by the blood in the superficial vessels of the skin.

Assuming that camouflage has failed to protect a frog there remain various ways which provide it with a chance of escaping an approaching enemy. Certainly it would be false to believe that every species has a great repertoire of escape mechanisms, for really each one seems to possess only one or two. However the array of defence possibilities is quite extensive in frogs as a whole.

In many cases it is possible to gain an impression of the sort of defence behaviour that a frog will employ simply by looking at its shape or skin. For example, those that rely upon their ability to avoid capture by prodigious feats of jumping have very long hind limbs with long feet. When they jump the limbs extend in a concertina fashion providing a tremendous initial spring. I do not know of any rivals to the South African champions that can clear ten metres in one leap; about three metres is the maximum for Australian and New Guinea species. Bearing in mind that even this involves a single spring equivalent to at least thirty times the body length of the frog, it is nevertheless a noteworthy effort.

On the whole the longer legged frogs tend to be timid animals. I think that this is a fair description because they are all likely to leap away at the slightest hint of danger. Any naturalist will testify that it is just not possible to approach the 'jumpers' in the same way as other frogs, and it is my impression that it takes far less to alarm those that can jump great distances than those that cannot. Obviously this form of defence is of value only in the right surroundings: streamside dwellers, for instance, can reach the safety of water without the need for feats of athletic excellence.

Almost all frogs have two types of glands in their skin secreting either mucus or poisonous materials which are not involved solely in defensive behaviour. However some species are definitely capable of releasing slimy mucus quite copiously when they are grasped. *Litoria aurea* and its close relatives are particularly prone to do this, and become so slippery that restraining them is very difficult.

Assuming that a frog is faced with such direct confrontation with an enemy that capture is imminent, there remains the possibility of attempting to convince the predator that the intended victim is too big to be eaten. At first consideration it seems a ludicrous activity, but the elaborate nature of some of the performances of frogs suggests that these antics do have a genuine survival value. For example the rotund bullfrogs increase their girth by inflating their lungs to maximal capacity, so that they become distended like balloons. Obviously the predator has to assess whether or not it can swallow the frog, and any sudden increase in size may cause the enemy to assume that the prey is simply too large for it to tackle.

Some toads undergo a quite elaborate behavioural display to achieve the same result. It is sheer bluff, but it is practised in such a consistent fashion that we must assume that it is often effective. Cott (1940) has described the curious actions of *Bufo marinus* in great detail because the success of its survival initially relies upon appearing larger than it really is, but by a far more elaborate method. What *B. marinus* does is to drop the side of the body nearest to the predator and raise the side furthermost from it. In effect it displays the greatest possible surface area to the view of the predator. Cott was impressed by the toad's virtual insistence that it was a large animal, and was amused by its reactions. He noted: 'I have more than once walked around and approached the animal from the opposite side, when, like a ship rolling heavily in the ocean swell, the body is made to rock over until it is again orientated over at right angles to the observer'. As Cott points out, the intention of the toad is simply to dishearten the predator by an increase in size which is partly real and partly due to an optical illusion.

Having been approached or even chased by an enthusiastic predator, feigning death seems a ludicrous activity. However, the fact that a few frog species do this at least indicates that the habit is of potential survival value. When flipped over upon their backs many of the little *Pseudophryne* toadlets will remain absolutely motionless with their legs extended. In this posture they are completely defenceless, and it seems likely that they are trying to convince the investigating predator that they are really dead and not worthy of further interest (Plate 3).

A possible defence mechanism which has not been explored by zoologists is the possession by different species of frogs of distinct odours produced by secretions released by glands in the skin. Most species have quite characteristic odours; some skin odours are faint and difficult to describe, others are exceptionally strong. For example the odour released by *Litoria aurea* is quite overpowering and distinctly resembles thyme. Several frog skin odours are comparable to culinary herbs, but there are others that are much like curry powder. In fact, with a little experience of what different species smell like, a sniff is almost as good as a glimpse as an aid to identification.

Admittedly the primary purpose of the characteristic odours may be to assist frogs to recognize their own kind, and be really another pre-mating isolating mechanism like the mating call: they may aid both sexes in their quest for mates. However the intensity of the odours from skin secretions does increase when a frog is antagonized and distressed. Hence it is quite possible that to their natural enemies a sudden waft of a smell which does not represent food may deter them from eating the frog.

Odour may be a useful ploy, but the skin secretions of many frogs are undoubtedly highly toxic. Collectors have found that placing other species in collecting bags containing *L. aurea* has resulted in the death of the other frogs, and these secretions are harmful to at least some of the enemies of frogs. The skin glands producing these substances are widely distributed throughout the skin, but are occasionally also aggregated together to form large glands, of which the parotoid glands of *Bufo marinus* (Fig. 12) are the best known examples. However, of our native species *Litoria*

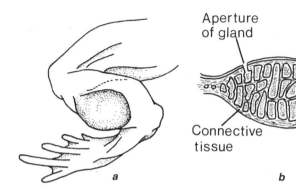

Aperture of gland

Connective tissue

Poison

FIG. 28 Calf gland of the bullfrog *Limnodynastes dumerili*. *a*. gland seen as raised lump on outer surface of calf; *b*. section through the gland showing it to be a series of compartments.

caerulea has similar structures; many species have glands on their backs, and bullfrogs have glands upon their legs (Fig. 28).

The leg glands of bullfrogs are most curious structures, forming large oval, protrusions on the skin. When sections of these glands are studied (Fig. 28) they can be seen to comprise a series of compartments which in life are distended with a creamy fluid. Each of the compartments communicates to the outside by a narrow duct through which the poisonous secretions can be released.

Quite recently a warning was issued that at least some of the Western Australian species of *Heleioporus* are potentially dangerous to man and other animals. Softly and Nairn (1975) learned of two instances in which humans were affected, one report involving a zoologist who after handling some frogs, inadvertently contaminated an antacid tablet with material released from their skins. When he later sucked the tablet he experienced a number of quite profound symptoms which lasted for about half an hour. Softly and Nairn found that *Heleioporus* species have large glands on the back and flanks. When extracts from these glands were injected into laboratory animals (guinea pigs, rats and mice), into native frogs and *Bufo marinus*, the subjects died after a few days.

The whole concept of survival in the face of so many enemies involves the methods by which frogs avoid attention, escape when detected or convince their enemies that they are dead or un-palatable. There is also the role of aggression in survival, and it is relevant for two reasons. Firstly because there are frogs which do react to interference by attacking their enemy and, secondly, because rivalry between individuals and species can become so intense that it affects survival.

Aggressive frogs are in the minority, but there is one species in New Guinea and another in the Solomon Islands known to lunge at the hand of anyone trying to pick them up.

Aggression between different species of frogs is poorly docu-mented. However, several years ago I watched some small *Ranidella signifera* adults in one of my vivaria cause the death of a tadpole of *Limnodynastes dumerili* by what was very clearly antag-onistic behaviour towards it. The *Ranidella* were the sole occupants of a flat rock surrounded by water. The tadpole of *L. dumerili* had reached the stage at which its fore limbs had erupted, its tail was being absorbed and its future survival depended upon its ability to leave the water and obtain refuge upon the rock. However, whenever it attempted to climb out of the water, one or two of the *Ranidella* would approach it and strike if forcefully on the head with the tips of their snouts. They repeated this performance upon numerous occasions and, irrespective of the portion of the rock that the tadpole approached, its efforts to climb up were immedi-ately rebuffed. The frogs succeeded in their efforts, and by morning the tadpole had drowned.

In captivity two closely related *Limnodynastes* species, *L. fletcheri* and *L. tasmaniensis*, may demonstrate the dominance of one species over another. I have noticed that when food is dropped into a vivarium the *L. fletcheri* chase away any *L. tasmanien-sis* in the vicinity before approaching the food.

Pengilley (1971) made a study of the aggressive behaviour of several species of toadlets, which not only utter threatening calls but physically attack other toadlets that enter their burrows. He describes the occupant making a lunge forward when uttering threats. Pengilley found that the *P. corroboree* living in the Snowy Mountains would 'butt the intruder vigorously'. If the intruder persists in its attempts to invade the burrow 'the occupant will crawl under the trespasser and attempt to throw the latter up and out of the burrow by flexing its fore and hind limbs'.

13   Parasites of Frogs

JUST MENTION OF THE WORD parasite probably results in two rather conflicting responses. On the one hand there may be a sense of disgust at the idea of an animal surviving and gaining benefit entirely at the expense of its unfortunate host. On the other hand we may have to admit grudging admiration for the initiative and skill that permits a parasite to harness successfully another animal's resources to its own benefit.

Frogs are hosts to a very wide variety of parasites which can occur in almost any part of their bodies. At any one time the lungs, intestine, bladder and body wall of one frog may harbour a variety of quite large and substantial parasites. It would seem that the presence of one or more kinds is almost inevitable, and those that live on the outside of the body (ectoparasites) and, to a greater extent, the internal ones (endoparasites) are virtually a fact of life. No account of frog natural history would be complete without a reasonably detailed account of the variety of these parasites.

The most important internal parasites are the parasitic worms (helminths): they comprise the Nematoda, better known as roundworms or threadworms, the Trematoda (flukes), Cestoda (tapeworms) and the Acanthocephala which are popularly called 'spiny-headed' or 'thorny-headed' worms.

There are many different nematode parasites of Australian frogs. The majority of them have been found living in the rectum, where they presumably feed upon the unwanted waste material. Others live in the stomach, within the intestine or free within the body cavity. In terms of the size of the host, the parasites can be quite large, female worms reaching as much as 8 mm in length, but males within the range of 2–4 mm. When alive the nematodes are quite transparent, and their digestive and reproductive organs appear in the form of dark areas through their outer lining. When dissected from preserved frogs they are quite white and resemble stiff and gently curved threads, easily recognizable amongst the dark contents of the digestive tract.

Some of the nematodes pass their life-histories entirely within the one host and for this reason are classified as monogenetic. The adult nematode lays eggs which reach the outside of the frog when the faecal matter is discharged. Quite how the frogs are infected with the eggs is uncertain because none of the life-cycles of the nematodes parasitic on Australian frogs are known. If the waste material is dropped on land there seems little chance of the eggs being eaten by another frog. However, if dropped in water, they could quite possibly be swallowed by tadpoles and the chain of events restarted by this means.

When the frog acts only as an intermediate host, the parasite has what are really two separate arenas of development and is said to be digenetic. The way in which the egg enters the host is probably the same as in a monogenetic nematode. However, the first of the intermediate stages concludes with the parasite enveloping itself as a cyst in the muscles of the body wall, the wall of the stomach or intestine, or perhaps in the thin membranous tissue anchoring the gut to the body wall. For the nematode to complete its development into an adult stage the frog has to be eaten by a snake.

The adult trematodes are broadly flattened and described as leaf-like because they are roughly oval, usually broader at one end than the other (Fig. 29a). They are commonly less than 5 mm long but reach 10 mm on occasions. Most species found in frogs have two suckers; one at one end and the other in the middle, or one at each end. *Polystoma* is one of the exceptions amongst the Australian and New Guinea trematodes, having a row of six suckers at one end surrounding a broad, circular disc.

Trematode life-cycles are often quite complicated, involving the passage of various stages in up to three intermediate hosts. The adult parasites are most commonly found in the bladder or lungs and can be seen readily through the transparent walls of these organs during dissection. Johnson (1912) provided an extensive account of the trematodes known to parasitize Australian frogs at that time, noting that some also occur in the duodenum, intestine and rectum. Quite recently I found numerous specimens attached to the floor of the mouth of many *Litoria caerulea* collected at the

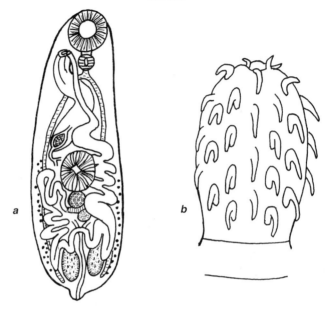

FIG. 29 Internal parasites (highly magnified). *a.* trematode or fluke; *b.* barbed end of an acanthocephalan or hookworm (after Johnston and Angel 1940, and Edmonds 1971).

Valley of the Eagles in the Northern Territory. To avoid being dislodged by food or movements of the tongue obviously required a most secure hold and in fact their suckers had raised wart-like blobs on the mouth floor.

In much the same fashion as some of the digenetic nematodes, some of the trematodes form cysts in the body wall of frogs, and complete their development only if the frogs are eaten by snakes. Johnston and Angel (1940) report a wide variety of snakes infected as a result of this unfortunate habit.

Frogs are the intermediate hosts for spargana, the larvae of a group of tapeworms of the genus *Spirometra*. The life-cycle of the parasite is a complex one (Fig. 30). An egg passed out of the body in the faeces of a carnivorous animal such as a cat or a dog has to reach water where it hatches to release a small larva called a coracidium. The coracidium has to be eaten by one of the small aquatic crustaceans, such as *Cyclops*, to proceed further in the path of development. Once within this animal the parasite burrows through the wall of the intestine and out into the haemocoel, or blood cavity, where it develops into the procercoid stage. The fate of the *Cyclops* determines the future of the parasite. If the *Cyclops* lives its normal lifespan and dies a natural death the parasite is doomed; in fact the *Cyclops* has to be eaten by a suitable small vertebrate host to carry on its development. If the *Cyclops* falls victim to a frog, the parasite bores through the intestine wall and enters the muscular or connective tissue of the host, developing into the sparganum stage.

The frog provides the 'second intermediate host' for *Spirometra*, and again the nature of the fate of the frog is vital to the parasite's life-history. To proceed any further the frog has to be eaten by a cat or dog (Bennett 1968).

On paper the chances seem weighted heavily against a *Spirometra* completing its life-cycle. In practice however, the likelihood of it reaching the second intermediate (sparganum) stage is quite high. Bennett found that five per cent of the *Bufo marinus* and one per cent of the *Limnodynastes tasmaniensis* that he examined were infected. In other parts of the world the incidence of sparganum in frogs may be even higher. Smyth (1962) mentions that humans in Vietnam, China and Japan become infected from the bizarre habit amongst the local inhabitants of applying to gaping wounds and to inflamed eyes poultices of frogs that have been split open for the purpose. In the course of this treatment the spargana enter the human tissues, causing the disease sparganosis which can be treated only by surgery.

The Acanthocephala or 'thorny-headed' or 'spiny-headed' worms gain their name from their protusible proboscis equipped with a formidable array of spines (Fig. 29) enabling these parasites to be readily recognized.

The first intermediate host in the acanthocephalan life cycle is usually a small crustacean or insect, and the frog (or possibly the tadpole) becomes infected when it eats them. Some thorny-headed worms have a second stage in another intermediate host before reaching adulthood.

So far the adult stages of only two species of acanthocephalans have been found in Australian frogs collected at Mount Wellington in Tasmania and at Rockingham near Perth. Only the encysted

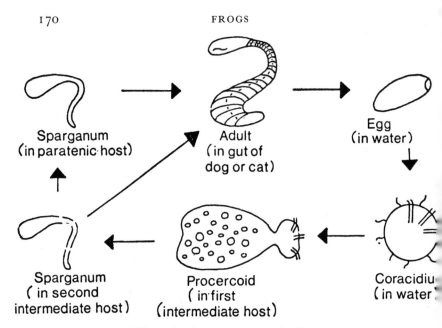

FIG. 30 Life cycle of a tapeworm (after Bennett 1968).

or intermediate stage of the acanthocephalan *Porrochis hylae* has ever been found in frogs, and the adult stage occurs only in birds. Here it is obvious that the frog has to be eaten by a bird for the parasite to complete its life-cycle. Cysts of the *Porrochis* have been located in the muscles of the body-wall of frogs and the thin transparent membrane (mesentery) anchoring the gut to the deeper tissues. The same parasite extends far beyond Australian shores, the adult having been found in birds in Formosa.

Mites are probably the smallest frog parasites that can be seen with the naked eye, but the chances of finding one are remote, for in Australia the only known infestations in frogs involve mites entering the nostrils. The practice may seem rather bizarre but there is in fact a whole family of mites which specialize in living in the nostrils of mammals, birds and other vertebrates. To date three species of these mites of the genus *Lawrencarus* have been discovered in Australia, a fourth in New Guinea. A complete list of the local frogs that are known to be hosts of mites can be obtained by referring to the papers of Womersley (1953), Domrow (1960), and Fain (1961).

Blood-sucking leeches are very widely distributed in Australia and New Guinea; from the rainforests to artificial dams they constitute an enemy to the frog. Because leeches normally attach themselves to the outside of the body of the host they are termed ectoparasites. They remain on the surface of the host only for as long as is required for them to gorge themselves with blood. Despite the relatively short duration of this attachment it is not uncommon to see one or more attached to a single frog. Observations on *Limnodynastes dumerili* at Kangaroo Island, South Australia, indicate the extreme that this form of parasitism can take when for breeding purposes frogs enter what happens to be a heavily infested pond. Waite (1925) writes: 'Leeches abound in the water, and every frog I saw had several of these annelids attached to it. Pairing frogs, being unable to rid themselves of the temporary parasites, had, literally, scores of leeches attached to their bodies, like so many streamers'.

In the New Guinea mountains, leeches called *Cedbdella* have evolved a habit (unique amongst leeches) of entering the body of the frog host. The route of entry is the cloaca (vent) and from that site they then either force their way into the space between the skin and the muscles of the body, or else penetrate the body cavity and feed from the liver or heart. Plate 20 shows a frog which has been partly dissected to reveal an enormous leech that lay beneath the skin of its back. The size of that particular leech is such that it is estimated to have been capable of taking almost the entire blood that the frog possessed in one meal. The leeches may indeed kill their hosts, for there are more recent records of leeches emerging from the cloacas of dead and dying frogs.

About twelve species of New Guinea frogs are known to be parasitized by leeches in the above way, but the habit is unknown in Australia. With the exception of one species, which is the aquatic frog *Rana grisea*, all of the hosts are tree-frogs (*Litoria* and *Nyctimystes* species), and the habits of these frogs may indicate why the many microhylids occurring in the same area of New Guinea appear to be immune from attack. Certainly the most obvious difference is that the microhylids are not so closely associated wi'' water and do not lay their eggs there. Hence it may simply be that the leeches congregate around the waterways and parasitize any frog that approaches or enters the water. They may not be at all selective in their choice of particular species of frogs as hosts because, from their point of view, the inside of one frog is probably much like that of another.

The habit of entering the body of the host would normally result in the *Cedbdella* leeches being termed endoparasites, as opposed to the normal ectoparasitic habit. However, it is quite clear that they are exercising little, if any, care and may in fact always cause the death of the host. For these reasons they may really be predators and not parasites at all.

Throughout the world there are certain kinds of flies which somehow manage to approach frogs without being detected and lay their eggs beneath the skin of the frogs' backs. Australia has its own unique type of fly for which W. S. Macleay coined the name *Batrachomyia*, literally meaning 'frog flies'. To date about ten species of *Batrachomyia* are known and, although only three have actually been reared from infested frogs, it seems likely that such a specialized habit will prove to be common to all of the parasites.

The *Batrachomyia* larvae live just beneath the skin on the back, particularly just behind the head. They can move about very slowly, shifting their position slightly from day to day. Their presence is indicated by a large oval hump often with an aperture at one end through which the larva breathes.

The host frogs are a mixed bunch, and it is quite possible that some of the *Batrachomyia* species are fairly selective in their choice of host. However what may be significant is that, with the exception of *Ranidella signifera*, all of the known hosts have rather glandular skins suggesting that they possess something that is particularly attractive to the parasites.

Within my own experience the most commonly parasitized frogs are *Litoria citropa* and *Pseudophryne bibroni*. In the former species it is not uncommon to find three or four larvae beneath the skin of one of them. A plate on page 391 of the *Australian Museum Magazine* (1955) shows an individual *L. citropa* infested with six larvae.

There are numerous parasites which commonly infect frogs but are so small that they cannot be seen without the aid of a microscope. Many are single-celled organisms living in various parts of the body, and not known to harm the host in any way at all. Whilst working at the University of Papua and New Guinea,

Ewers (1962) found that out of 96 frogs that he examined 34 harboured parasites in their blood. These blood parasites (haematozoa) may be transmitted to frogs by mosquitoes in much the same way that man contracts malaria, for Marks (1960) has watched mosquitoes taking a blood meal from frogs.

Reichenbach-Klinke and Elkan (1965) have written a 600-page textbook on the major diseases of lower vertebrate animals, and they describe a very wide variety of diseases of frogs. It comes as somewhat of a surprise to learn that even tuberculosis and cancers occur in these animals. There is no suggestion that frog diseases can be transmitted to man, with the exception perhaps of the notorious bacterium *Salmonella*. However, in that case the frog simply seems to run the risk of harbouring *Salmonella* if it lives near man.

Australian species of frogs have been known to suffer the misfortune of hernia, and even the presence of a stone in the bladder has been reported. The list of the odd conditions is quite extensive and it serves as a reminder that man is not the only creature to be plagued by injury and disease.

Teratology is the study of monsters or animals which are in some way abnormal, and is a topic which could be ignored in a book of this kind. Nevertheless it is worth mentioning because there are situations in which the occurrence of abnormal frogs could indicate contamination of water in which they were reared. Frogs are exceptionally sensitive to chemicals such as some insecticides, and the field naturalist should be equipped to recognize what may be an instance of pollution and be prepared to report his observations to the relevant State department.

Abnormalities probably occur in the populations of every animal species, and it is only amongst domestic animals that the grossly malformed are painlessly destroyed by man when they are discovered. Hence the sort of question that needs always to be posed is whether the incidence of abnormalities is higher than that which can be reasonably expected.

By far the most common naturally occurring abnormalities are an additional limb, limbs or portions of limbs (Plate 19). Museums have been regarded by the general public as the natural repositories for these monsters, with the result that most museums in Australia have at least one or two preserved specimens. The lack of one or more toes, or the presence of additional ones, is rarely noticed in the field, but is in fact of much more common occurrence than is generally appreciated. Kinghorn (1924) has a drawing of the foot of a frog from Kangaroo Island with this sort of abnormality.

The highest incidence of abnormalities that I have seen appeared in collections of several species taken in 1963 from cotton plots at Kununurra on the Ord River irrigation system, in the Kimberley Division of Western Australia. The cotton plots had been sprayed repeatedly with extremely high concentrations of insecticides. Some dead frogs and large numbers of dead fishes had been seen floating on the surface after those sprayings and most of those that survived had malformations of some kind. There is obviously no conclusive evidence that the insecticide had caused the malformations, nevertheless an environmental factor is required to explain abnormalities in different species that had little in common except that they happened to share the same breeding site.

14 Dispersal

FROGS REQUIRE ACCESS TO MOISTURE throughout the year, have limited ability to tolerate changes in temperature outside their own particular optimal ranges and generally have a rather low tolerance to salt water. These factors greatly inhibit their ability to travel far and have a profound influence upon their capability of colonizing new areas. The result is that tracts of dry country, mountain ranges and seas are the most obvious major barriers to their dispersal.

Prior to the advent of man in Australia active dispersal in undisturbed areas was probably a continual process, with some species gaining new ground possibly at the expense of territorial loss by other species. The enormous changes that man has wrought, by drainage of swamps, clearing of forests and scrub means that several species have suffered. Many are now almost certainly less widely distributed than in former times.

For most frogs active dispersal is probably a very slow process, favoured by climatic shifts towards moister conditions and changes in sea levels uniting offshore islands with the mainland: events that occupied tens of thousands of years. It does not mean that frogs lined up on the edges of the deserts and coastlines impatiently waiting for conditions that would enable them to cross to the other side, and it could be argued that 'migration' is a rather misleading word when used to describe these movements of populations. All that really happened over long periods of time was that as the barriers reduced in size so the populations expanded their territory until they ultimately occupied the entire area of what was formerly a barrier.

It is perhaps fortunate that frogs disperse across major barriers other than by their own efforts. This so-called passive dispersal is a fascinating study prompted by the evidence of the results. For example, there are frogs on the small islands in the Pacific, even in the most remote ones such as Fiji. Most of the islands have not been connected by land bridges to the larger land masses at any time in their history. They arose from the ocean bed through volcanic or other activity and their faunas resulted from dispersal of animals across the seas. No one was around to see them arrive, so we may always lack real proof of just how they reached these tiny outposts.

To cross a sea barrier an animal has to be able to fly or swim, or be carried in some way by air or sea. None of the species of frogs on islands can even glide, let alone fly, but swimming is not completely out of the question. This does not mean that to travel from one island to another is an active marathon effort, but frogs are undoubtedly accidentally carried far out to sea in the massive discharges from the mouths of some rivers. When the volume of fresh water entering the sea is considerable, there is little dilution with salt water at the surface, even at distances several kilometres from the river mouth. In 1957 a Netherlands naval party in a small boat, 10 km from the mouth of the Sepik River off the north coast of New Guinea, was surprised to find a large specimen of the tree frog *Litoria infrafrenata* swimming on the surface. The likelihood of the survival of that frog must have been remote, the chances being that eventually it would have perished from exposure to salt water or would have provided a tasty morsel for a fish. However slender the chances may appear of the survival of not one but two individuals of one species, and of them reaching and breeding upon a remote island, the fact of the matter is that frogs do enter sea water in this way, probably in their thousands. In the space of thousands of years two may be successful in reaching and colonizing new territory.

Some species of frogs actually live on the seashore and others are rare visitors there. For example, in 1969 an adult *Litoria ewingi* was found beneath a pile of seaweed on the beach at Victor Harbour in South Australia, but in New Britain the ranid *Platymantis papuensis* is a common beachcomber. On the Willaumez Peninsula jutting out from the north coast of the island, lush, moist vegetation grows right up to the high tide mark. When disturbed from their home in this fringe area the frogs often leap straight into the sea, swim out for a couple of metres and then dive to hide beneath shells, seaweed or debris on the floor. There they remain for several minutes before emerging. To enter the sea upon slight provocation indicates that this frog may have a reasonable tolerance to salt water.

Frogs do vary considerably in their ability to survive in pure sea water. As a general rule size is a determining factor, for large species can survive for longer periods than small species. Unfortunately the survival time of *P. papuensis* is unknown, but in fifteen other species I studied in 1972 it ranged from less than fifteen minutes to more than twenty-four hours.

Voyages on rafts are probably the usual means by which many different kinds of animals cross seas to reach and eventually colonize remote islands. The word 'raft' can conjure up the mental picture of a number of trunks lashed together in true Robinson Crusoe fashion, but in reality these rafts are vast masses of tangled grass, shrubs and trees, frequently rising high above the surface of the water. Rafts often become formed during the passage of debris down swollen, flooded rivers. On a minor scale the method by which they grow and take shape can be seen in any small creek following a downpour. A few branches washed from the banks become jammed at some point, and vegetation floating down behind them becomes trapped to form a sort of suspended dam. Eventually the whole lot breaks free and flows on in a jumbled pile. In parts of New Guinea, where as much as 500 mm of rain can fall in 24 hours, the erosion of soils is substantial and entire trees fall into rivers. Add broken branches, torn free in accompanying gale-force winds, and the rafts can become very large indeed.

The celebrated nineteenth-century zoologist and economist Arthur Russell Wallace reported seeing in the South Seas a floating raft including trees with earth still attached to their roots. In South America a giant raft bore a number of cheetahs who reached land when it drifted to a bank of the Amazon. They celebrated their fortunate disembarkation by terrorizing the inhabitants of a nearby village.

Mr J. I. Menzies wrote to tell me his observations of a raft that, during a flash flood, became jammed on a bridge spanning the Kerevat River at Kerevat in New Britain. When the flood waters had subsided the raft was left suspended in the air and he examined it carefully looking for animal life. He found several species of frogs and lizards which, but for the presence of the bridge, would have been carried into the open sea.

It is evidence of this kind which has led zoologists to conclude that rafting is probably the most common vehicle of transport of frogs to islands. McCann (1953) considers that this applies equally well to the dispersal of the gecko lizards within the Pacific area.

It is fairly well known that many insects are carried for vast distances in turbulent winds several kilometres above the earth's surface. What is not so frequently appreciated is that vertebrate animals such as frogs and fishes are also unwilling passengers and that there are numerous reports of these creatures falling from the skies. Gilbert Whitley of the Australian Museum made a particular study of these strange phenomena and prepared a list of the reported sightings that have been published in Australian newspapers, magazines and scientific journals. He managed to trace fifty-three reports between 1879 and 1971, including details of one occasion when thousands of frogs rained down at Ewingsdale near Lismore in New South Wales, and another when frogs landed on a roof at Coff's Harbour and simultaneously upon the deck of a naval vessel off the New South Wales coast.

The majority of the sightings traced by Whitley occurred in New South Wales, and in the most densely populated parts of that State. As he points out, not all of the rains that have actually occurred in Australia will have been seen, whilst others that were seen may not have been reported in the press and so placed on permanent record. The source of these rains of animals is almost certainly miniature whirlwinds or similar atmospheric disturbances. Anyone who has watched a 'whirly' plucking up branches, debris and dust from the ground can appreciate how, on a larger scale, numbers of small animals can be lifted up and carried for long distances by the wind.

In northeastern and northwestern Australia, where cyclones are of regular seasonal occurrence, the winds may well transport frogs for very great distances, but whether the frogs can survive the journeys is dubious. Inger (1954) suggested that winds may be the principal means of transport of the microhylid genus *Oreophryne*, which has reached the Philippine Islands from New Guinea. The suggestion is attractive simply because the members of this genus have been found in bulbous plants growing on the trunks of trees: material likely to be torn off and carried away by high winds.

It has often been suggested that wading birds inadvertently assist the dispersal of frogs. Certainly they do stand in water, but the idea of them unconsciously carrying frog spawn wound around their legs from one pond to another seems a little too bizarre. To become attached to their legs the spawn would conceivably need to be in a chain-like form. The spawn of *Bufo marinus* meets these requirements, but there are no odd distribution records of that species that cannot be explained by a less complex process such as a deliberate introduction by man.

Pelicans sometimes carry food in their beaks whilst in flight, and there is a report in the *Sydney Morning Herald* of 21 April 1956 of fish up to 250 grams in weight falling on Forbes in New South Wales whilst a flock of pelicans passed overhead. The existence of this sort of record means that pelicans, as consumers of frogs, must be considered potential distributors. However, to believe that they are making a tangible contribution to dispersal by providing a convenient aerial distribution service is, unlike frogs, hard to swallow.

Throughout the world there are numerous occasions when frogs are carried vast distances amongst freight, particularly in consignments of fresh fruit and vegetables. From the Adelaide Fruit Market I have received two species of living tree frogs that had been found inside crates of bananas despatched from northern Queensland. This sort of dispersal is completely accidental and is hardly likely to result in species becoming established in new areas (other than temporarily within the restricted confines of banana warehouses). Successful establishment is most likely to result from the small boy collecting frogs whilst holidaying with his family in Queensland, and later releasing them in a stream at the bottom of his garden which may be in an outer suburb of Sydney.

Two foreign species have been deliberately introduced into Australia. The first was the African clawed toad *Xenopus laevis* used in medical science and now kept in captivity in several research laboratories in the eastern and southern States. The second involved the introduction and release of *Bufo marinus*, described in detail in Chapter 6.

Far less publicity has been given to the expatriate Australian species, for Australian frogs have been released in other countries for various reasons and have usually become successfully established in their new homes. Probably the first attempt to extend the range of an Australian species involved the efforts of settlers in New Zealand. There existed on each of the islands in the Dominion so-called 'acclimatization' societies whose object appeared to include making good any apparent deficiencies in the fauna and flora of New Zealand. With only three species of native frogs in existence a concerted effort was made to introduce a few more (McCann 1961).

In 1867 and 1868 the Auckland Acclimatization Society imported and released a number of *Litoria aurea* which had been collected in Sydney. On the South Island in 1868 the Southland Acclimatization Society introduced spawn of the same species that had been collected in Tasmania. However, the southern introduction did not meet with immediate success, and from 1888 onwards frogs were repeatedly transferred from the North Island to the South Island. These efforts resulted in *L. aurea* being firmly established throughout much of the Dominion.

Litoria ewingi entered New Zealand in 1875 when Mr W. Perkin released, in a ditch at Greymouth on the South Island, several frogs that he had obtained in Tasmania. Extension of the species to the North Island occurred as recently as 1948 and it is now to be found at many localities.

Litoria caerulea was introduced into New Zealand from Australia by the Department of Agriculture in 1897 and 1899. Specimens were released at several sites on both islands, but nowhere has the species become entrenched. In fact it is now nearly twenty years since a frog was last sighted.

Just when, how or why *L. aurea* was introduced into New Caledonia is uncertain. Sarasin (1926) was the first person to record it there, and Neill (1964) has suggested that it may have arrived there as a stowaway amongst produce shipped from an Australian port. However it is highly likely that French planters would regard the frog as a natural means of controlling mosquitoes and insect pests of economic importance, and for these reasons they possibly deliberately introduced *L. aurea* into islands formerly lacking frogs altogether.

There is similarly no record of how *L. aurea* entered the islands of the New Hebrides group situated to the east of New Caledonia. The first record of its presence there was made by the parasitologists Fischthal and Kuntz in 1967, and enquiries made by members of the Royal Society Expedition in 1971 indicate that it was obtained from New Caledonia by planters in about 1960. It is now present in enormous numbers on the New Hebridean islands of Efate, Malekula and Espiritu Santo.

Litoria aurea was introduced into Hawaii by Mr E. M. Ehrhorn in 1929 but according to Tinker (1941) the attempt to establish it there proved a failure.

The process of importing and releasing animals in England has almost achieved the status of being a national sport, and Frazer (1964) lists no less than thirteen introduced species of frogs. An Australian one was included in that total, for about a dozen *Litoria ewingi* were released in Cornwall in 1951. They thrived and bred for several years in a small artificial pond but were totally destroyed in 1963–64 by the exceptionally severe winter.

The only species of frog from New Guinea introduced elsewhere is the largest member of the Hylidae: *Litoria infrafrenata*. Its presence on the island of Java in Indonesia is far to the west of its normal geographic range, and Van Kampen (1907) states that it was introduced by man. The introduction was certainly an early one because it was first reported there in 1857. For many years *infrafrenata* could be found in the Botanical Gardens at Bogor, but the population appears to have died out.

15   Geographical Distribution

STUDY OF THE DISTRIBUTION of animals (zoogeography) is a fascinating topic involving not just where the different kinds happen to occur, but why they are not elsewhere. Interest lies in two spheres: the limiting factors of the present distribution of animals and, for the purpose of interpretation of the evolutionary history, the routes of communication and the former dispersal of them and their ancestors.

The fact that each of the major continents has its own distinctive fauna is discovered by everyone during early childhood. The seeds are sown by children's alphabets, which almost without exception favour associating many letters with animals. Hence the first attempts to communicate involve recognizing that the letter L stands for Lion and Z for Zebra. As we grow older we may remain uncertain about the geographic distribution of zebras, but somehow the lion and Africa become inseparable as related bits of information that are stored away. In later life the average person's impression of any continent remains restricted to its most spectacular examples of fauna.

As a field of science zoogeography had a comparable upbringing, for the earliest attempts to recognize differences between different parts of the world were founded upon the presence or preponderance of particular groups of animals in those areas.

The present scheme was proposed by Arthur Russell Wallace in 1876, and includes uniting Australia with New Guinea and adjacent islands as one Region. A century of great progress in zoogeography has modified his scheme only in minor points of detail.

The Australian Region has proved to be one of the most difficult to separate as a unit. Although it was isolated for millions of years, it is no longer isolated from the adjacent Oriental Region by a vast ocean, and there is a chain of islands leading up to New Guinea.

Many of the Oriental animals have taken advantage of them and moved southwards from one island to another, and New Guinea animals have similarly used these same islands to extend northwards into Indonesia. Hence although the major components of the two areas are vastly different, a few creatures are common to both, and it is impossible to draw a line on a map to show where one Region ends and the other begins.

Of all of the terrestrial animals frogs are probably the best subjects for zoogeographical studies. What makes them so suitable are their dependence upon moisture, limited powers of locomotion and other limitations to their dispersal. Where frogs are found on offshore islands separated from the mainland by shallow seas it is probable that they arrived there originally by land at a time when the seas were lower.

Sea-level changes have to be placed in their correct perspective. These are not just minor differences that took place millions of years ago, but tremendous contrasts, some of which have occurred within the life of the species we call modern man and many of the other species of animals that inhabit the world today. The biblical description of a great flood reported in the Book of Genesis has parallels in Babylonian scriptures, Hindu legends and Australian Aboriginal mythology. It is easy enough to argue that it is just a story conjured up by religious leaders to demonstrate the existence of an all-powerful deity, but to suggest that several priests in different parts of the world simultaneously hit on the same ruse is carrying matters too far. As it happens the study of geology provides quite conclusive evidence of changes in sea-level, and it is now appreciated that these were associated with the existence of ice-caps. During the so-called glacial periods when the ice-caps were more extensive and when glaciers existed in southeastern Australia and almost covered Tasmania, a good deal of the world's water supplies were tied up in the form of ice. Today the Australian glaciers have disappeared and the small remnants in New Guinea are rapidly melting. Nevertheless their potential impact on current sea-levels is fantastic. It has been estimated that if the ice-caps of Greenland and Antarctica were to thaw, sea-levels would rise by about 100 metres. Almost all of the Australian coastal cities would be submerged; in Sydney only the top floors of a few multi-storey buildings would remain above the surface.

FIG. 31 Australia and New Guinea as they were united by lower sea-
levels. The rows of dots between the land masses indicate the
position of a river system envisaged by Darlington (1957).
Remainder of figure derived from Doutch (1972).

In the reverse situation, when the glacial periods were at their
peak, sea-levels were about 200 metres lower than they are today.
The Australian continental shelf was exposed, and Australia and
New Guinea were united as a single land-mass. Tasmania,
Kangaroo Island and other similar islands were an integral part
of the Australian continent (Fig. 31).

The glacial periods were separated by periods when the glaciers
waned (inter-glacials). The climate became drier, seas rose,
drowning vast areas of land, and isolating the portions of hills and

mountains at the edge of the drier continental shelf to form separate islands. Our lifetime is being spent during an interglacial period, and studies of frogs and their distribution can help to establish such details as whether this period has been any drier than it is today.

Within the Australian sub-region the fauna can be separated into three major components (provinces) shown in Figure 32. The central Australian or Eyrean province is an arid zone, inhabited by frogs which have managed to overcome the problems of life in areas of low and unreliable rainfall. In the southeast the Great Dividing Range separates the Eyrean province from the moister and cooler Bassian which has proved to be a major area of frog evolution. The northern and northeastern coastal zone is termed the Torresian province and contains many species shared with New Guinea or closely related to New Guinea animals.

No scheme of provinces is going to satisfy all zoologists, and the

FIG. 32 The zoogeographic provinces of Australia.

situation occurring in the south of the continent is a prime example of the sort of problem that exists. While the southwest has many unique species of frogs, their nearest relatives – little more than distant cousins – are found in the southeast, so that the most satisfactory answer might be to regard the southeast and southwest corners as districts of the Bassian province.

In Australia the frog faunas of three areas have received considerable attention: the southwest of Western Australia; the southeast including Tasmania; and the portion of Australia and New Guinea flanking Torres Strait. Of these Tasmania and New Guinea have something in common: lower sea levels abolished the present sea barriers now isolating them from the Australian mainland. At the same time the moister climates in Australia would have rendered the now arid section of southern Australia a good deal wetter than it is today. Hence the frogs of the southwest would have been in no way cut off from the southeast.

In the southwest of Western Australia there are twenty-five species of frogs. Eight of these are very closely related to species found in southeastern Australia (Littlejohn 1967). Of the remaining seventeen some are more distantly related to southeastern ones, but it is clear that their ancestry is in some way intimately associated with the Bassian fauna. Hence, without reference to any other scientific discipline, the southwestern frog fauna seem to indicate at least two periods of contact between that part of western Australia and the southeastern portion of the continent.

Main, Lee and Littlejohn (1958) suggested that within the last one million years there had been three periods during which moist climatic conditions existed in the now arid intervening zone, so permitting frogs to roam at will into and out of the southwest.

Several zoologists think that it is best to visualize the route used by ancestral frogs travelling between the southwest and the southeast as the shortest route possible. This would have been the southern fringe of the continental shelf, now submerged beneath the sea. The Nullarbor Plain adjacent to this shelf must have been fairly wet at that time, but so far no fossils of really moist-dependent animals have been found there. In caves on the western border of the Nullarbor Plain, Lundelius (1963) reported remains of animals such as the koala which, although in our lifetime has been confined to the forests of eastern Australia, was once extensively distributed in the southwest. In its present barren form the Nullarbor is a barrier to many animals, but whether it was wet enough for frogs to live there remains unknown.

Of all of the members of the southwestern frog fauna with intimate relatives in the southeast, the toadlet *Pseudophryne occidentalis* is probably the one which is least dependent upon moist conditions (Main 1968) and extends far into the more arid zone to the east. Its southeastern partner *P. bibroni* is also perfectly capable of surviving short dry spells, reaching the Flinders Ranges in South Australia.

Until recently these two species were believed to be separated from one another by a distance of 1600 km, but a chance discovery has disturbed ideas about frog migration routes, and may have cast light upon past climatic history. In November 1970 Dr E. Mathews, an entomologist on the staff of the South Australian Museum, visited the Everard Ranges in the far northwest of South Australia to collect insects. He was particularly interested in collecting dung beetles which are important creatures that help to fertilize the soil by burying animal droppings. One of his collecting techniques involved sinking into the ground traps which were nothing more than steep-sided, cardboard drinking cups, claimed by their manufacturers to provide the 'longest drink in the world'. He was unsuccessful in his attempts to collect beetles, but into the cups fell six frogs. One was *Neobatrachus centralis*, formerly known to exist at that locality, but the others found were *Pseudophryne occidentalis* previously unknown in South Australia.

The population of *Pseudophryne occidentalis* in the Everard Ranges is 880 km east of the southwestern population, and is the only known link between the southwest and southeast partner species. Perhaps the most important feature about the site of the finding (Fig. 33) is the fact that it lies so far north of the route that the 'migrating' populations of frogs are supposed to have used during the moist glacial periods.

How this particular species can testify to the past climate in the Everard Ranges hinges upon its requirements for survival. During dry periods *Pseudophryne* species do not aestivate in cells beneath the surface of the ground, and it is probably this inability more than any other factor that inhibits their ability to extend further into arid areas. Sheltering beneath rocks is a successful

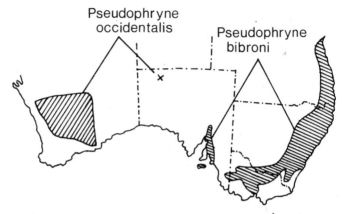

FIG. 33 Distribution of two species of *Pseudophryne* toadlets in southern Australia (from Tyler 1971).

survival mechanism for short, dry periods but little more. Hence a prolonged drought would probably wipe out the adults, and the population would expire for this reason rather than through lack of opportunity to breed. That *P. occidentalis* exists today in the Everard Ranges indicates that the population there has not been exposed to prolonged droughts. The presence of these frogs at least suggests that during the present arid period we are experiencing in our lifetime, that portion of South Australia has not been significantly drier than it is today.

Tasmania has little that is obviously similar to the southwestern portion of the mainland, but it would seem that its frog fauna can be shown to have developed its own peculiarities through basically similar events. Tasmania is very much a part of the Bassian province, and it and the islands in Bass Strait were united with Victoria during periods of substantially lower sea levels. When the seas rose Tasmania and the islands became isolated from one another and the mainland, and it was this splitting up of populations of animals which may have initiated the evolution of new kinds.

At the times when sea-levels were lower than they are today, Australia and New Guinea were completely united with one another. The sea now separating them is exceptionally shallow and, at Torres Strait where they are nearest to one another, the ιast land communication may have been broken by rising waters only about 6500 years ago (Jennings 1972). The site of Torres Strait was a vital link between Australia and New Guinea, and there is in fact a remarkably close similarity in the frog fauna of the now opposing shores.

To date forty-five species of frogs are known to live on the Cape York Peninsula, and thirty-three on the adjacent part of New Guinea extending north to the Fly River. Included in these totals are thirteen species which are common to both land masses. This is not a high number and one of the most intriguing questions is just why the frog faunas of the opposing shores differ from one another as much as they do. It is the species which are confined to one land mass or another that attract particular interest. For example in Australia the bullfrogs occur in the southwest of the continent, and in eastern Australia right up the coast to the very tip of the Cape York Peninsula. Another widespread species is *Cyclorana australis* which extends completely along the northern coastline and the closely related *C. novaehollandiae* which goes down into northern New South Wales. The total geographic ranges of these species involve thousands of kilometres and yet none occurs in New Guinea.

By far the simplest explanation is that these species did not exist on the Cape York Peninsula when Australia was connected to New Guinea. Alternatively that they did, but the land link did not provide the sort of environment suitable for them and so they did not venture out on it. Many diverse kinds of frog did cross the land link, and because the bullfrogs and *C. australis* range throughout a wide variety of habitats, the idea that the land communication was unsuitable for them seems most unlikely. Hence their absence from New Guinea implies that they have occupied the Cape York Peninsula after the seas separated it from New Guinea. The direction of the movement of *C. australis* (whether it evolved in the northwest of the continent and then ventured to the southeast or vice versa, or even in opposing directions from a central site) is immaterial. The implication remains that the species has travelled thousands of kilometres since Australia was isolated from New Guinea only a few thousand years ago.

Compared with our own lifespan 'a few thousand years' seem

an enormous period of time, but the idea that species of frogs can move thousands of kilometres in possibly no more than 5000 years is of tremendous importance. It provides a sort of brake to be borne in mind when reading speculative interpretations of the history of frogs, involving dispersal and isolation expressed in tens of millions of years. If populations really can move so rapidly it means that these interpretations have to be viewed with very great caution. Focusing attention upon the species which are widely distributed and yet have failed to cross certain geographic barriers is probably the most fruitful source of information.

Torres Strait assumes particular importance in interpreting just what the exposed surface of the Sahul Shelf between Australia and New Guinea may have been like when the sea-level was so low that these land masses formed one gigantic continent. Darlington (1957) has suggested that the major rivers of northern Australia and southern New Guinea merged together on the Sahul Shelf and flowed out as one giant river going in a westerly direction (Fig. 31). Gill (1970) envisaged that the Sahul Shelf bore a rich and diverse vegetation, and so there would be every reason to suppose that it was populated by an equally rich and diverse frog fauna. Species from New Guinea would have been free to live there and pass across into Australia, and Australian species would have intermingled with them and passed on to New Guinea.

Fortunately there are a few islands left in the now flooded area (the Kei, Aru and Tenimbar Islands) and so the frogs living on them today are probably relics of the Sahul fauna surviving on what were the highest portions of land on the shelf, and now the only existing remnants. Unfortunately no one has ever visited these islands with the specific intention of collecting frogs, and those that have been found there were obtained by experts in other fields of zoology.

If the Sahul Shelf really was hospitable to frogs throughout its length it is hard to understand why there are not some species common to just northwestern Australia and New Guinea. There are several species which do inhabit this segment of Australia and yet fail to reach the Cape York Peninsula in the northeast. This special Australian component which includes the small rock-hole dweller *Litoria meiriana* and the larger species *L. coplandi* and *L. wotjulumensis* failed to venture into New Guinea or the intermediate islands. Amongst the many explanations that can be offered to explain their restriction to the northwest is that the Sahul Shelf may not have been a zone uniformly suitable for frogs. Every species which is shared by Australia and New Guinea occurs on the Cape York Peninsula. There is the implication that there was something rather special about the area around Torres Strait, and it was only there that frogs made successful crossings.

The frog fauna of the numerous islands in Torres Strait, such as Thursday Island, Horn Island and Murray Island, confirm the fact that Torres Strait was a route for dispersal. None of the islands is known to have more than five species, and the total fauna from six islands in the Strait is ten species. Nine of these are forms which are common to both Australia and New Guinea; the tenth is *Limnodynastes ornatus*, one of the most abundant Torresian frogs which has failed to reach the New Guinea mainland.

With a few exceptions the boundaries that separate the Australian States from one another are little more than straight lines drawn on maps. Animals simply do not recognize political boundaries, with the result that the frog fauna of each State contains both unique elements and ones shared with other States. Because zoologists travel far and wide, data important for State surveys have become dispersed amongst institutions throughout the Commonwealth. Naturalists living near State boundaries are often placed at a particular disadvantage because they not only need to become acquainted with the fauna of their own State, but be equally aware of publications about the fauna of the adjacent one to be able to recognize creatures formerly unreported from their own. New State checklists have been included as an Appendix.

Maps showing the distribution of particular species can be invaluable, but inevitably maps can show only where those species have been found. The blank areas may represent portions where searches for the species proved unsuccessful and where they can be assumed not to occur, or places where it just happens that no one has searched.

Many new species of frogs undoubtedly still await discovery: some may have been already collected and are now wrongly included in the distribution maps of other species, whilst others have genuinely yet to be found for the first time. In the final assessment when the fauna is completely known and every detail of every distribution pattern established, it is quite possible that the ideas of recognizing provinces will change.

New Guinea presents a much more difficult problem when attempts are made to split the mainland up into components in any way comparable with provinces in Australia. There is no question of wanting to divide it up for convenience. There is simply the real benefit of learning more about the relationships of the dispersed animals and, in the process, perhaps something about the sequence of events that occurred during the turbulent geological history of the island itself.

It is easy to recognize the similarity with Australia at the southern coast of New Guinea, and the fauna of what is termed the Oriomo Plateau there could just as well be called Torresian. Basically however New Guinea is dominated by the incredible chain of towering ranges of mountains extending from the Vogelkop Peninsula in the far west to the tip of the opposing peninsula in the far southeast. Throughout the length of the island there is an absolute paradise for frogs with a high rainfall, a rich and luxuriant vegetation, and only on the southeastern shoreline any suggestion of a really dry season.

There are no geographic barriers in New Guinea comparable to the Nullarbor Plain: areas where frogs are simply unable to survive. The barriers are perhaps more subtle and reflect the problems faced by frogs when they commit themselves to a particular way of life. For example there are very few lakes in the highlands and most of the rainfall is soaked up by the soil or flows off in the fast currents of creeks leading to rivers. Hence to exist in the mountains, frogs must either be able to dispense entirely with the free-swimming tadpole stage as the microhylids have done or, if they persist in having tadpoles, so modify them that these can survive in the fast currents. In the Hylidae it does not matter whether the species of frog happens to be what we recognize to be a *Nyctimystes* species or a *Litoria* species, for as far as is known all of the mountain-dwellers of these genera have the same sort of thick-coated egg and flattened, sucker-mouthed tadpole. In the lowland areas nearer to the coast the members of this family breed in static or slowly flowing water and their tadpoles are much like

Hawkesbury Toadlet *Pseudophryne australis*

17 CAMOUFLAGE

Peron's tree frog *Litoria peroni*

ABOVE RIGHT: Alpine stream in N.S.W.
ABOVE LEFT: Temporary swamp in N.S.W.
LEFT: An artificial dam in N.S.W.

18 AUSTRALIAN HABITATS

LEFT: Permanent stream in N.S.W.
BELOW LEFT: Central Australian gorge
BELOW RIGHT: Mary River, N.T. in
the wet season

their Australian counterparts. The fragile spawn clumps and more delicate tadpoles of lowland hylids simply could not survive in mountain streams.

It is certainly quite likely that New Guinea frogs are just as variable in their tolerances to extremes of temperature as Australian species, and at different altitudes in the mountains there are quite distinct zones, each with its own peculiarities in terms of frog faunas. The little that has been discovered so far suggests that the altitude of 1000 metres above sea-level is about the upper limit of most of the lowland species.

When sea-levels were lower during glacial periods, many of the off-shore islands were connected to the mainland of New Guinea, and they were as much a part of New Guinea as Tasmania was a continuous portion of Australia. However New Britain to the east of New Guinea remained isolated, for the narrow Vitiaz Strait between them is almost 1000 metres deep. New Britain suffered badly in consequence and only three species of hylid frogs, two microhylids and a variety of ranids have crossed the water barrier. The mountainous island may resemble a broken-off portion of the chain extending throughout New Guinea, but it would have a very rich frog fauna if a land communication had existed when frogs abounded in New Guinea as they do today.

Zoogeographically the Solomon Islands even further east are quite unique in their frog fauna, but why there should be more kinds there (21 species) than in New Britain (13), which probably provided the stepping stone for them and their ancestors, is the sort of unanswered question that makes the study of animal distribution so interesting.

16   Frogs and Man

THROUGHOUT THE WORLD frogs provide man with a minor source of food. In western countries the attitudes towards eating frogs range from considering frog meat as a gastronomic delicacy to absolute revulsion at even contemplating eating them. Perhaps the uninitiated are unaware that in Europe only the large muscles on the two long bones of each hind leg are eaten. When dusted with flour, gently fried in butter and served with salad, the taste is much like that of the delicate, white meat of breast of chicken.

In most countries the frogs that are eaten are species of *Rana*, probably because the members of this genus are not only edible but abundant and of a sufficiently large size for a few pairs of legs to provide an adequate meal. For some reason the frog-eating habit has not extended to Australia. Certainly I am not suggesting that in Europe every Saturday night the average family dines on a meal of frogs. But it is a fact that in countries where frogs are a food item and there are native edible species, imports of additional supplies run into countless millions of pairs of frogs' legs. In Australia frogs' legs are rarely marketed at all. Our one species of Australian *Rana* is confined to northern Queensland, and the demand for frogs' legs has not reached the stage to induce anyone to examine the palatability of frogs of other genera that exist nearer to the main cities.

It is in parts of New Guinea that the eating of frogs is of daily occurrence, but the situation there is quite different from our own. In the absence of many particularly large native mammals the daily diet, in many areas, has always been low in animal protein. There frogs have alleviated the deficiency.

To hunt and capture animals with the minimum of effort it is necessary to know much about their habits, refuges, activity, etc. However, it is only recently that professional zoologists have realized that the knowledge of many of the indigenous people of

New Guinea is vastly superior to theirs in depth and detail.
The most intensive study of this new field of ethnozoology
commenced in 1960 when Ralph Bulmer, now Professor of
Anthropology at Auckland University, visited the remote
Kaironk Valley of the Western Highlands to make contact with
the Karam people there. He became accepted by them, won their
confidence, and was able to introduce over a period of years
specialists in anthropology, zoology, sociology, linguistics and
other sciences. As a result of this long and respected contact he
learned of the existence of a refined system of using names for
frogs and other animals. It was my pleasure to collaborate with
him for several years, and much of what I report here is the result
of those studies, first published by us in an anthropological
journal in 1969.

Frog-hunting by the Karam is an almost perpetual activity
involving adults and children of both sexes, but particularly
women and girls who are the recognized experts. The Karam are
well aware of the places where frogs are most likely to be found,
and concentrate their efforts near streams. There during the
daytime they search amongst vegetation, sometimes beating it
with sticks to cause the frogs to jump out. At other times the
streamside vegetation is cut down in a broad swathe up to
40 metres long as a prelude to night collecting. On moonlight
nights, with the aid of burning torches of bundles of dry plant
stems, they search the surface of the cut vegetation to capture the
exposed frogs.

Tadpoles are collected in large numbers by small boys. The
children build long stone weirs across shallow sections of the
Kaironk River to provide static water to ease their job of finding
and catching them.

Preparation and methods of cooking the frogs are often quite
elaborate. The frogs are killed by biting them just behind the
head. The long bones of the hind legs are then removed and the
body is thrown on the hot coals of a fire and cooked for about
one minute on each side. It is then taken from the fire partially
cooked and the intestines are removed. After this procedure the
remainder is cooked until crisp and eaten immediately. There is
also a method of preserving frogs which involves putting them in a
row on a split stick and smoking them over a fire. When required

for a meal the smoked frogs are cooked on a bed of greens in a submerged earth oven. The cooking of tadpoles includes roasting on hot embers, cooking with cultivated herbs in an earth oven or baking in small packages of leaves. Brongersma (1958) reports that at the Wissel Lakes in Irian Barat tadpoles of *Lechriodus* are eaten in the form of stew.

The capture of the larger, meatier and more desirable (but more elusive) frogs requires a different approach and the co-operation of several adult hunters. In New Britain, where *Discodeles* can approach 250 mm in length and weigh nearly one kilogram, the frogs provide substantial food. I have watched the frogs being located, and driven from their hiding places at the edge of streams by the hunters' scrawny dogs. The men then took over and captured the frogs with their hands in a frantic mêlée that they obviously enjoyed very much indeed and regarded as sport.

Dogs are also used to hunt large frogs in the Western Highlands of New Guinea. In May 1960 I learned of the technique as a result of making a trek from the Waghi Valley to the small village of Tarar located above the small rivers that feed the headwaters of the Sepik River. Near Tarar there is claimed to be a giant species of frog as big as a human baby. By the inhabitants' estimates the frog is about 300 mm in length. They were familiar with the large *Rana arfaki* which occurs in their district and is up to 200 mm long. They name *R. arfaki* 'week', and use the name 'carn-pnay' for the unknown giant.

The villagers at Tarar state that the technique for locating 'carn-pnay' is to use dogs to drive them from the steeply sloping river banks, down to the boulder-strewn river beds below. There the frogs are shot with arrows and beaten to death with sticks, after which there is sufficient meat on one large frog for it to be shared by several people. The efforts of seventy hunters were unsuccessful, and my search for it was a fruitless one. I reported the visit in a journal in 1962 and, if the present inclusion of the name 'carn-pnay' (as possibly the largest frog in the world) in the *Guinness Book of Records*, is to be judged the hallmark of approval, the existence of this unsubstantiated animal seems to have become accepted.

In Australia the greater abundance of other vertebrate animal food such as marsupials, birds and reptiles, probably almost eliminated the need for Aborigines to eat frogs. Fletcher (1891) records an instance when the frog *Notaden bennetti* was eaten more as a delicacy than of necessity. He cites a correspondent in Western New South Wales who wrote: 'I myself saw an old gin seemingly enjoy as a dainty morsel the muscular thighs of the frog, eating them quite raw with a little salt'. Moore (1842) reported that Aborigines at Swan River in Western Australia were particularly partial to 'wurgyl', a swamp frog, when it was full of eggs.

During times of early contact with Aborigines of Central Australia, European explorers were impressed by the use of frogs as a source of water. Spencer (1928) sampled the water squeezed out of unearthed *Cyclorana platycephalus* and declared it 'perfectly pure and fresh'. Johnston (1943) provides a valuable summary of the information gleaned by Europeans since 1844 on the use of frogs by Aborigines.

Location of buried frogs is obviously difficult, but an ingenious method was observed at Roper River in the Northern Territory by Dr N. B. Tindale of the South Australian Museum. The Aborigines visited dry lagoon beds and stamped on the ground. The subterranean frogs responded to the stamping by croaking. From comparison of the volume of sound detected at different sites in a bed, the greatest density of specimens was located prior to any digging taking place. Spencer's observations were quite different, for he watched boys examining the surface of the ground to detect the minute marks that indicated the exact point that frogs had burrowed down.

Frog-eating is not entirely indiscriminate, and finding out just why some are excluded is an interesting area of investigation. To a certain extent there is the association of particular kinds of frogs with tribal myths and sorcery, but in New Guinea the Karam never eat the fat, globular-bodied, short-legged microhylids such as *Barygenys*, *Phrynomantis* and *Xenobatrachus*, and avoid touching them if they possibly can. The thick skin of these frogs is densely packed with glands. The secretion released from these glands is quite likely to be poisonous if eaten, and the Karam are wise to leave such frogs well alone.

Dietary prohibitions are extended to other frogs for a variety of reasons not quite so comprehensible to the European. For example, there is a total prohibition by the Karam against the eating of any frogs or tadpoles by boys, for a period of one to three years between the act of nose-piercing and the final completion of initiation rites. Other perfectly edible frogs such as *Rana grisea* are avoided by all men, either because of prohibitions inherited from the ancestors of their particular families or because the swollen shape of the belly is said to induce similar belly growth in those who eat them. Children are denied some of the tree frogs because the skin and limbs of these frogs are likened to those of elderly people and, it is claimed, would cause children not to flourish.

The tremendous interest in frogs as a source of food for the people of New Guinea makes knowledge of just where and when frogs are to be found most important. It becomes of value to be able to recognize the calls of those frogs that are sought after as food items and to distinguish the calls of the smaller species that provide a less substantial meal.

The depth of knowledge of the Karam is considerable and accurate to points of minute detail. Gi, a young Karam informant of Bulmer, illustrates this well with his account of a man of the Kaironk Valley who intended to lure a girl he fancied into the seclusion of some long cane-grass. He lay in wait whilst she was out one night collecting frogs and, to attract her to his hiding place, he imitated the call of 'kwlek', a kind of tree frog. Unfortunately his imitation was not quite right. To the girl's expert ear it did not resemble 'kwlek' or any other frog's call, and she fled screaming, in fear that a witch was abroad. Her screams brought a male relative to the scene and he shot the man in the shoulder.

The Karam identify any frog by a variety of characteristics. They take into consideration its size, colour, texture of the skin, its smell and where it lives. They distinguish frogs by the same sort of means that we use, and they differ and argue about identification in a way that is reminiscent of a group of our naturalists on a field excursion.

There is a fairly close association between our concept of kinds of animals as species and to the natural kinds of the Karam that Bulmer and I have termed 'speciemes'. However, to the 120 frogs collected by Bulmer considered one species (*Litoria angiana*), the Karam gave no less than thirteen names. In another instance involving *Nyctimystes kubori* we were in almost total agreement of their being one kind, because the Karam excluded only one of 43 frogs from the category 'kwlek'. If we can agree so closely over *N. kubori*, why should there be such disharmony over *L. angiana*? The answer lies at the very root of our different conceptions of kinds of animals. We have only one name for a species which is a population of animals of which the individuals may differ from one another in their size and colour. To us the important issue is the ability of the members of the population to breed together to produce offspring capable of perpetuating the species. What the Karam are doing is to recognize as different entities some of the individuals of a species that do not in fact look alike: the more variable any species is in its appearance the more names the Karam are likely to have for it.

It is easy to jump to the conclusion that we have discovered a fault in the Karam system, but actually there are deficiencies on both sides. Certainly the Karam fail to attribute any more importance to kinds that are reproducing populations than differently coloured or patterned members of just one population. However, a limitation of our own system is the lack of any provision for the *L. angiana* sort of situation in which animals can have any one of a number of patterns and colours.

In 1968 I reported the results of a study of 690 *L. angiana* collected throughout New Guinea. It turned out that there were four quite different forms of appearance and a variety of intermediates between them. I referred to the four clearly distinguishable forms as 'variants'; some people use the word 'morphs' to achieve the same end. I needed a means of saying, 'there is a green sort; a brown sort, with a patch on its head, etc. etc.' The Karam have separate names.

The only other major difference between the Karam system and our own involves the situation where one Karam name is applied in an uncharacteristically and seemingly unusual way to a wide variety of different species. 'Gwnm' is a good example, for it has been applied to six different species. This is not a failure to recognize these species as distinct. 'Gwnm' is the forbidden group and it probably serves a very useful purpose to lump together in this way the potentially harmful animals. It resembles our use of the sign DANGER which we display whenever there exists a hazard to our safety. We could have different signs saying HIGH VOLTAGE or DEEP WATER, or CRUMBLING CLIFF EDGE. DANGER is universally used in the English language, and is a sign which is respected. 'Gwnm' achieves the same end by the same means.

Many plants and animals are the source of drugs used by man, and within the last few years numerous scientists have begun to look to frogs as possible sources of previously unknown substances. Study of the Australian fauna has been particularly rewarding: one new drug resulting from these investigations is already on the market and others may be forthcoming.

In 1964 investigation of the Australian fauna was started by a group of Australian and Italian scientists. The Australian contributors were led by Dr R. Endean of the Department of Zoology at the University of Queensland. One of the first species that they examined was *Litoria caerulea*. Dr Endean felt that there was likely to be something unusual about the secretions of its skin, simply because he had noticed previously that his dog, which often ate other species of frogs, would pick up *L. caerulea* in its mouth but drop it rapidly as though the frog was distasteful.

As a first step a number of frogs were collected and killed. The skins were removed from the frogs, dried and then sent to Italy by air mail. There the skins were soaked in alcohol and a yellow extract was recovered and subjected to intensive study in which the various chemical components were separated from one another, analysed and identified. Many of the components proved to be well-known substances that occur in many animals, but one was totally unknown to science. The investigators named it Caerulein after the donor animal.

Caerulein rapidly proved to be of very great interest. It was tested on various tissues and upon anaesthetized animals, and it was found that when injected into a vein it produced a fall in blood pressure. Because high blood pressure (hypertension) is such a common complaint, any substance that might prove a suitable drug to control hypertension is clearly investigated very thoroughly. Caerulein excited attention because of the way in which blood pressure remained at a low level for a particularly long period after the administration of a very small dose.

With the assistance of many Brisbane schoolchildren about 2000 *L. caerulea* were collected for the extraction of more Caerulein for investigation. However, in 1968 its chemical structure was discovered and, with the entry of the Italian drug company Farmitalia as a manufacturer of artificial Caerulein, no more frogs were needed.

Caerulein is now being prepared by several biochemical manufacturers, and it is being distributed throughout the world. The main clinical use at present is as a drug to cause relaxation of the bile duct, so aiding X-Ray investigation of conditions such as the presence of stones in the gall bladder. Caerulein is so effective that only minute doses are needed and it has been calculated that one frog could provide doses for use in this technique on between 5000 and 10,000 human subjects. Other possible uses of Caerulein are still being explored.

In 1966 Erspamer, de Caro and Endean reported the discovery of another interesting substance, this time the warty and rather glandular skin of the little *Uperoleia* species. They named it Uperolein, and investigations now in progress indicate that this substance may have a role to play in the treatment of hypertension.

The material present in skins has been used for other purposes. In 1971 it was reported that drug users in Queensland were smoking the chopped up dried skins of *Bufo marinus*, because they had discovered that they were able to obtain the hallucinogenic effects that they sought in this way. The habit caused concern, not because of a loophole in a law, but because there are so many poisonous substances in the skin of *B. marinus* that the smokers may have been unaware that they faced a very real risk of taking the longest trip of all.

Native frogs and the toad *Bufo marinus* are used extensively as subjects in the teaching of biology, in research in the biological and medical sciences and for a few other experimental purposes of direct benefit to man. Prior to about 1940 the largest of the native frogs, such as *Litoria aurea* of the eastern States and its relatives such as *L. moorei* in Western Australia, were used exclusively to demonstrate the basic principles of anatomy in universities, colleges and secondary schools. These frogs were also bjects for the first investigations of the actions of some of the ilian snake venoms, and pioneering investigations that led to a closer understanding of the structure and methods of function of nerve and muscle tissues.

The swing towards the use of *Bufo marinus* started in about 1940 when it was already abundant. It was used for studies on topics such as the actions of anaesthetics on the heart and the methods by which various drugs act. It was shown that many of the muscles of toads are extremely sensitive to minute traces of drugs such as the chemical messenger acetylcholine, and toads continue to be used for this sort of experimental purpose.

The use of frogs and toads in experimental biology may have declined over the past ten years or so. Changing research interests amongst the contributors of scientific articles, new techniques, improved supplies of conventional laboratory animals such as mice, rats, guinea pigs and rabbits are factors that may be involved in causing this decline. However, the demand for frogs and toads for teaching purposes is on the increase (Chapter 6).

One recent and quite new use for native frogs has been reported by Gooden (1973) who was interested in decompression sickness in humans. Better known as 'the bends' decompression sickness is a hazard faced by divers who return to the surface too rapidly from great depths, resulting in the formation of gas bubbles in blood vessels and surrounding tissues.

It is obviously helpful to be able to study this process of gas-bubble formation actually taking place, but the ideal experimental animal for exposure to artificial decompression would have to have a transparent skin and equally transparent muscles. Gooden found that the tail of the tadpole of *Litoria ewingi* fulfilled these criteria perfectly. His studies led to the discovery that gas bubbles outside blood vessels were in fact formed by the rupturing of the vessels, so releasing the bubbles they contained.

The African clawed toad *Xenopus laevis* used to be maintained in several Australian laboratories to provide a reliable means of confirmation of pregnancy in humans. However *Bufo marinus* was an equally suitable subject and many toads were used for this purpose. The test relied on the ability of hormones present in the urine of pregnant women to induce a female toad to lay eggs. The procedure was a simple one in which a small quantity of urine from a sample provided by the patient was injected via a hypodermic syringe into a female toad. If the patient was pregnant the toad laid eggs within a few hours. A false alarm produced no response.

Within the past few years the toad has been superseded by special test kits marketed by several drug companies that give results more rapidly. However, the parents of many readers within the age group of about fifteen to thirty probably first had confirmation of his or her forthcoming arrival by courtesy of *Bufo marinus*.

There is one area of man's interest in frogs which is divorced from the practical implication of most of the previous examples. This is the representation of the frog in demonstrations of his artistic abilities. In the case of the European the subject has had little appeal beyond the atrocious concrete effigies that adorn the lawns of so many suburban homes. An exception did occur in April 1968 when the Department of Posts and Telegraphs of what is now Papua New Guinea produced a set of four postage stamps depicting native frogs.

In Aboriginal art, reptiles and marsupials predominate their magnificent rock engravings and bark paintings. The artists' attempts to represent frogs have been particularly poor. Cox included two frog motifs in some bark paintings obtained at Essington Island and displayed at a meeting of the Linnean Society of New South Wales in 1879. Unlike reptile illustrations, which Bustard (1970) claims are so well executed that he has no difficulty in identifying the subjects, the frogs shown by Cox are most odd in their appearance and I've never seen anything like them. Both have slender necks; one has been generously endowed with external genital organs (Fig. 34), and it takes a considerable stretch of the imagination to accept that the animals really are frogs.

The Australian Aborigines have a rich background of tribal lore and myths in which frogs have a particular place. At the end of the last century Baldwin Spencer, then Professor of Zoology at the University of Melbourne, travelled widely in northern Australia watching and recording Aboriginal life. Fortunately Spencer was interested in frogs and the name *Limnodynastes spenceri* of Central Australia fittingly records this fact.

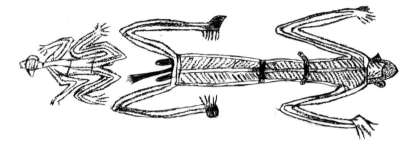

FIG. 34 Frogs in Aboriginal bark paintings at Essington Island
(from Cox 1879).

In 1895 Spencer travelled to Alice Springs to witness the prolonged Engwura ceremony being held there by the Arunta people. He describes the proceedings in his 1889 book with F. J. Gillen, and reports the same account in various other books published between 1912 and 1928.

Amongst the many spectacular proceedings was the Frog Ceremony performed by the leader of the Engwura. The purpose of this ceremony was to convey to the young men of the tribe the importance and reverence attached to the headman who had lived and died at a place called Imanda on the Hugh River. Because the banks of the Hugh River were inhabited by frogs, the new generation was taught that there were now human frog spirits residing there.

The preparations for the ceremony lasted five hours. Firstly a great turban was created on the head of the performer by binding round and round lengths of string woven from human hair. This helmet provided a centrepiece for a long, wooden, vertical pole or 'churinga' tipped with owl feathers, and other sticks bearing the tips of the tails of rabbit bandicoots. The pole and the sticks, and the head, body and limbs of the performer were then covered with a layer of pink and white down. The down was stuck on with human blood in a carefully prepared pattern of bands and bars representing the legs of frogs. Spencer likened the costume to a tightly fitting eiderdown quilt which would have been hot and uncomfortable to wear under any circumstances. He pointed out that in addition the air temperature that day reached a stifling 60°C.

When all was in readiness the young men were brought forward to view the impressive frog totem for the first time. For a few minutes the men circled round and round the totem crying 'Wha! Wha!' whilst the performer, squatting in the sand, swayed and wriggled his body. Within five minutes the ceremony was over. The impression had been made and, hopefully, the young men would remember what they had seen, to ensure perpetuation of this detail of tribal lore. Unfortunately the Aboriginal people involved in this ceremony rapidly vanished or dispersed, and there is now no tribe to maintain it (Strehlow 1971).

There are several Aboriginal myths which illustrate perfectly the familiar association of frogs with rain. Even the great deluge that followed the droughts of prehistoric times are attributed to frogs. Thomas (1906) recorded one of them: 'The natives at Lake Tyers tell of a time when there was no water to be found on the earth, and all the animals met in council to discover the cause of this extraordinary drought. At last they discovered that a gigantic frog had swallowed all the water, and would only disgorge it if he were made to laugh. So they set themselves to amuse him, and various animals danced and capered in front of him, but to no purpose; he remained just as stupid and impassive as any ordinary frog. At last the eel began to wriggle and distort itself, and this was too much for the frog's gravity; his jaws opened, out rushed the water, and a great flood overspread the land'.

There are a number of State and Commonwealth laws and regulations which involve the 'protection' of animals, control their import and export from and between States and from Australia. The naturalist needs to be aware of current restrictions in the areas where he proposes to study or collect animals.

I think that anyone interested in our native fauna would hope that State laws would operate in such a way that the rare animals would gain complete protection against exploitation or any other action that would endanger their abundance or very existence. Hopefully, too, the most abundant and widely distributed species should be accessible for study by any child or adult irrespective of the person's standing in the community.

Unfortunately the achievement of the ideal policy is a pipedream. For a start it is rarely practicable to discriminate between different species of animals, protecting some and not others, because it requires the collector to distinguish the protected from the unprotected. (Birds are one of the few exceptions.) It becomes an extremely difficult policy to administer in such a way that the rare animals, those really needing protection, would be recognized and left alone.

It is obviously simplest either to prohibit totally the collection of animals or to do absolutely nothing at all about it. Basically this is what the various States have done. The only real area of uniformity in Australia involves the National Parks and the Fauna Reserves where theoretically every native creature living there is totally protected. The States are virtually declaring that these little bits of Australia will remain untouched for the benefit of the present and the (hopefully grateful) future generations. At the same time there is the implication that native animals that have lived on this continent for thousands of years before it was colonized by Aborigines or Europeans have a right to life as much as we have. Hopefully these refuges will ensure it.

In his book on Australian lizards Bustard (1970) was highly critical of conservation policies generally, and particularly the place of reptiles in them. Several State Acts have been reviewed since his book was published, affording reptiles a greater degree of protection, but there remain as many holes for exploitation as in the proverbial block of Swiss cheese.

Frogs have never been specifically protected to the extent that no one has secured protection for any of our rarer species. A few of the rare species certainly do exist in National Parks and Fauna Reserves, but as a whole they shelter beneath the cloak of total embargoes, such as those existing in Western Australia, and the Northern Territory, where all animals are protected. Tasmania has pursued a quite unique isolationist policy where the most obvious activity has centred around the prevention of unauthorized import of animals from the mainland.

The sort of question that has to be asked is whether frogs need to be protected. To answer it properly requires a detailed background knowledge of the nature of the frog fauna and its distribution throughout Australia. At present there are a few areas where that fauna is sufficiently well known to be able to answer accurately. Without this information conservation arguments become weak, inaccurate and sometimes purely emotive. Certainly there are many species which do not merit or require man's assistance to ensure their perpetuation in great numbers. It is those species which are apparently restricted to specialized habitats that need to be examined carefully. Here in fact lies the crux of the problem, for the habitat has to be preserved for the animal to survive. It would be absolutely ridiculous to declare any animal a protected species and then permit land clearance and possibly housing development to occur where it lives.

Conservationists are well aware of this basic problem and so we find a price being placed against their efforts. The price is the extent to which we are prepared to inhibit 'development' and all that is declared to be good for the future of Australia. We hear of 'rationalization' of conservation policies, implying that it is irrational to argue too strongly in the face of progress.

Happily not all of the threats to the existence of a few species of frogs are quite so radical, and it is the more indirect ones that deserve and require immediate attention.

Rheobatrachus silus, the brooding frog of Queensland, is a good example of a species which probably needs to be the subject of special legislation. In its structure and habits it is so unusual that Australian collectors are keen to obtain specimens, and zoologists in every country want some too. *Rheobatrachus* will undoubtedly become the subject of considerable scientific research from which, of course, its relationships to other frogs may be established. Obviously there are benefits to be gained for zoology as a whole to have these studies undertaken. However, the sobering thought is that there may be more zoologists than *Rheobatrachus*; even restricting access to contributors with a plausible reason for examining living or preserved specimens may not curtail the collecting sufficiently.

Fortunately *Rheobatrachus* does occur in at least one reserve, but preventing collecting from taking place there may prove difficult. I believe that unless it can be demonstrated that *Rheobatrachus* is genuinely abundant and not just confined to two or three localities, the animal should be protected by State law providing a high penalty to deter deliberate contravention. The fact that there is no precedent in Australia is immaterial. The New

Zealand Government legislation protecting the native species of *Leiopelma* is rigorously enforced, and applications from resident and foreign zoologists are carefully scrutinized to establish whether approval should be granted or refused. Much the same sort of system may be needed to protect *Rheobatrachus*, and it is a pity that the initiative, responsibility and burden of enforcement rests solely in the hands of a State Government.

The control of the export of frogs from Australia is the province of the Australian Government, and its enforcement the duty of the Department of Police and Customs. Export is permitted only under a licence system which bars financial transactions, so outlawing the pet trade, but permits despatch to scientists and institutions such as zoos.

There really is no restriction on the overseas zoologist who wishes to undertake studies on Australian species. For example, a colleague of mine in the Department of Physiology and Cell Biology at the University of Kansas asked me to send him twenty or thirty South Australian frogs for his studies on methods of water uptake. He had already examined the responses of species sent to him from several other continents, and access to Australian species was needed to complete his survey. I had no trouble in obtaining the licence. The frogs were sent by air freight within inflated polythene bags inside a lightweight box, and they all arrived at Kansas in perfect condition.

The total embargo on the export of frogs by pet dealers is not a situation unique to Australia. However, it is hard to justify, and I see no harm if export of at least the abundant species could be permitted under a licence system, requiring inspection and approval of the method of transport.

The regulation of the export of frogs, or in fact any living creature, from Papua New Guinea is an example of bureaucracy in its most petty and ludicrous form, but fortunately conflict between scientists and bureaucrats is not that common.

There are happily areas of interest divorced from the official arena. For example, from time to time frog jumping competitions are reported in newspapers. Events of this kind had their beginning in 1863 at Angel's Camp, then a thriving city in Calaveras County in California. The local miners held regular, weekend frog-jumping events, and betting on favourites resulted in small

Albino marsh frog *Limnodynastes fletcheri* from the River Murray

Tree frog with an extra pair of arms

New Guinea tree frog with leech which was under its skin

Rana jimiensis collected for food at Telefomin, New Guinea

fortunes being won and lost. Mark Twain had a cabin near Angel's Camp and his visits to the mining community inspired the book *The Jumping Frog of Calaveras*.

Frog jumping contests are held in many parts of the world, and often provide the Junior Chambers of Commerce and similar organizations with a popular and successful source of funds for charities. For example the Annual Jumping Frog Jamboree held at the San Diego County Fairlands in Del Mar has raised thousands of dollars for cancer research.

The competition rules are as follows: the frog is allowed thirty minutes in which to make its first jump, and the measured distance on which it is judged extends from the middle of the launching pad to the point where the frog lands on its third leap.

The organization involved in American frog jumping competitions is quite elaborate. Angel's Camp remains the site of the controlling body and, to gain official recognition, a contest has to meet the requirements and receive the approval of the 'International Board of Frog Jumping' and the 'Mayor of Frogtown' at Angel's Camp.

In Australia the organizers of frog jumping competitions seem unaware of the international code of conduct, and gaming laws loom their ugly heads. As a result Australian events are certainly novelties but do not imitate their American counterparts as serious attempts to raise funds for charities. In 1973 allegations were made that some of the Australian competitions permitted the doping of frogs by pouring whisky into their mouths to act as stimulants. In Australia frogs are not protected by Acts of Parliament to prevent cruelty to animals, so permitting any abuse that ingenious idiots care to perpetrate.

17 Herpetology in Australia

LONG BEFORE THE FIRST EUROPEAN COLLECTORS visited Australia and New Guinea the Aboriginal peoples of these lands were able to distinguish different kinds of frogs, possessed data about their habits, caught them for food or the water they contained and recorded their appearance in paintings and carvings. The reports of the collectors obtained by the European naturalists who invariably accompanied the voyages of discovery, only introduced a new dimension to the study of these animals in enabling data to be recorded in a printed form and in providing an internationally recognized method of naming creatures.

In reading some of the studies of modern zoologists who have needed to re-examine specimens in some of the collections that were made, it is commonplace to detect a sense of frustration, irritation and even ridicule at what, by modern standards, are interpreted to be errors of description resulting from slipshod work. This veiled criticism is most unfair, for the only reasonable way of assessing early contributions is to appreciate the quality of the techniques of study in vogue in those times, the great difficulty of communication between herpetologists, the absence of specialist journals, the enormous array of new animals demanding attention and concepts of species.

The first Australian frog to be described by a European was the large tree frog now called *Litoria caerulea*. It was one of several frog species from Australia donated to the Royal College of Surgeons in London, and formed a part of the nucleus of the collection assembled there by John Hunter. In the late 1790s Dr George Shaw of the college prepared a manuscript catalogue of the contents in which there is the following preface.

The New Holland Division, as Dr Shaw has named it, stood first, and consists of specimens collected by Sir Joseph Banks, during his voyage with Captain Cook; and in 1792 Sir Joseph divided all his Collection of

Zoological specimens between Mr Hunter and the British Museum; Mr Hunter had a new set of Cases and Shelves made for their reception which occupied one end of the Museum; and they were all put into new Spirit or the old Spirit distilled by R. Haynes and W. Clift during the summer of 1792. Those given to the British Museum were sent down into the Basement store of the British Museum and allowed to take care of themselves; or spoiled if they preferred it.

By good fortune the Australian frogs were not destined for the British Museum basement. An entry in Shaw's catalogue in his own handwriting briefly lists the salient features of *caerulea* tallying fairly well with one published two years previously by White:

Blue frog speckled beneath with greyish; the feet divided into four toes, the hind-feet webbed. Size of the common frog.

A plate accompanying White's book depicts a hideously shrivelled frog sitting in a pool of water (reproduced here in the endplates). Its dreadful condition clearly accounted for White's error in assuming that it had four and not five toes.

Jessie Dobson, who until recently was Curator of the Hunterian Museum, and I tried to locate this frog for sentimental as much as scientific reasons. We studied many manuscripts, plates by Miss Susan Stone who prepared illustrations for White, and various letters. We confirmed that the specimen was in the collection until the present century, but that it was destroyed with a great portion of Hunter's collection when a bomb hit a corner of the Museum during the Second World War.

In 1795 George Shaw described '*Rana australiaca*' (now *Heleioporus australiacus*), the second species of frog to be found in Australia, and this probably was another of Sir Joseph Banks's specimens since destroyed. It would appear that it too was a misshapen specimen, for Shaw writes: 'Its rarity must, therefore, apologize for its deformity.'

During the early part of the nineteenth century when the first collections of Australian frogs reached Europe, Paris was one of the major centres of research into herpetology, promoted there to a great extent by the collaboration of two distinguished and highly respected workers: André Duméril and Gabriel Bibron. They received rich and varied collections of Australian frogs and reptiles from several naturalists including François Péron and his close friend, the scientific artist Charles-Alexandre Le Sueur.

Péron and Le Sueur arrived in Australia in 1802 as members of a voyage of discovery under the command of Captain Nicolas Baudin. Péron and his colleague amassed a collection of over 100,000 specimens of animal life, and their success is reflected by the large numbers of Australian animals named *peroni* or *lesueuri* in their honour.

Many nineteenth century museum workers were secretive about their collections until they had published their observations. There may have been justification, because one zoologist is known to have visited a colleague, scribbled down details of a creature in his host's care while the host was out of the room, and published them as his own findings. Duméril and Bibron provided access to a number of their co-workers whilst they were actually engaged in the preparation of their nine-volume treatise on amphibians and reptiles. One of these collaborators was a young Swiss student, Johann Tschudi, destined to become equally famous. Tschudi spent several months in Paris and in 1838, when twenty years of age, produced a masterpiece entitled, 'Classification der Batrachier'. In that work Tschudi coined the names *Litoria* and *Crinia* that are now so well known, but he also changed some of the names being used by Duméril and Bibron and published others that they had apparently chosen. The controversy that these actions touched off are mentioned by Mertens in a biographical introduction inserted in a 1967 facsimile edition of Tschudi's monograph.

The published work of Tschudi and particularly the volumes of Duméril and Bibron (1841–1845) are important hallmarks in the development of knowledge of Australian frogs. They placed under single covers the names of the majority of the known species with brief descriptions, and established for the benefit of contemporary zoologists the extent and variety of the Australian fauna known at that time.

By the middle of the nineteenth century herpetologists in France began to concentrate their attention on the fauna of the French colonies and, with Australia being settled by immigrants principally from the United Kingdom, the majority of collections of frogs were directed to the British Museum in London. These were reported in two catalogues. The first was the work of Albert Gunther and was published in 1858. Scanning the lists of names of the collectors of the Australian frogs that had reached him demonstrates that settlers and transient visitors contributed to the task of such early zoologists. For example, *Litoria aurea* was received from Sir Arthur Smith, Mr R. Gunn, Mrs Rowden, The Earl of Derby and many others, including even Charles Darwin. It was an exciting era when the chances of finding new animals was very high indeed, and the study of natural history and the collection of specimens was a popular pastime.

Gunther was responsible for admitting to the British Museum the herpetologist who must rank as the most productive worker of all time. His name was Georges Albert Boulenger (1858–1937). A Belgian, he left Brussels in 1881 and, with Gunther's encouragement, prepared a new catalogue of all the frogs in the British Museum collection. By the following year the 503-page work was completed and published. Although Boulenger has been criticized for his frequently superficial approach, the majority of his decisions, diagnoses and intimations have stood the test of time; it is only within the last few years that his opinions have been questioned. Boulenger went on to publish over 600 zoological papers and books.

The trend of exporting vast collections of frogs and other animals to museums in Europe and also America continued through to the present century. Most museums in Australia were grossly understaffed (as many remain today), the work load of curators of vertebrate collections was enormous and the financing of Australian institutions was absolutely pitiful in comparison with their overseas counterparts.

The first moves to establish a museum in Australia were made in Sydney in 1827, and The Australian Museum became a reality when it occupied its first home in 1836. In 1860 Gerard Krefft, a German naturalist, was appointed Curator (Director) and devoted his research activities to various forms of vertebrate animals. He established great fame for himself by reporting the first discovery in Australia of the lungfish, a virtual living fossil.

Krefft also holds the distinction of being the first resident zoologist to describe a species of frog believed to be new to science. Unfortunately the subject was not new at all and his six other publications on Australian frogs appearing between 1862 and 1876 are marred by many erroneous spellings of their Latin names. There was something lacking in his expertise at writing about frogs but he will be remembered as the first collector of many species. As it was there were greater deficiencies in his relationship with the Museum Board and, following numerous disagreements, he was dismissed from his post in 1874. Such was the antipathy between the parties that he ignored the decision and remained in office until a bailiff carried the Curator's chair and its seated occupant out into the street (Whitley 1962).

During Krefft's term of office the Museum Board was joined by Sir William Macleay who became one of Sydney's greatest scientific benefactors. Sir William was responsible for elevating the Linnean Society of New South Wales to the status of the foremost scientific society in Australia. In 1885 he presented the society with a meeting house and provided it with such extremely substantial endowments that its assets today are undoubtedly far greater than any comparable body in Australia. Through Sir William's generosity it became possible to establish a permanent position of Secretary and general administrator. The study of Australian frogs was placed on an entirely new footing as a result, for the first appointee, Mr J. J. Fletcher, was extremely interested in frogs and after fulfilling his official duties had adequate time to pursue his own research activities.

Fletcher's horizons extended far beyond the concept of many contemporary contributors. He was deeply interested in the habits of frogs and details of geographic distribution. In a series of five papers between 1890 and 1898 he reported which species occurred in which particular areas. He explored the reasons that might account for the differences in the distribution of the many species he encountered, and his papers included numerous digressions about the causes of abundance and scarcity, and delightful anecdotes about burrowing frogs.

Fletcher's papers are so liberally interspersed with acknowledgements to those who sent him specimens or accompanied him on collecting trips, that it is quite obvious that he must have been an enthusiastic researcher with a wide circle of friends and acquaintances.

In the other Australian States there was little activity in the nineteenth century. C. W. de Vis of the Queensland Museum published a couple of papers describing new species; Spencer of

Melbourne University contributed valuable observations on the frogs of Central Australia, but there was little else of any impact. Australian herpetology suffered a tremendous loss with the tragic death of Dene B. Fry at the age of twenty-three. Fry joined the staff of the Australian Museum as a Cadet in 1908 and wrote eleven papers between 1912 and 1914. He interrupted his university studies to enlist for service in the First World War and was killed in action in France. The last of his contributions, published posthumously in 1916, typifies the superb quality of his research and demonstrates an assurance of a brilliant and already mature zoologist.

It was Dene Fry who indicated that *Limnodynastes dorsalis* was really a complex of species and geographic races, whilst his work on the microhylid frogs of northern Australia (1912, 1915) remained the sole reference works for more than fifty years. Throughout all his contributions his dissections and illustrations were superb, and much of his research on anatomy has not been bettered.

Fry was one of the first Australian herpetologists to make any contribution to knowledge of the frog fauna of New Guinea. There were a number of reasons for the lack of activity of Australians in this area, of which the most obvious is the abundance of work to be done on their own fauna. Initially at least, the division of New Guinea into colonies administered by Holland, Britain and Germany meant that most of the collections made there were by members of expeditions mounted by these countries.

There were a few Australian forays into New Guinea in the nineteenth century, one of which was the *Chevert* expedition of 1877 of which Sir William Macleay was a member. He obtained some frogs when the *Chevert* visited Katow on the south coast, and described several new species upon his return to Australia.

The gleaning of knowledge of the kinds of frogs that inhabited New Guinea suffered from the fact that there were magnificent birds of paradise, incredibly beautiful butterflies and a host of other spectacular creatures to attract the attention of collectors. In fact many privately financed expeditions set out with the intention of obtaining birds of paradise and nothing more. The collection of other animals was commonly of secondary importance, to be undertaken as time permitted. This sort of background of the intentions of the collectors explained how it was that by 1858 Sclater was able to list no less than 158 species of birds then known to occur in New Guinea, whereas Bleeker (1859) could produce a tally of only six species of frogs.

New Guinea presented a tremendous challenge to the survival of often ill-equipped and inexperienced Europeans. It was commonly the case that adventurous individuals achieved considerably more than the less mobile, large parties. A classic example is Luigi D'Albertis who over a century ago successfully navigated the upper reaches of the great Fly River and on another visit penetrated the Arfak Mountains in the far west of the island. D'Albertis was completely unscrupulous in his methods and collected everything he could lay his hands on or shoot with his rifle. His boat was equipped with a cannon to subdue any resistance to his presence. He obtained quite a number of frogs which he preserved and sent to the Museo Civico di Storia Naturale at Genoa in Italy. There W. Peters teamed with Count Doria to produce in 1878 a substantial publication describing many species formerly unknown. D'Albertis wrote a book describing his experiences, and chose for it a title that was quite explicit about the topic and the nature of the contents: *New Guinea. What I Did and What I Saw.*

Of the herpetologists who specialized in the description of the New Guinea frogs that reached Europe, G. A. Boulenger dominated the scene in much the same way that he did the Australian fauna. Between 1882 and 1920 Boulenger wrote 26 papers that included information about New Guinea frogs, and in them were the description of 35 species that he considered new to science.

In Holland P. N. Van Kampen was by far the major contributor, describing 23 new species in twelve works published between 1906 and 1923. His swan song was a superb collation of condensed descriptions of the 119 species recognized at that time.

Following the retirement of Boulenger and Van Kampen the frog fauna of New Guinea was almost entirely neglected for about 25 years. It was the Second World War which revived zoological interest in the island. It happened that amongst the Allied forces were a few zoologists incapable of neglecting their pre-war training. It was particularly fortunate that the U.S. personnel should include Dr P. J. Darlington and that he should become the first professional zoologist to reach the Western Highlands District. His collections of frogs eventually reached the Museum of Comparative Zoology at Harvard University stimulating A. A. Loveridge (1948) to compile a new checklist of New Guinea frogs and descriptive notes of all the species represented at Harvard.

Loveridge's contributions to the frog fauna of New Guinea had the effect of creating a challenge to other zoologists to become interested in working on New Guinea frogs. He expressed opinions on whether some of the names that were being used genuinely represented different kinds of animals. Whether he was ultimately proved to be correct or incorrect does not detract from the great service that he had performed in assessing and reviewing all the available information. In 1935 Loveridge had undertaken a similar task in assembling a list of the Australian frog fauna and commenting on those species available to him. Such an ambitious effort had not been attempted by an Australian zoologist.

No account of the history of the herpetology of Australia and New Guinea would be complete without reference to what has taken place within the last few years, but listing the respective roles and achievements of the current contributors is a very difficult and extremely hazardous task. If the survey is to be comprehensive, no one can really be omitted, and there is the risk of failing to give credit where it is due.

The development of Australian herpetology during the period 1920–1953 was reviewed in considerable detail by Copland (1953) in his Presidential Address to the Linnean Society of New South Wales. For the more recent years it seems fairest, and most diplomatic, to single out for particular attentions only those contributors who provided the foundation studies for the vast number of folk engaged in research today.

If anything there were three initiators. At the University of Western Australia A. R. Main was one, for in the early 1950s he commenced a study of the frogs of the southwestern part of the State, a project involving a large number of collaborators and resulting in a totally new concept of frogs as populations of animals. It was largely through their efforts that some frog species were found to be only subtly distinguished from one another by biological features such as the mating call of males. As a result of their studies the number of species known from southwestern

Australia was doubled over a period of only ten years.

One of Main's colleagues was Murray Littlejohn who later moved to Melbourne, and there inspired and led a number of zoologists in a detailed study of the frog fauna of southeastern Australia. In the space of about ten years they added fifteen species and sub-species to the known fauna of Victoria.

The third major stimulator of studies of frogs in Australia was J. A. Moore, a visiting American. The results of most of his studies were incorporated in a monograph published in 1961 long after his return to the U.S.A. Although he was mainly concerned with the frogs of the eastern portion of New South Wales, his publication included lists of all names used for Australian frogs, lists of the fauna of each State, a general discussion of patterns of distribution and a complete synthesis of the literature. It provided a greater stimulus than anything that preceded it. That his State faunal lists are now hopelessly incomplete, and many of his concepts of species demonstrably false, is a tribute to the incentive that he provided.

For New Guinea R. G. Zweifel at the American Museum of Natural History led the way with a series of publications from 1956 onwards. Zweifel had access to the vast unidentified collections assembled by the numerous Archbold Expeditions, and has periodically published contributions that have greatly increased the number of known species.

There has always been a number of amateur naturalists but it was not until 1950 that any move was made to form their own specialist associations. The initiative was taken in Sydney in February of that year, resulting in the formation of the Australian Herpetologists' Society. There are now comparable organizations in most States, either existing quite independently like the Queensland Herpetological Society, or as sections of larger organizations. Hence the latest addition, the Herpetology Study Group, was founded in 1971 as a section of the long-established Field Naturalists' Society of South Australia. Most of these groups produce their own newsletters or magazines and have achieved a good deal in the short period of their existence. Several place curbs and restraints upon the collecting activities of their members to avoid endangering the existence of small populations of animals. Some have lobbied State Governments to introduce or tighten controls involving the protection of animals. They organize field excursions, undertake surveys and are providing vital information on the biology and distribution of Australia's frog and reptile fauna.

In 1964 the professional herpetologists, working mostly in museums and universities, banded together with a few amateur workers to form their own society: The Australian Society of Herpetologists. This society holds annual meetings but a large proportion of its membership is now composed of zoologists living overseas. Throughout Australia the membership of this and all other groups totals about 500, of whom 350 are school students down to the age of around eleven.

18   Study of Frogs

THE ENJOYMENT of the study of any aspect of natural history is really a progressive process of discovering information. To progress involves gleaning facts by personal observation, by reading, through discussion with fellow enthusiasts and by a host of other ways. Whether the naturalist ends up by concentrating his interest on birds, beetles, flowers, frogs or any other particular form of life, or maintains a broad interest, the immense satisfaction that can be gained from discovering something quite new can be appreciated only by those who have been fortunate enough to experience it. Whether this discovery involves finding an animal in an area where it has not been found previously, or perhaps clarifying a little detail about an animal's life, it represents establishing a new fact. However, if this information is not placed on permanent record and so made known to other naturalists and specialists, the naturalist adds nothing to the field of science from which he derives pleasure.

In Australia and New Guinea the study of frogs is greatly in need of a large number of extra amateur enthusiasts, for there are many incredible gaps in our knowledge that naturalists are quite capable of filling. The following sections of this chapter are intended principally to assist and generally guide the newcomer, but some parts may be of help to naturalists already interested in frogs, seeking sources of practical information not included in the preceding chapters.

Identification

Gaining the ability to identify frogs is the first and most vital need. Unfortunately there are very few handbooks that have been written specifically for beginners, and it is rather a matter of luck whether there is anything available that describes the frogs that occur in the geographic area you are interested in.

By far the most comprehensive introductory text is the 73-page handbook on the frogs of the southern part of Western Australia written by Main (1965). This work is unfortunately now out of print and is obtainable only on loan from libraries. Main provides brief descriptions, includes details of colour in life, notes on biology, keys which make it possible to identify adults, tadpoles and eggs, and has photographs of each of the species.

A booklet on the frogs of New South Wales was prepared by Cogger (1960) who included keys to identify adults and had line-drawings of each species. Tyler (1966) tackled the frog fauna of South Australia in a similar fashion but added photographs of each species found in that State. Copies of these booklets can be obtained from the Australian Museum and the South Australian Museum respectively.

The rich frog fauna of Victoria has been studied in greater detail than the faunas of New South Wales and South Australia, but the vast amount of published information has yet to be condensed into a single field guide for the entire State. In the 1971 *Victorian Year Book*, Littlejohn gives a broad summary of the fauna, discusses its biology and distribution and includes superb colour plates of thirteen species. It is only in the vicinity of Melbourne that details of the frog fauna have been presented in a form designed to be of value to the field naturalist. Most of the information is to be found in series of publications in the *Victorian Naturalist*. Littlejohn (1963) gives brief descriptions of the frogs there with notes on biology and a key to their identification. Martin (1965) treats the tadpoles in a similar fashion, and Martin, Littlejohn and Rawlinson (1966) produced a key to the eggs of the same species.

There are no comparable publications for the frogs of Tasmania, Queensland, the Northern Territory and the central and northern parts of Western Australia, but Clyne (1969) has included representatives from these and other areas of Australia in an illustrated handbook.

In the past five years a vast number of names used for frogs have been changed, affecting many of those used in each of the publications referred to above. A note of these changes is given with a list of all Australian frogs in Appendix 1.

The naturalist living in a city suburb may decide to join a Field

Naturalists' Club where he can make contact with more experienced amateur herpetologists and identify his finds by this
means. Many State museums have on their staff Information
Officers with a very broad knowledge of natural history capable
of identifying the most commonly occurring animals in their
State. This sort of staff position was often created to relieve the
specialist curators of the bulk of the inquiries being received from
the general public. The demand now being placed upon the
services of Information Officers is truly enormous; this is in many
ways an encouraging sign for it reflects the current interest in
natural history amongst the general public.

To the naturalist possibly working on his own, the Museum
provides a source of free information and particularly, when it is
needed, access to expert opinions from curators. Until comprehensive field guides are available in each State or a reasonably
priced field guide for all species of Australian frogs is published,
a museum may be the only place where he can identify his finds.
Nevertheless, a distinction can be drawn between an ordinary
member of the general public who is fascinated by a frog he has
found, wants to know what it is and something more about it, and
the enthusiastic naturalist. I am always happy to provide assistance but, when the enquiries are from naturalists, I remain much
more impressed with ones from those who have first referred to
available publications and then approached the Museum because
other sources of information have proved to be inadequate for their
purpose.

Naturalists living in country districts, and particularly those in
New Guinea, are placed at a considerable disadvantage but are
by no means prevented from undertaking a serious study of frogs.
I correspond on a fairly regular basis with over one hundred
amateur frog enthusiasts scattered throughout Australia and New
Guinea. Some of these are teachers, others are housewives,
farmers, doctors, students, missionaries and park rangers. They
usually make notes about the living or preserved specimens that
they send to me, and I send back identifications, details of which
of their finds are particularly interesting and news about whether
amongst their collection there is anything not previously known
to occur in their districts. Almost every museum department
probably has an equally large band of 'corresponding naturalists'

contributing specimens and information and receiving aid and advice in return. Certainly no naturalists living in remote areas should feel inhibited about approaching a museum, for it is recognized that their contribution is potentially of very great value in the quest for a better understanding of the Australian fauna.

Collecting

There are no real secrets about collecting frogs, just the need for different approaches when searching for them in their hiding places in the daytime, or intercepting them when they are wandering around at night. It becomes largely just a matter of knowing when and where to look. From season to season and locality to locality these times and places will change. For example, in seasonally arid, hilly country frogs tend to congregate around the creeks draining them, and remain there throughout the summer. As the water supply to the creeks lessens and the creeks stop flowing, they diminish to a chain of small pools amongst the boulders on the floor. Curiously enough, I know of many localities where it is much easier to observe and catch frogs during this, the most unsuitable period of the year for them, than it is in the moister months. It is simply that roughly the same number of frogs exist, but that in the summer the vast majority are concentrated in an area of a few square metres. Hence summer collecting can become a straightforward, but back-breaking exercise of 'boulder-rolling'. Perhaps the only point worth remembering is the need to replace the boulder snugly back in the cavity you levered it from. Left precariously balanced at any odd angle, it can represent a hazard to the next naturalist who passes by. Added to that is the possibility of depriving the animals that you study of a potential life-saving refuge.

When conditions are moister frogs are likely to be more widely and so more evenly distributed throughout a locality. Streamside searches involving lifting stones and beating overhanging vegetation are always likely to expose or flush out the odd one or two, but it is at night that the same spots can become almost overrun by frogs.

Catching an active frog at night is a quite different proposition from picking up an inactive one that has been suddenly exposed whilst it is hiding away during the daytime. A powerful torch (preferably a waterproof one) or miner's type of headlamp that leaves both hands free are essential aids, and success often depends upon spotting a frog before it has been disturbed and alarmed. Collectors tend to walk very slowly, treading with care and continually scanning the vegetation around them. What they look for at night is just a glimpse of a bright red flash caused by reflection of the torchlight from a frog's eyes ('eye-shine'). In fact if it becomes possible to approach a frog in such a way that both eyes are held in the light beam, the animal may behave as though in a trance, remaining absolutely motionless and apparently totally oblivious of any noise and movements taking place around it. When collecting frogs at night in marshes and pools, the ripples that are made as the collector wades forward may be enough to cause the frog to bob up and down. Nevertheless, provided that the light is maintained shining on both of the subject's eyes, the frog is unlikely to attempt to escape even when jogged about in this way. However, just as soon as one eye is left out of the light's beam the 'spell' seems to be broken and the frog leaps away.

Quite often male frogs can be heard calling readily enough, but finding them is a totally different matter. It is not that the frogs are ventriloquists as frustrated collectors suggest, but simply that it is often genuinely difficult to accurately pinpoint the exact source of a sound. What the naturalist needs are two companions, so that the three collectors can create a triangle around the general area from which the call seems to be coming. Each time that the frog calls, each of the listeners then moves forward a little towards the position that he thinks the sound is coming from. If all of the listeners are correct in their sense of direction, the frog will be found at the intersection of their paths, but almost inevitably there is argument and indecision before arriving at the frog. This technique of triangulation is fine when there is adequate help around. However, only too often the collector will be out on his own, inching forward and experiencing the frustration of getting very close, but just not close enough.

In addition to a powerful torch there are a few other useful items of collecting equipment. The containers to hold specimens need not be elaborate. If travelling out within walking distance of home, there is need for little more than a few plastic bags which are long enough to be sealed by tying a knot in one end and, if this is not possible, rubber bands to seal them off. If frogs have to be kept alive for several days, and space for equipment is at a premium, ideal containers are bags of calico, linen or a similar cloth material. When rolled up they occupy little space in a pocket and will remain moist for long periods if soaked in water before use. A useful size of bag measures about 25 cm × 15 cm and has a pair of long linen tapes sewn near the open neck for sealing it off. The only thing to bear in mind when making them is that the free threads of the material at the seams on the inside of the bag are trimmed down before use. They should also be checked at regular intervals. The reason is simply that it is very easy for a frog's arm or leg to become snagged if the threads form loops, and there have been several examples of limbs becoming cut and quite badly mutilated when the frog struggled to free itself.

Most of the frogs collected by naturalists are destined for their own vivaria where they can be observed at leisure. Just a few of these same frogs will ultimately end up in museum collections as preserved specimens where their value will partly hinge upon the field data recorded by the collector. In fact because accurate locality data are so vital in many studies of animals, there is often little merit in a museum devoting any of its precious space to a specimen of unknown or uncertain origin. Hence naturalists should get into the habit of making good notes in the field and maintaining at home perfect records of the source of the animals in their care.

The field information about the actual location of the specimen may be expressed in the form of metres or kilometres from the nearest well-known landmark; as the distance from a known position on a major highway or secondary road, or perhaps in the form of a map grid reference. The date of collection is particularly important when the frogs are preserved straight away. The dates matter to the extent that when several specimens taken on different dates are compared, and it is found out whether each one is an adult with or without eggs, or perhaps juvenile, it may become possible to predict fairly accurately spawning periods and other unconfirmed details about the life of the species.

Frogs in captivity

It seems hard to imagine that anyone is going to establish a vivarium to provide a home for frogs, obtain a food supply for them and then, when all is in a final state of readiness, go out and catch some frogs. If anything, it is the chance capture of a frog which will lead to seeking out a temporary home for it and then finding a source of food. However as quarters go, the plastic washbowls and glass jam jars have their limitations for frogs and their observers. Eventually the day is reached when the decision is made to either release the captive or obtain for it more suitable permanent accommodation.

Ask for a vivarium at some pet shops or departmental stores and the chances are that there will be uncertainty about your requirements. Hence it is best to request an aquarium and fail to mention that it is not your intention of keeping fish in it. The first need is to provide a lid that will keep the frogs in, and yet will not block off their air supply. Some herpetologists do use a sheet of glass for a lid and separate it from the metal frame by sticking a matchstick or sliver of wood to the frame at each corner. This creates a space of only two or three millimetres, and ensures a fairly humid atmosphere inside. However, every time the lid is removed there is always the risk of breaking the glass or, if the edges have not been milled smooth, of cutting yourself. A simpler and safer lid can be made from stretching a sheet of plastic coated (and hence rustproof) fly wire across a wooden framework of 2 cm × 2 cm 'quad' or a similar material.

Irrespective of the type of environment that you may wish to reproduce faithfully inside the vivarium, the long-term problem of providing food for the inhabitants is of paramount importance. Hence a totally wet vivarium with a pool of water at one end and saturated vegetation at the other may be fine for frogs but quite unsuitable for the insect and other life available and intended to be the major source of food. If the insects being provided for food will drown within minutes of being dropped into the vivarium, the frogs are hardly likely to thrive.

Certainly some frogs do live in very wet places, but the insect or other living food found there is going to be of a special kind: one perfectly designed for this sort of soggy environment. The slaters, cockroaches and other creatures that are most likely to be trapped by naturalists just do not fall into this category. Hence there normally has to be some sort of compromise between constructing and arranging a vivarium that looks most appealing to human observers and yet fulfils the requirement of being equally suitable to the food items that are going to be available. Some herpetologists overcome the problem by suspending a low wattage light globe over a funnel above the tank, arranged in such a way that winged insects attracted to the light fall down the funnel and into the vivarium through a hole in its lid. This 'automatic' feeding device can deliver an abundance of food if the tank is sited on a verandah, or perhaps indoors but near an open window, and so works on the basis of providing such a quantity of food that the loss of a few insects through drowning is of no consequence.

Only too often this ideal is quite impractical and an alternative supply of food has to be provided, involving more effort than just having a light on for a period each night. By far the most common practice is to establish a colony of an insect such as the pale yellow, glossy-skinned mealworm which is the immature larval stage of the beetle *Tenebrio molitor*. Mealworms feed on flour and other milled or crushed grain products and are a major pest threatening flour mills. As a result government entomologists in many countries have devoted a great deal of time, effort and money into establishing knowledge of the insect's life-cycle and the food, temperature range and humidity it prefers. This information about the habits of their enemy proved vital in the battle to control infestations in stored food. This same information became available to herpetologists, bird keepers and other naturalists who now use it with the reverse objective: successfully rearing large numbers of mealworms for their pets. Pamphlets describing the arts of establishing and maintaining thriving colonies of these insects can be obtained in pet shops and museums. For example: *Keeping Mealworms* by R. F. Brown (South Australian Museum Education Booklet No. 2). Initial stocks of mealworms can be purchased in batches of hundreds or even thousands from pet shops, and particularly those catering for the requirements of bird enthusiasts.

The mealworms that are on sale are inevitably fully grown, measuring about 30 mm long and 3 or 4 mm in diameter. This size is fine for the large frogs but is far too big for some of the smaller ones. Finding adequate quantities of food for the more diminutive frogs can become a major problem, and it is the young mealworms, perhaps only 10 mm long, that are absolutely ideal. To obtain a regular supply at this stage of their development is really possible only if the naturalist keeps his own colony.

Gentles, the maggots which are used as fishing bait and sold by such suppliers, will be eaten by frogs. Similarly the blowflies into which the maggots eventually develop are pursued and devoured by tree frogs. However, blowflies and their offspring are not the sort of insects that should be brought into a home if there is even the slightest risk of one escaping from a vivarium.

Rearing Tadpoles

Free-swimming tadpoles have such tenacity for life that 'rearing' them really involves little more than avoiding making errors that will prevent them from successfully completing this phase of development. For example, there is no hard and fast rule about the maximum number of tadpoles that can live together in a jar or aquarium. The total mass of tadpoles in terms of their bulk will be important to ensure that they are going to be able to obtain adequate oxygen from the water. Hence at any time it is best to restrict the number to the sort of density seen in the wild and by this means avoid any suggestion of overcrowding that could result in all of the tadpoles dying.

Tadpoles have to be given an excess of food because, if they find themselves running short, they will eat one another. To avoid pollution of the water in which the tadpoles are living, the food provided needs to be of a kind which will not rapidly decompose or putrify. Hence the food needs to be of a rather special kind and there are two readily available items which meet the requirements. The first is the dried fish-food sold by aquarist suppliers and the other is lettuce leaves which have been boiled for about five minutes – so reduced to a sloppy, soggy mass. The nutritional value of lettuce is usually considered to be rather low, but tadpoles thrive on it and will complete their life-cycle on a diet of boiled lettuce leaves and nothing else. Cabbage is no substitute because it contains substances which can retard the development of tadpoles into frogs.

Left to their own devices tadpoles will eventually transform into frogs and leave the water. Imprisoned in jam jars or aquariums there is the very real risk that, when they decide that the time has come to start their life out of water, they won't be able to. Scrambling against the steep sides of the container they may well drown if they cannot find a way out. Hence it really is extremely important to watch them carefully and, when their arms emerge and they can be seen to be transforming, to either transfer them to a shallow dish with gently sloping sides, or else to put a rock inside the container on which they can crawl when they want to.

If the very young frogs are particularly small rearing them calls for large supplies of tiny insects such as the fly *Drosophila*. It is not an impossibility by any means, but unless good stocks of this food are assured, the frogs' chances of survival are remote, and it is much more humane to release the juveniles at the very spot where the spawn or tadpoles were collected.

Killing and Preservation

Whether a frog is to be killed because it has been found to be diseased and suffering, or whether it is important to preserve it because of its potential scientific value in a personal, school or museum collection, it is essential that it be destroyed humanely. In recent years a good deal of effort has been directed into finding techniques that will enable frogs to be killed without causing them to suffer, or to experience any pain at all in the process.

It is extremely unfortunate that many of the chemical substances which are perfect for painlessly destroying frogs, are drugs subject to abuse by man. As a result of this abuse or other dangers associated with their use, the sale of some of the most ideal ones is banned other than for approved therapeutic purposes, or to recognized scientific institutions. However, State Government regulations still permit the sale of a few quite suitable solutions from retail pharmacists. For example it is at present legally permissible to purchase from a pharmacy a solution of chloral hydrate of up to 5 per cent concentration. As it happens this is in excess of that needed for killing frogs, and naturalists should seek 3 per cent. The point should be made that this needs to be an aqueous solution, so avoiding the possibility of ending up with it in the form of the usually dispensed sugary syrup.

A 3 per cent solution of chloral hydrate can be used in small quantities and re-used over a long period. The technique employed could not be simpler: just put the frog in a small glass jar and add sufficient chloral hydrate solution to form a film covering the bottom of the jar. The frog absorbs the chloral hydrate through its skin and very slowly becomes more and more lethargic before finally dying. It dies in a relaxed, limp state and rarely gives any indication that it is aware that it is not sitting in water.

An alternative to chloral hydrate is a solution of urethane (ethyl carbamate), but the satisfactory concentration varies between 5 per cent and 10 per cent. Most frogs succumb to 5 per cent but a few seem to be rather tolerant and require a higher concentration. For this reason it is best to prepare or obtain a 10 per cent solution, dilute part of it to 5 per cent by adding an equal volume of water, retaining the remaining 10 per cent stock for use if needed. As with chloral hydrate the technique of killing a frog with urethane involves allowing the frog to maintain contact with the solution for a few minutes. Tree frogs may quickly climb up the side of the jar, but tilting the jar to one side about once a minute to splash the frog with the solution is usually enough to cause the frog to die just as quickly as one sitting in the solution.

Just cooling a frog sufficiently can cause its death, and Brattstrom's (1970) experiments on just how low each species can go suggests that some of the inhabitants of the warmer areas can be killed very quickly by surrounding the bag containing them with crushed ice, or by placing it in a refrigerator.

There is always the chance of finding a frog in a remote area when quite unprepared for it, or perhaps at a quite unexpected time when the ideal chemical substances are not available and there is no access to ice or a refrigerator for cooling. In this sort of situation it is probably best to keep the frog alive and if these efforts are unsuccessful, to preserve it immediately.

One of the advantages of the use of chloral hydrate or urethane is that the frog dying from the absorption of either of these substances is in a completely relaxed state. Hence before the process of after-death rigidity (rigor mortis) sets in, it is possible to arrange the limbs in a natural pose, and so avoid permanent distortion. For this reason it is helpful to transfer the freshly killed frogs to a shallow enamel baking dish or plastic tray where, in the preservative solution, their body and limbs can be gently adjusted to the desired positions.

Quite a variety of preservative solutions are known to be suitable for frogs and the Society for the Study of Amphibians and Reptiles has published a 22-page booklet on this topic which it sells at a nominal cost.[1]

The two most popular frog preservatives for long-term storage are solutions of formalin and ethanol. Formalin is itself a solution of the gas formaldehyde which is usually sold in a 40 per cent stock solution. For frog preservation this basic stock has to be reduced to about one-thirteenth, i.e. one volume of formalin plus twelve volumes of water to produce a solution of approximately 3 per cent. This is considerably less than the concentration quoted in many publications, but I have found the results to be just as good as those from the use of higher concentrations. Unfortunately formalin has a most obnoxious odour, is unpleasant to handle because it can cause hardening and cracking of the skin of the fingers and sometimes can produce allergies amongst those handling it. However, where it does have an advantage over other preservatives lies in the economy of space, weight and volume on field trips. Because of the low concentration in which it is actually used, a little of the concentrated solution goes a long way.

In the shelter and refuge of the home or laboratory, long-term preservation is best catered for by using a 60 per cent solution of industrial alcohol. Seventy per cent is usually recommended, but it can result in specimens that are slightly too dehydrated and hence tend to become hard and rather unpliable. This is a disadvantage when there is a need to examine them.

The carriage of concentrated alcohol by aircraft is often completely prohibited because of the safety hazard involved in the event of fire on board. Bearing in mind the extent of the alcohol content of some of the beverages on sale to passengers, the total embargo is rather inconsistent. Nevertheless it exists and, for this reason, naturalists travelling vast distances to collect specimens favour the use of formalin.

[1] *A Guide to Preservation Techniques for Amphibians and Reptiles*, by George R. Pisani, 1973, Society for the Study of Amphibians and Reptiles; Miscellaneous Publications; Herpetological Circular No. 1. Single copies U.S. $0.35 each ($0.10 for orders of 25 or more). Orders to Dr. Henri Seibert, Dept. of Zoology, Ohio University, Athens, Ohio 45701, U.S.A.

Tadpoles can be killed in much the same way as frogs, but successful preservation is slightly more difficult to achieve. The trouble is that the thin outer layer of the young tadpole skin is so very delicate and liable to damage. The formula of a tadpole preservative was described in The Australian Journal of Science in 1962, and some of my friends have delighted in naming this solution 'Tyler's Fluid.'

Using a Library

The larger libraries can tend to be rather awe-inspiring institutions. In asking the question, 'Have you tried the famous echo in the Reading Room at the British Museum?', Gerard Hoffnung illustrated just how revered these temples of knowledge can become. There is no doubt that a little effort is required by users to shatter the spell and so restore libraries to their proper status as workshops.

Using a library to the very best advantage certainly requires a little skill, involving knowledge of the various ways in which books and periodicals are catalogued, organized and separated into units.

There really are few mysteries to solve to discover techniques of library systems, and in any case the professional librarian can advise and guide the newcomer. However, it is equally important to appreciate that the resources of any library extend far beyond its own walls, and that through one library you can gain detailed information about the possessions of other libraries in Australia and overseas.

Publications fall broadly into the categories of serial and non-serial. The serial ones are journals or other publications appearing in a series at either regular or irregular intervals. In contrast books published as separate units fall into the non-serial category. The Commonwealth Scientific and Industrial Research Organisation produces a hefty three-volume loose-leaf catalogue of the scientific serials available locally ('Scientific Serials in Australian Libraries'). From a few moments' examination of these volumes it is possible to establish whether any published journal is held by any Australian library. If it is, the name of the library and exact details of the volumes possessed are provided. Collaboration between the National Library of Australia in Canberra and 600 other libraries scattered throughout Australia has resulted in the preparation of a list of the non-serial works, called The National Union Catalogue.

Finding out just what has been written about the frogs of Australia and New Guinea is a fairly straightforward task. This is because the titles of a large proportion of the literature on the Australian frogs (and certainly all that is really significant) are to be found at the back of the publications by Copland (1957) and Moore (1961). New Guinea frog literature published prior to 1972 was listed by Tyler (1973) who provided notes against each entry indicating the field or fields of interest of the contents; for example, whether it is concerned with ecology, anatomy or perhaps parasites.[1]

For the more recently published papers on the frogs of Australia and New Guinea it is necessary to refer to the *Zoological Record*, an annual listing of the zoological literature of the world, published by the Zoological Society of London. Each year the literature is listed and cross-referenced in such a way that it is possible to look up special topics or to pick out a particular species and discover exactly what was written about that species by anyone in that year.

There can be a delay of as much as three or four years between the publication of an article in a journal and the appearance of its title in the *Zoological Record*. As a result the *Zoological Record* is useful as a means of finding out just what has been written about any particular species or about frogs in general, but is necessarily behind the times. The bringing together of topics under one cover is invaluable but it is not a substitute for the more tedious task of regularly checking journals as they are put on display in libraries.

Roughly one-half of what is written about the frog fauna of Australia and New Guinea ends up being published in Australia. The remainder is published overseas, principally in Europe and the U.S.A. The titles of the Australian journals most favoured by

[1] Available free of charge from the University of Papua New Guinea, P.O. Box 4820, University, Papua New Guinea.

contributors to the study of frogs (and so worth checking on a regular basis as they appear) are:

Australian Journal of Zoology
Memoirs of the Queensland Museum
North Queensland Naturalist
Proceedings of the Linnean Society of New South Wales
Proceedings of the Royal Society of Queensland
Proceedings of the Royal Society of Victoria
Records of the South Australian Museum
South Australian Naturalist
Transactions of the Royal Society of South Australia
Victorian Naturalist
Western Australian Naturalist.

Appendix

CHANGES IN FROG NAMES

As an aid to the use of the State handbooks detailed on page 221, note of the following name changes will update the contents.

Crinia: Of the Western Australian species in this genus only *Crinia georgiana* remains unchanged. *Crinia rosea, C. leai* and *C. lutea* are now called *Geocrinia* species (*Geocrinia rosea* etc.), and all of the remaining species in Western Australia are now referred to *Ranidella*. In South Australia *Crinia riparia* and *C. signifera* have become *Ranidella* species. In Victoria and New South Wales *C. haswelli* remains unchanged, the species *laevis* and *victoriana* are now referred to *Geocrinia*, and all of the remaining species are now called *Ranidella* species (Blake 1973).

Cyclorana: What was called *Cyclorana alboguttatus* in New South Wales (and Queensland) has been shown to be really a *Litoria* species and so is now named *Litoria alboguttata* (Tyler 1974).

Heleioporus: The name *Heleioporus australiacus* is now used only for the species occurring in Victoria and New South Wales. The frogs in Western Australia formerly known by this name are now called *H. barycragus* (Lee 1967). *Heleioporus pictus* in Cogger (1960) is now termed *Neobatrachus pictus*.

Hyla: All of the species that were formerly referred to *Hyla* are now called *Litoria* species. For example *Hyla caerulea* has become *Litoria caerulea* (Tyler 1971a).

Limnodynastes: The supposedly wide-ranging *Limnodynastes dorsalis* has been shown by Martin (1972) to be several different species and sub-species that had been wrongly lumped together. Ignoring the sub-species, the necessary changes are *L. dumerili* for the South Australian and Victorian frogs, whilst the New South Wales ones represent *L. dumerili, L. interioris* and *L. terraereginae* respectively.

Metacrinia: The solitary member of this genus, *M. nichollsi* has been shown to be best associated with the *Pseudophryne* toadlets. Hence its name is now *P. nichollsi* (Blake 1973).

STATE CHECKLISTS

Western Australia

Crinia georgiana
Cyclorana australis
Cyclorana cultripes
Cyclorana dahli
Cyclorana platycephalus
Glauertia mjobergi
Glauertia russelli
Heleioporus albopunctatus
Heleioporus barycragus
Heleioporus eyrei
Heleioporus inornatus
Heleioporus psammophilus
Limnodynastes dorsalis
Limnodynastes ornatus
Limnodynastes spenceri
Litoria adelaidensis
Litoria bicolor
Litoria caerulea
Litoria coplandi
Litoria cyclorhynchus
Litoria inermis
Litoria meiriana

Litoria microbelos
Litoria moorei
Litoria nasuta
Litoria rothi
Litoria rubella
Litoria wotjulumensis
Myobatrachus gouldi
Neobatrachus centralis
Neobatrachus pelobatoides
Neobatrachus sutor
Neobatrachus wilsmorei
Notaden nichollsi
Pseudophryne douglasi
Pseudophryne guentheri
Pseudophryne nichollsi
Pseudophryne occidentalis
Ranidella glauerti
Ranidella insignifera
Ranidella pseudinsignifera
Ranidella subinsignifera
Uperoleia marmorata

South Australia

Cyclorana platycephalus
Geocrinia laevis
Limnodynastes dumerili
Limnodynastes fletcheri
Limnodynastes peroni
Limnodynastes spenceri
Limnodynastes tasmaniensis
Litoria aurea
Litoria caerulea
Litoria ewingi

Litoria peroni
Litoria rubella
Neobatrachus centralis
Neobatrachus pictus
Pseudophryne bibroni
Pseudophryne occidentalis
Pseudophryne semimarmorata
Ranidella parinsignifera
Ranidella riparia
Ranidella signifera

Victoria

Crinia haswelli
Geocrinia laevis
Geocrinia victoriana
Heleioporus australiacus
Limnodynastes dumerili
Limnodynastes fletcheri
Limnodynastes interioris
Limnodynastes peroni
Limnodynastes tasmaniensis
Litoria aurea
Litoria citropa
Litoria ewingi
Litoria jervisiensis
Litoria lesueuri

Litoria maculata
Litoria paraewingi
Litoria peroni
Litoria phyllochroa
Litoria verreauxi
Mixophyes balbus
Neobatrachus centralis
Neobatrachus pictus
Philoria frosti
Pseudophryne bibroni
Pseudophryne dendyi
Pseudophryne semimarmorata
Uperoleia marmorata
Uperoleia rugosa

New South Wales

Adelotus brevis
Assa darlingtoni
Bufo marinus
Crinia haswelli
Cyclorana australis
Cyclorana cultripes
Cyclorana platycephalus
Geocrinia victoriana
Heleioporus australiacus
Kyarranus sphagnicolus
Lechriodus fletcheri
Limnodynastes dumerili
Limnodynastes fletcheri
Limnodynastes interioris
Limnodynastes ornatus
Limnodynastes peroni
Limnodynastes salmini
Limnodynastes spenceri
Limnodynastes tasmaniensis
Limnodynastes terraereginae
Litoria alboguttata

Litoria aurea
Litoria booroolongensis
Litoria brevipalmata
Litoria caerulea
Litoria chloris
Litoria citropa
Litoria dentata
Litoria ewingi
Litoria freycineti
Litoria glandulosa
Litoria glauerti
Litoria gracilenta
Litoria jervisiensis
Litoria latopalmata
Litoria lesueuri
Litoria nasuta
Litoria paraewingi
Litoria peroni
Litoria phyllochroa
Litoria rubella
Litoria verreauxi

New South Wales

Mixophyes balbus
Mixophyes fasciolatus
Mixophyes iteratus
Neobatrachus pictus
Notaden bennetti
Pseudophryne australis
Pseudophryne bibroni
Pseudophryne coriacea

Pseudophryne corroboree
Pseudophryne dendyi
Ranidella parinsignifera
Ranidella signifera
Ranidella sloanei
Uperoleia marmorata
Uperoleia rugosa

Tasmania

Geocrinia laevis
Limnodynastes dumerili
Limnodynastes peroni
Limnodynastes tasmaniensis
Litoria aurea
Litoria burrowsi

Litoria ewingi
Pseudophryne bibroni
Pseudophryne semimarmorata
Ranidella signifera
Ranidella tasmaniensis

Queensland

Adelotus brevis
Assa darlingtoni
Bufo marinus
Cophixalus exiguus
Cophixalus neglectus
Cophixalus ornatus
Cyclorana australis
Cyclorana brevipes
Cyclorana dahli
Cyclorana novaehollandiae
Kyarranus loveridgei
Lechriodus fletcheri
Limnodynastes convexiusculus
Limnodynastes dumerili
Limnodynastes fletcheri
Limnodynastes ornatus
Limnodynastes peroni
Limnodynastes salmini

Limnodynastes spenceri
Limnodynastes tasmaniensis
Limnodynastes terraereginae
Litoria alboguttata
Litoria bicolor
Litoria brevipalmata
Litoria caerulea
Litoria chloris
Litoria dayi
Litoria eucnemis
Litoria ewingi
Litoria freycineti
Litoria glandulosa
Litoria glauerti
Litoria gracilenta
Litoria inermis
Litoria infrafrenata
Litoria latopalmata

Queensland

Litoria lesueuri
Litoria nannotis
Litoria nasuta
Litoria nigrofrenata
Litoria nyakalensis
Litoria pearsoni
Litoria peroni
Litoria phyllochroa
Litoria rheocolus
Litoria rothi
Litoria rubella
Mixophyes fasciolatus
Mixophyes schevilli
Neobatrachus pictus
Notaden bennetti
Notaden melanoscaphus
Nyctimystes hosmeri
Nyctimystes tympanocryptis

Nyctimystes vestigea
Pseudophryne bibroni
Pseudophryne coriacea
Pseudophryne major
Rana papua
Ranidella parinsignifera
Ranidella signifera
Ranidella tinnula
Rheobatrachus silus
Sphenophryne fryi
Sphenophryne pluvialis
Sphenophryne robusta
Taudactylus acutirostris
Taudactylus diurnus
Taudactylus eungellensis
Taudactylus rheophilus
Uperoleia marmorata
Uperoleia rugosa

Northern Territory

Cyclorana australis
Cyclorana cultripes
Cyclorana dahli
Cyclorana platycephalus
Glauertia orientalis
Glauertia russelli
Limnodynastes convexiusculus
Limnodynastes ornatus
Limnodynastes spenceri
Litoria bicolor
Litoria caerulea
Litoria coplandi
Litoria inermis

Litoria meiriana
Litoria microbelos
Litoria nasuta
Litoria rothi
Litoria rubella
Litoria wotjulumensis
Neobatrachus centralis
Notaden melanoscaphus
Notaden nichollsi
Ranidella sp.
Sphenophryne robusta
Uperoleia marmorata

References

Chapter 1 *Introduction*

BLAKE, A. J. D. 'Taxonomy and relationships of myobatrachine frogs (Leptodactylidae): A numerical approach.' *Aust. J. Zool.*, vol. 21, pp. 119–149, 1973.

DUKE ELDER, S. *System of Ophthalmology. Vol. 1.* 'The Eye in Evolution.' 843 pp. Henry Kimpton, London, 1958.

FLETCHER, J. J. 'Contribution to a more exact knowledge of the geographical distribution of Australian Batrachia. No. II.' *Proc. Linn. Soc. N.S.W.*, 2nd Series, vol. 6, pp. 263–276, 1891.

GORHAM, S. W. 'The comparative number of amphibians in Canada and other countries III.' *Canadian Field Nat.*, vol. 77, pp. 13–48, 1963.

LYNCH, J. D. 'The transition from archaic to modern frogs.' *In:* J. L. Vial (Ed.), *Evolutionary Biology of the Anurans* (pp. 133–82). University of Missouri Press, Columbia, 1973.

SAVAGE, J. M. 'The geographic distribution of frogs: patterns and predictions.' *In:* J. L. Vial (Ed.), *Evolutionary Biology of the Anurans* (pp. 351–445). University of Missouri Press, Columbia, 1973.

TYLER, M. J. 'A new genus for the Australian leptodactylid frog *Crinia darlingtoni*.' *Zool. Meded.*, vol. 47, pp. 193–201, 1972.

TYLER, M. J. 'First frog fossils from Australia.' *Nature*, vol. 248 (5450), pp. 711–712, 1974.

VIAL, J. L. (ED.). *Evolutionary Biology of the Anurans.* 470 pp. University of Missouri Press, Columbia, 1973.

Chapter 2 *The Tree Frogs: Hylidae*

DUELLMAN, W. E. 'The hylid frogs of Middle America.' *Monogr. Mus. Nat. Hist. Univ. Kansas*, vol. II (1), pp. 429–753, 1970.

NOBLE, G. K., and JAECKLE, M. E. 'The digital pads of the tree frogs. A study of the phylogenesis of an adaptive structure.' *J. Morphol.*, vol. 45 (1), pp. 259–92, 1928.

PYBURN, W. F. 'Breeding behaviour of the leaf frogs *Phyllomedusa callidryas* and *Phyllomedusa dacnicolor* in Mexico.' *Copeia* 1970, pp. 209–18, 1970.

SAVAGE, R. M. *The ecology and life history of the Common Frog (Rana temporaria temporaria).* Pitman, London, 221 pp., 1961.

ZWEIFEL, R. G. 'Results of the Archbold Expeditions. No. 78. Frogs of the Papuan hylid genus *Nyctimystes*.' *Amer. Mus. Novit.* (1896), pp. 1–51, 1958.

Chapter 3   *Frogs of the Land and Water: Leptodactylidae*

BLAKE, A. J. D. 'Taxonomy and relationships of myobatrachine frogs (Leptodactylidae): A numerical approach.' *Aust. J. Zool.*, vol. 21, pp. 119–149, 1973.

FRY, D. B. 'On a collection of reptiles and batrachians from Western Australia.' *Rec. W.A. Mus.*, vol. 1, pp. 174–210, 1914.

LEDO, W., and TYLER, M. J. 'The type locality of the leptodactylid frog *Neobatrachus centralis* Parker.' *S. Aust. Nat.*, vol. 47 (4), pp. 75–6, 1973.

LEE, A. K. 'Studies in Australian amphibia II. Taxonomy, ecology, and evolution of the genus *Heleioporus* Gray (*Anura:* Leptodactylidae).' *Aust. J. Zool.*, vol. 15, pp. 367–439, 1967.

LITTLEJOHN, M. J. 'The breeding biology of the Baw Baw Frog *Philoria frosti* Spencer.' *Proc. Linn. Soc. N.S.W.*, vol. 88 (3), pp. 273–6, 1963.

MAIN, A. R. *Frogs of Southern Western Australia.* Handbook No. 8, Western Australian Naturalists' Club, Perth, 1965.

MARTIN, A. A. 'Emergence from hibernation in an Australian burrowing frog.' *Copeia* 1969, (1), pp. 176–8, 1969.

MOORE, J. A. 'Geographic and genetic isolation in Australian Amphibia.' *Amer. Nat.*, vol. 88, pp. 65–74, 1954.

NOBLE, G. K. *The Biology of the Amphibia.* McGraw-Hill, New York, 577 pp., 1931.

PARKER, H. W. 'The Australasian frogs of the family Leptodactylidae.' *Novit. Zool.*, vol. 42, pp. 1–106, 1940.

ZWEIFEL, R. G. 'A review of the frog genus *Lechriodus* (Leptodactylidae) of New Guinea and Australia.' *Amer. Mus. Novit.* (2507), pp. 1–41, 1972.

Chapter 4   *Conquerors of the Mountains: Microhylidae*

ZWEIFEL, R. G. 'Results of the Archbold Expeditions No. 72. Microhylid frogs from New Guinea, with descriptions of new species.' *Amer. Mus. Novit.* (1766), pp. 1–49, 1956.

ZWEIFEL, R. G. 'Results of the Archbold Expeditions No. 97. A revision of the frogs of the subfamily Asterophryinae, Family Microhylidae.' *Bull. Amer. Mus. Nat. Hist.*, vol. 148 (3), pp. 411–546, 1972.

Chapter 5   *The Island Colonists: Ranidae*

ALCALA, A. A. 'Breeding behaviour and early development of frogs of Negros, Philippine Islands.' *Copeia* 1962, vol. 4, pp. 679–726, 1962.

BOULENGER, G. A. 'Diagnoses of new reptiles and batrachians from the Solomon Islands, collected and presented to the British Museum by H. B. Guppy Esq., M.B., H.M.S. 'Lark'.' *Proc. Zool. Soc. Lond.*, pp. 210–13, 1884.

FLEURIEU, M. *Discoveries of the French in 1768 and 1769, to the south-east of New Guinea with the subsequent visits to the same lands by English Navigators, who gave them new names.* Stockdale, London, 323 pp., 1791.

GANS, C. 'A bullfrog and its prey.' *Nat. Hist.*, vol. 70 (2), pp. 26–37, 1961.

GORHAM, S. W. 'Fiji Frogs. Life history data from field work.' *Zool. Beitrage.*, vol. 14, pp. 427–46, 1968.

GUPPY, H. B. *The Solomon Islands and their natives.* Swan, Sonnenschein, Lowrey & Co., London, 384 pp., 1887.

Chapter 6   *The Cane Toad: Bufo marinus*

ADAMS, N. G. K. '*Bufo marinus* eaten by *Rattus rattus*.' *N. Qd. Nat.*, vol. 34 (143), p. 5, 1967.

ARNOLD, H. L. *Poisonous plants of Hawaii.* Tongg Publ. Co., Honolulu, 71 pp., 1944.

BALDWIN, P. H., SCHWARTZ, C. W., and SCHWARTZ, E. R. 'Life history and economic status of the mongoose in Hawaii.' *J. Mammalogy*, vol. 33 (3), pp. 335–56, 1952.

BELL, J. H. 'How frequently do giant toads produce eggs?' *Cane Growers' Quart. Bull.*, 1937, p. 12, 1936.

BRONGERSMA, L. D. *The Animal World of Netherlands New Guinea.* J. B. Wotters, Gronginen, pp. 41–2, 1958.

CAIN, A. J., and GALBRAITH, I. C. J. 'Correspondence.' *Ibis*, vol. 99, pp. 128–30, 1957.

CASSELLS, M. 'Another predator of the Cane Toad.' *N. Qd Nat.*, vol. 37 (151), p. 6, 1970.

CASSELLS, A. J., and ST. CLOUD, S. F. 'Disembowelled toads near water.' *N. Qd Nat.*, vol. 34 (141), p. 6, 1966.

DEXTER, R. R. 'The food habits of the imported toad *Bufo marinus* in the sugar cane sections of Puerto Rico.' *Bull. Int. Soc. Sugar Cane Techn.*, vol. 74, pp. 1–6, 1932.

FROGGATT, W. W. 'The introduction of the Great Mexican Toad *Bufo marinus* into Australia.' *Aust. Nat.*, vol. 9 (7), pp. 163–4, 1936.

FULLWAY, D. T., and KRAUSS, N. L. H. *Common insects of Hawaii.* Tongg Publ. Co., Honolulu, 228 pp., 1945.

HINCKLEY, A. D. 'Diet of the Giant Toad, *Bufo marinus* (L), in Fiji.' *Herpetologica*, vol. 18 (4), pp. 253–9, 1962.

ILLINGWORTH, J. F. 'Feeding habits of *Bufo marinus*.' *Proc. Hawaiian. Ent. Soc.*, vol. 11 (1) (1940), p. 51, 1941.

KINGHORN, J. R. 'The Giant Toad *Bufo marinus* in Australia.' *Aust. Mus. Mag.*, vol. 6, pp. 410–11, 1938.

MUNGOMERY, R. W. 'A short note on the breeding of *Bufo marinus* in captivity.' *Proc. Int. Soc. Sugar Cane Techn.*, 1935, pp. 589–91, 1935.

MUNGOMERY, R. W. 'A survey of the feeding habits of the Giant Toad (*Bufo marinus* L)., and notes on its progress since its introduction into Queensland.' *Proc. Qd. Soc. Sugar Cane Technologists*, 1936, pp. 63–74, 1936.

OLIVER, J. A., and SHAW, C. E. 'The amphibians and reptiles of the Hawaiian Islands.' *Zoologica*, New York, vol. 38 (2), pp. 65–95, 1953.

ORMSBY, A. I. 'Notes on the Giant Toad (*Bufo marinus*).' *Proc. R. Zool. Soc. N.S.W.* (for 1955–56), pp. 54–5, 1957.

PEMBERTON, C. E. 'Local investigations on the introduced tropical American Toad *Bufo marinus*.' *Hawaiian Planters' Rec.*, vol. 38, pp. 186–92, 1934.

Chapter 7 *Diet and Feeding Habits*

ALEXANDER, T. R. 'Observations on the feeding behaviour of *Bufo marinus* (Linne).' *Herpetologica*, vol. 20 (4), pp. 255–9, 1965.

BOULENGER, G. A. 'Diagnoses of new reptiles and batrachians from the Solomon Islands, collected and presented to the British Museum by H. B. Guppy, Esq., M.B., H.M.S. 'Lark'.' *Proc. Zool. Soc. Lond.*, 1884, pp. 210–13, 1884.

CALABY, J. H. 'The food habits of the frog, *Myobatrachus gouldi* (Gray).' *W. Aust. Nat.*, vol. 5 (4), pp. 93–6, 1956.

CALABY, J. H. 'A note on the diet of Australian desert frogs.' *W. Aust. Nat.*, vol. 7 (3), pp. 79–80, 1960.

COTT, H. B. 'The effectiveness of protective adaptations in the hive-bee, illustrated by experiments on the feeding reactions, habit formation and memory of the common toad *(Bufo bufo bufo)*.' *Proc. Zool. Soc. Lond.*, 1936, pp. 111–33, 1936.

DODD, J. M. 'Ciliary feeding mechanisms in anuran larvae.' *Nature (Lond.)*, vol. 165, p. 283, 1950.

FLEAY, D. 'Frogs devour snakes.' *Vic. Nat.*, vol. 52 (6), pp. 122–3, 1935.

FRANCIS, E. T. B., and EISA, E. A. 'Salivary diastases of the frog and toad.' *Nature (Lond.)*, vol. 167, p. 281, 1951.

GANS, C. 'A bullfrog and its prey.' *Nat. Hist.*, vol. 70 (2), pp. 26–37, 1961.

HEATWOLE, H., and HEATWOLE, A. 'Motivational aspects of feeding behaviour in toads.' *Copeia* 1968, vol. 4, pp. 692–8, 1968.

KENNY, J. S. 'Feeding mechanisms in anuran larvae.' *J. Zool. Lond.*, vol. 157, pp. 225–46, 1969.

MAIN, A. R. 'Studies in Australian amphibia I. The genus *Crinia* Tschudi in south-western Australia and some species from south-eastern Australia. *Aust. J. Zool.*, vol. 5, pp. 30–55, 1957.

MOORE, J. A. 'The frogs of eastern New South Wales.' *Bull. Amer. Mus. Nat. Hist.*, vol. 121 (3), pp. 151–385, 1961.

PENGILLEY, R. K. 'The food of some Australian anurans (Amphibia).' *J. Zool. Lond.*, vol. 163, pp. 93–103, 1971.

SAVAGE, R. M. 'Ecological, physiological and anatomical observations on some species of anuran tadpoles.' *Proc. Zool. Soc. Lond.*, vol. 122, pp. 467–514, 1952.

SEVERTSOV, A. S. 'Food-seizing mechanism in anura larvae.' *Doklady Biol. Sci., Proc. Acad. Sci., U.S.S.R.*, vol. 187 (1), pp. 530–2, 1969.

Chapter 8 *Obtaining Water and Avoiding Heat*

BENTLEY, P. J. 'Adaptations of amphibia to arid environments.' *Science*, vol. 152 (3722), pp. 619–23, 1966.

BRATTSTROM, B. H. 'Thermal acclimation in Australian amphibians.' *Comp. Biochem. Physiol.*, vol. 35, pp. 69–103, 1970.

FLETCHER, J. J. 'Contributions to a more exact knowledge of the geographical distribution of Australian Batrachia. No. II.' *Proc. Linn. Soc. N.S.W. 2nd Series*. vol. 6, pp. 263–76, 1891.

HUNTER, J. 'Of the heat and cold of animals and vegetables.' *Phil. Trans. R. Soc. Lond.*, vol. 68, pp. 7–8, 1778.

JOHNSON, C. R. 'Aggregation as a means of water conservation in juvenile *Limnodynastes* from Australia.' *Herpetologica*, vol. 25 (4), pp. 275–6, 1969a.

JOHNSON, C. R. 'Water absorption response of some Australian anurans.' *Herpetologica*, vol. 25 (3), pp. 171–2, 1969b.

KAMPMEIER, O. F. *Evolution and Comparative Morphology of the Lymphatic System.* C. C. Thomas, 620 pp., 1969.

LASIEWSKI, R. C., AND BARTHOLOMEW, G. A. 'Condensation as a mechanism for water gain in nocturnal desert poikilotherms.' *Copeia*, 1969, pp. 405–7, 1969.

LEE, A. K., and MERCER, E. H. 'Cocoon surrounding desert-adapted frogs.' *Science*, vol. 159, pp. 87–8, 1967.

LOVERIDGE, J. P. 'Observations on nitrogenous excretion and water relations of *Chiromantis xerampelina* (Amphibia, Anura).' *Arnoldia*, vol. 5 (1), pp. 1–6, 1970.

MAIN, A. R., and BENTLEY, P. J. 'Water relations of Australian burrowing frogs and tree frogs.' *Ecology*, vol. 45, pp. 379–82, 1964.

NEILL, W. T. 'An unusual habitat for frogs and lizards.' *Copeia* 1946, (4), p. 258, 1946.

RUIBAL, R. 'The adaptive value of bladder water in the toad, *Bufo cognatus*.' *Physiol. Zool.*, vol. 35 (3), pp. 218–23, 1962.

SCHOLANDER, P. F., HARGENS, A. R., and MILLER, S. L. 'Negative pressure in the interstitial fluid of animals.' *Science*, vol. 161, pp. 321–8, 1968.

SHOEMAKER, V. H., BALDING, D., RUIBAL, R., and MCCLANAHAN, L. L. 'Uricotelism and low evaporative water loss in a South American frog.' *Science*, vol. 175, pp. 1018–20, 1972.

SLEVIN, J. R. 'Notes on Australian amphibians.' *Proc. Calif. Acad. Sci.*, vol. 28, pp. 355–92, 1955.

STRAUGHAN, I. R., and LEE, A. K. 'A new genus and species of leptodactylid frog from Queensland.' *Proc. R. Soc. Qd*, vol. 77 (6), pp. 63–6, 1966.

STROMME, S. B., MAGGERT, J. E., and SCHOLANDER, P. F. 'Interstitial fluid pressure in terrestrial and semiterrestrial animals.' *J. Appl. Physiol.*, vol. 27 (1), pp. 123–6, 1969.

TYLER, M. J., and ANSTIS, M. A. 'Taxonomy and biology of frogs of the *Litoria citropa* complex (Anura: Hylidae).' *Rec. S. Aust. Mus.*, vol. 17 (5), pp. 41–50, 1975.

WALPOLE, J. R. B. 'Observations on the burrowing toad: *Neobatrachus pictus*.' *S. Aust. Nat.*, vol. 39 (2), 1964.

WARBURG, M. R. 'On thermal and water balance of three Central Australian frogs.' *Comp. Biochem. Physiol.*, vol. 20, pp. 27–43, 1967.

WARBURG, M. R. 'Water economy and thermal balance of Israeli and Australian amphibia from xeric habitats.' *Symp. Zool. Soc. Lond.*, 31, pp. 79–111, 1972.

Chapter 9 *Breathing*

CZOPEK, J. 'The vascularization of the respiratory surfaces of some Salientia.' *Zool. Polon.*, vol. 6, pp. 101–34, 1955.

DE JONGH, H. J., and GANS, C. 'On the mechanism of respiration in the Bullfrog, *Rana catesbeiana*: A reassessment.' *J. Morph.*, vol. 127 (3), 1969.

FOXON, G. E. H. 'Blood and respiration.' *In:* Moore, J. A. (Ed.), *Physiology of the Amphibia.* Academic Press, New York and London, 3, pp. 151–209, 1964.

GANS, C., DE JONGH, H. J., and FARBER, J. 'Bullfrog (*Rana catesbeiana*) ventilation. How does the frog breathe?' *Science*, vol. 163, pp. 1223–5, 1969.

GRADWELL, N. 'The respiratory importance of vascularization of the tadpole operculum in *Rana catesbeiana* Shaw.' *Canad. J. Zool.*, vol. 47 (6), pp. 1239–43, 1969.

GRADWELL, N. 'The function of the ventral velum during gill irrigation in *Rana catesbeiana*.' *Can. J. Zool.*, vol. 48 (6), pp. 1179–86, 1970.

GRADWELL, N., and PASZTOR, V. M. 'Hydrostatic pressures during normal ventilation in the bullfrog tadpole.' *Can. J. Zool.*, vol. 46 (6), 1169–74, 1968.

LILLYWHITE, H. B. 'Thermal modulation of cutaneous mucus discharge as a determinant of evaporative water loss in the frog, *Rana catesbeiana*.' *Z. vergl. Physiol*, vol. 73, pp. 84–104, 1971.

NOBLE, G. K. 'The value of life history data in the study of the evolution of the Amphibia.' *Ann. New York Acad. Sci.* vol. 30, pp. 31–128, 1927.

NOBLE, G. K. *The Biology of the Amphibia.* McGraw-Hill, New York, 577 pp., 1931.

PARKER, H. W. 'The amphibians of the Mamfe Division, Cameroons, 1. Zoogeography and systematics.' *Proc. zool. Soc. Lond.*, pp. 135–63, 1936.

SAVAGE, R. M. *The Ecology and Life History of the Common Frog (Rana temporaria temporaria).* Pitman, London, 221 pp., 1961.

SEYMOUR, R. S. 'Energy metabolism of dormant Spadefoot Toads (*Scaphiopus*).' *Copeia* 1973, (3), pp. 435–45, 1973a.

SEYMOUR, R. S. 'Gas exchange in Spadefoot Toads beneath the ground.' *Copeia* 1973, (3), pp. 452–60, 1973b.

STRAWINSKI, S. 'Vascularization of respiratory surfaces in ontogeny of the Edible Frog, *Rana esculenta* L. *Zool. Polon.*, vol. 7, pp. 327–65, 1956.

Chapter 10   *Communication by Sound*

BLAIR, W. F. 'Mating call in the speciation of anuran amphibians. *Amer. Nat.*, vol. 92, pp. 27–51, 1958.

COGGER, H. G. 'Reptiles and amphibians of Coburg Peninsula.' *Aust. Nat. Hist.*, vol. 17 (9), pp. 311–16, 1973.

DUELLMAN, W. E. 'The hylid frogs of Middle America.' *Monogr. Mus. Nat. Hist. Univ. Kansas*, vol. (1), pp. 1–753, 1970.

HARRISON, L. 'On the breeding habits of some Australian frogs.' *Aust. Zool.*, vol. 3 (1), pp. 17–34, 1922.

LEE, A. K. 'Studies in Australian amphibia. II. Taxonomy, ecology, and evolution of the genus *Heleioporus* Gray (Anura: Leptodactylidae).' *Aust. J. Zool.*, vol. 15, pp. 367–439, 1967.

LITTLEJOHN, M. J. 'Vocal communication in frogs.' *Aust. Nat. Hist.*, vol. 15 (2), pp. 52–5, 1965.

LITTLEJOHN, M. J. 'Frog calls and the species problem.' *Aust. Zool.*, vol. 14 (3), pp. 259–64, 1968.

LITTLEJOHN, M. J., and MARTIN, A. A. 'Mating call as an aid to the identification of the frogs of the Melbourne area.' *Vic. Nat.*, vol. 86, pp. 126–7, 1969.

LOFTUS-HILLS, J. J., and JOHNSTONE, B. M. 'Auditory function, communication, and the brain-evoked response in anuran amphibians.' *J. Acoust. Soc. Amer.*, vol. 47 (4), pp. 1131–8, 1970.

LOFTUS-HILLS, M. J., and LITTLEJOHN, M. J. 'Mating call sound intensities of anuran amphibians.' *J. Acoust. Soc. Amer.*, vol. 47 (4), 1327–9, 1971.

MOORE, J. A. 'The frogs of eastern New South Wales.' *Bull. Amer. Mus. Nat. Hist.*, vol. 121, pp. 149–386, 1961.

Chapter 11 *Reproduction*

COGGER, H. G. 'A reptile-collecting expedition to New Guinea.' *Aust. Nat. Hist.*, pp. 363–8, 1964.

LIEM, D. S. 'A new genus of frog of the family Leptodactylidae from S.E. Queensland, Australia.' *Mem. Qld. Mus.*, vol. 16 (3), pp. 459–70, 1973.

LITTLEJOHN, M. J. 'The breeding biology of the Baw Baw frog *Philoria frosti* Spencer.' *Proc. Linn. Soc. N.S.W.*, vol. 88 (3), pp. 273–6, 1963.

LOVERIDGE, A. 'Four new crinine frogs from Australia.' *Occ. Pap. Boston. Soc. Nat. Hist.*, vol. 8, pp. 55–60, 1933.

MARTIN, A. A., and COOPER, A. K. 'The ecology of terrestrial anuran eggs, genus *Crinia* (Leptodactylidae).' *Copeia* 1972, vol. 1, pp. 163–8, 1972.

STRAUGHAN, I. R., and MAIN, A. R. 'Speciation and polymorphism in the genus *Crinia* Tschudi (Anura: Leptodactylidae) in Queensland.' *Proc. R. Soc. Qld.*, vol. 78 (2), pp. 11–28, 1966.

TYLER, M. J. 'A new genus for the Australian leptodactylid frog *Crinia darlingtoni*.' *Zool. Meded., Leiden*, vol. 47, pp. 193–201, 1972.

Chapter 12 *In the Face of the Enemy*

BARBOUR, T. 'A new genus of Amphibia Salientia from Dutch New Guinea.' *Proc. biol. Soc. Wash.*, vol. 23, pp. 89–90, 1910.

CLELAND, J. B. 'The food of Australian birds. An investigation into the character of the stomach and crop contents.' *Sci. Bull. Dept. Agric. N.S.W.*, No. 15, pp. 3–112, 1918.

COTT, H. B. *Adaptive Coloration in Animals.* Methuen, London, 508 pp., 1940.

INGER, R. F. '*Bufo* of Eurasia.' *In: Evolution in the Genus Bufo.* (Ed. W. F. Blair). Univ. Texas Press, Austin and London, 1972.

LEA, A. M., and GRAY, J. T. 'The food of Australian birds. An analysis of the stomach contents.' *Emu*, vol. 34, pp. 275–92; vol. 35, pp. 63–98; vol. 35, pp. 145–78; vol. 35, pp. 251–347, 1935.

MCKEOWN, K. C. 'Vertebrates capture by Australian spiders.' *Proc. R. Zool. Soc. N.S.W.* (for 1942–43), pp. 17–30, 1943.

PENGILLEY, R. K. 'Calling and associated behaviour of some species of *Pseudophryne* (Anura: Leptodactylidae).' *J. Zool. Lond.*, vol. 163, pp. 73–92, 1971.

SOFTLY, A., and NAIRN, M. E. 'A newly reported toxic Australian frog (Genus *Heleioporus*).' *Med. J. Aust.*, vol. 1 (62nd year) (18), pp. 560–561, 1975.

TYLER, M. J., and PARKER, F. 'New species of hylid and leptodactylid frogs from southern New Guinea.' *Trans. R. Soc. S. Aust.*, 1974.

WORRELL, E. *Reptiles of Australia.* Angus and Robertson, Sydney, 1970.

Chapter 13 *Parasites of Frogs*

BENNETT, L. B. 'The immunological responses produced by mice and amphibians to spargana.' Ph.D. Thesis, University of Adelaide, 1968.

DOMROW, R. 'The family Speleognathidae in Australia (Acarina).' *Proc. Linn. Soc. N.S.W.*, vol. 85 (3), pp. 374–81, 1960.

EWERS, W. H. 'Blood parasites of some New Guinea reptiles and amphibia.' *J. Parasitol.*, vol. 54 (1). pp. 172–4, 1968.

FAIN, A. 'Observations sur les acariens de la sous-famille Lawrencarinae (Ereynetidae: Trombidifarmes) (note préliminaire).' *Bull. Ann. Soc. Roy. Ent. Belg.*, vol. 97 (9–10), pp. 245–55, 1961.

JOHNSON, S. J. 'On some trematode parasites of Australian frogs.' *Proc. Linn. Soc. N.S.W.*, vol. 37 (2), pp. 285–362, 1912.

JOHNSTON, T. H., and ANGEL, L. M. 'The morphology and life history of the trematode *Dolichopera macalpini* Nicoll.' *Trans. R. Soc. S. Aust.*, vol. 64, pp. 376–87, 1940.

KINGHORN, J. R. 'Reptiles and batrachians from south and south-west Australia.' *Rec. Aust. Mus.*, vol. 34 (3), pp. 163–83, 1924.

MARKS, E. N. 'Mosquitoes biting frogs.' *Aust. J. Sci.*, vol. 23 (3), p. 89, 1960.

REICHENBACH-KLINKE, H., and ELKAN, E. *The Principal Diseases of Lower Vertebrates.* Academic Press, London and New York, 600 pp., 1965.

SMITH, M. A. *The British Amphibians and Reptiles.* Collins, London, 322 pp., 1953.

SMYTH, J. D. *Introduction to Animal Parasitology.* English Universities Press, London, 470 pp., 1962.

WAITE, E. R. 'Field notes on some Australian reptiles and a batrachian.' *Rec. S. Aust. Mus*, vol. 3 (1), pp. 17–32, 1925.

WOMERSLEY, H. 'A new genus and species of Speleognathidae (Acarina) from South Australia.' *Trans. R. Soc. S. Aust.*, vol. 76, pp. 82–4, 1953.

Chapter 14 *Dispersal*

FISCHTHAL, J. H., and KUNTZ, R. E. 'Digenetic. trematodes of amphibians and reptiles from Fiji, New Hebrides and British Solomon Islands.' *Proc. Helminth. Soc. Washington*, vol. 32 (2), pp. 244–51, 1967.

FRAZER, J. F. D. 'Introduced species of amphibians and reptiles in mainland Britain.' *Brit. J. Herpetol.*, vol. 3 (6), pp. 145–50, 1964.

INGER, R. F. 'Systematics and zoogeography of Philippine amphibia.' *Fieldiana: Zoology*, vol. 33 (4), pp. 183–531, 1954.

MCCANN, C. 'Distribution of the Gekkonidae in the Pacific area.' *Proc. 7th Pacific Sci. Congress*, vol. 4, pp. 27–32, 1953.

MCCANN, C. 'The introduced frogs of New Zealand.' *Tuatara*, vol. 8 (1), pp. 107–20, 1961.

NEILL, W. T. 'Frogs introduced on islands.' *Q. J. Florida Acad. Sci.*, vol. 27 (2), pp. 127–30, 1964.

SARASIN, F. 'Uber die tiergeschichte der lander des Sudwestlichen Pazifischens Ozeans auf grund von forschungen in New-Caledonien und den Loyalty Inseln.' *Nova Caledonia* (A) (Zoologie), vol. 4, pp. 1–119, 1926.

TONKER, S. *Animals of Hawaii, a natural history of the amphibians, reptiles and mammals living in the Hawaiian Islands.* Tongg. Publ. Co., Honolulu, 190 pp., 1941.

TYLER, M. J. 'An analysis of the lower vertebrate faunal relationships of Australia and New Guinea.' *In:* D. Walker (Ed.), *Bridge and Barrier: The Natural and Cultural History of Torres Strait.* Dept. of Biogeography and Geomorphology, Publ. BG/3, Australian National University, Canberra.

VAN KAMPEN, P. N. '*Hyla dolichopsis* Cope von Java.' *Bull. Dep. Agric. Indes. neerl.*, (8), pp. 13–4, 1907.

WHITLEY, G. P. 'Rains of fishes in Australia.' *Aust. Nat. Hist.*, vol. 17 (5), pp. 154–9, 1972.

Chapter 15   *Geographic Distribution*

DARLINGTON, P. J. *Zoogeography: The Geographical Distribution of Animals.* Wiley, New York, 1957.

GILL, E. D. 'Current Quaternary shoreline research in Australasia.' *Aust. J. Sci.*, vol. 32 (11), p. 426, 1970.

JENNINGS, J. N. 'Some attributes of Torres Strait.' *In:* D. Walker (Ed.), *Bridge and Barrier: The natural and cultural history of Torres Strait.* Dept. of Biogeography and Geomorphology, Publ. BG/3, Australian National University, Canberra, 1972.

LUNDELIUS, E. L. 'Vertebrate remains from the Nullarbor caves, Western Australia.' *J. R. Soc. W. Aust.*, vol. 46, pp. 75–80, 1963.

MAIN, A. R. 'Ecology, systematics and evolution of Australian frogs.' *In:* J. B. Cragg (Ed.), *Advances in Ecological Research*, vol. 5, pp. 37–86, Academic Press, London, 1968.

MAIN, A. R., LEE, A. K., and LITTLEJOHN, M. J. 'Evolution in three genera of Australian frogs.' *Evolution*, vol. 12, pp. 224–33, 1958.

TYLER, M. J. 'Discovery in the Everard Ranges of a species of leptodactylid frog new to the fauna of South Australia.' *Trans. R. Soc. S. Aust.*, vol. 95 (4), pp. 215–7, 1971.

Chapter 16   *Frogs and Man*

ANASTASI, A., ERSPAMER, V., and ENDEAN, R. 'Isolation and amino acid sequence of caerulein, the active decapeptide of the skin of *Hyla caerulea*.' *Arch. Biochem. Biophys.*, vol. 125 (1), pp. 57–68, 1968.

BRONGERSMA, L. D. *The Animal World of Netherlands New Guinea.* J. B. Wolters, Groningen, 70 pp., 1958.

BULMER, R. N. H., and TYLER, M. J. 'Karam classification of frogs.' *J. Polynesian Soc.*, vol. 77, pp. 333–85, 1968.

BUSTARD, R. *Australian Lizards*. Collins, Sydney and London, 162 pp., 1970.

COX, J. C. 'Drawings by Australian aborigines.' *Proc. Linn. Soc. N.S.W.*, vol. 3 (2), pp. 155–60, 1879.

ERSPAMER, V., DE CARO, G., and ENDEAN, R. 'Occurrence of a physalaemin-like polypeptide (Uperolein) and other active polypeptides in the skin of *Uperoleia rugosa*.' *Experientia*, vol. 22, pp. 1–2, 1966.

FLETCHER, J. J. 'Contributions to a more exact knowledge of the geographical distribution of Australian Batrachia. No. II.' *Proc. Linn. Soc. N.S.W.*, 2nd Series, vol. 6, pp. 263–74, 1891.

GOODEN, B. A. 'The tadpole tail as a model for decompression studies.' *Aust. J. Exp. Biol. Med. Sci.*. vol. 51 (1), pp. 109–12, 1973.

JOHNSTON, T. H. 'Aboriginal names and utilization of the fauna in the Eyrean Region.' *Trans. R. Soc. S. Aust.*, vol. 67 (2), pp. 244–311, 1943.

MOORE, G. F. *Descriptive Australian Vocabulary*. 1842.

SPENCER, B. *Natives of the Northern Territory of Australia*. Macmillan, London, 1914.

SPENCER, B. *Wanderings in Wild Australia*. Macmillan, London, 1928.

SPENCER, B., and GILLEN, F. J. *The Native Tribes of Central Australia*. Macmillan, London, 671 pp., 1899.

SPENCER, B., and GILLEN, F. J. *Across Australia*. Macmillan, London, 1912.

SPENCER, B., and GILLEN, F. *The Arunta, Vol. 1–2*. Macmillan, London, 646 pp., 1927.

STREHLOW, T. G. H. *Songs of Central Australia*. Angus and Robertson, Sydney, 775 pp., 1971.

THOMAS, N. W. *Natives of Australia*. Constable, London, 256 pp., 1906.

TYLER, M. J. 'On the possible existence of a giant frog in New Guinea.' *Brit. J. Herpet.*, vol. 3 (2), pp. 28–30, 1962.

TYLER, M. J. 'The Frogs of South Australia.' *S. Aust. Mus.*, Adelaide, 40 pp., 1966.

TYLER, M. J. 'Papuan hylid frogs of the genus *Hyla*.' *Zool. Verhand.*, Leiden, vol. 96, pp. 1–203, 1968.

Chapter 17 Herpetology in Australia

BLEEKER, P. 'Verslag omtrent reptilien van Nieuw-Guinea, aangeboden door H. von Rosenberg.' *Natuurk Tijdschr*. Ned.-Ind., vol. 16 (2), pp. 420–3, 1859.

BOULENGER, G. A. *Catalogue of the Batrachia Salientia s. Ecaudata in the collection of the British Museum*. Second Edition, London, 1882.

COPLAND, S. J. 'Presidential Address. Recent Australian Herpetology.' *Proc. Linn. Soc. New South Wales*, vol. 78 (1–2), pp. 1–37, 1953.

DUMÉRIL, A. M. C., and BIBRON, G. *Erpétologie générale ou histoire naturelle complète des reptiles*. Roret, Paris, 1841–1854.

FLETCHER, J. J. 'Contributions to a more exact knowledge of the geographical distribution of Australian Batrachia. Nos. 1–5.' *Proc. Linn. Soc. New South Wales*, vol. 5–12, 1890–1898.

FRY, D. B. 'Description of *Austrochaperina*, a new genus of Engystomatidae from north Australia.' *Rec. Aust. Mus.*, vol. 9, pp. 87–106, 1912.

FRY, D. B. 'Herpetological notes.' *Proc. R. Soc. Qd*, vol. 27, pp. 60–95, 1915.

FRY, D. B. 'Description of *Aphantophryne*, a new batrachian genus from New Guinea.' *Proc. Linn. Soc. New South Wales*, vol. 41, pp. 770–85, 1916.

GUNTHER, A. *Catalogue of the Batrachia Salientia in the collection of the British Museum.* London, 1858.

LOVERIDGE, A. A. 'Australian Amphibia in the Museum of Comparative Zoology, Cambridge, Massachusetts.' *Bull. Mus. Comp. Zool.*, vol. 78, pp 1–60, 1935.

LOVERIDGE, A. A. 'New Guinean reptiles and amphibians in the Museum of Comparative Zoology and United States National Museum.' *Bull. Mus. comp. Zool.*, Harvard, vol. 101 (2), pp. 305–430, 1948.

MERTENS, R. *In:* Classification der Batrachier by J. J. Tschudi. Facsimile by *Soc. Study Amph. Rept.* Ann Arbor, Michigan, 1967.

MOORE, J. A. 'The frogs of Eastern New South Wales.' *Bull. Amer. Mus. Nat. Hist.*, vol. 121 (3), pp. 149–386, 1961.

PETERS, W., and DORIA, G. 'Catalago dei rettili e dei batraci raccolti da O. Beccari, L. M. D'Albertis e A. A. Bruijn nella Sotto-Regione Austro-Malese.' *Ann. Mus. Civ. Stor. Nat.*, vol. 13, pp. 323–450, 1878.

SCLATER, P. L. 'On the zoology of New Guinea.' *J. Proc. Linn. Soc.*, Zoology, vol. 2, pp. 149–70, 1858.

SHAW, G. A. *Nat. Misc.* 6 (lacks title), 1795.

TSCHUDI, J. J. 'Classification der Batrachier, mit Berucksichtigung der fossilen Thiere dieser Abtheilung der Reptilien.' *Mém. Soc. Sci. Nat.* Neuchatel, vol. 2, pp. 30–75, 1838.

TYLER, M. J., and DOBSON, J. 'On the identity, authorship and fate of the type specimens of *Rana caerulea*.' *Herpetologica*, 1973.

VAN KAMPEN, P. N. *Amphibia of the Indo-Australian Archipelago.* Brill, Leiden, 1923.

WHITLEY, G. P. 'The first hundred years.' *Aust. Mus. Mag.*, vol. 14 (4), pp. 111–15, 1962.

Chapter 18 *The Study of Frogs*

BLAKE, A. J. D. 'Taxonomy and relationships of myobatrachine frogs (Leptodactylidae): A numerical approach.' *Aust. J. Zool.*, vol. 21, pp. 119–49, 1973.

BRATTSTROM, B. H. 'Thermal acclimation in Australian amphibians.' *Comp. Biochem. Physiol.*, vol. 35, pp. 69–103, 1970.

CLYNE, D. *Australian Frogs.* Lansdowne Press, Melbourne, 1969.

COGGER, H. G. *The Frogs of New South Wales.* Australian Museum, Sydney, 1960.

COPLAND, S. J. 'Presidential address: Australian tree frogs of the genus *Hyla*.' *Proc. Linn. Soc. N.S.W.*, vol. 82, pp. 9–108, 1957.

LEE, A. K. 'Studies in Australian Amphibia II. Taxonomy, ecology and evolution of the genus *Heleioporus* Gray (Anura: Leptodactylidae).' *Aust. J. Zool.*, vol. 15, pp. 367–439, 1967.

LITTLEJOHN, M. J. 'Frogs of the Melbourne area.' *Vict. Nat.*, vol. 79 (10), pp. 296–304, 1963.

MAIN, A. R. *Frogs of Southern Western Australia.* Handbook No. 8, Western Australian Naturalists' Club, Perth, 1965.

MARTIN, A. A. 'Tadpoles of the Melbourne area.' *Vict. Nat.*, vol. 82 (5), pp. 139–49, 1965.

MARTIN, A. A. 'Studies in Australian Amphibia. III. The *Limnodynastes dorsalis* complex (Anura: Leptodactylidae).' *Aust. J. Zool.*, vol. 20, pp. 165–211, 1972.

MARTIN, A. A., LITTLEJOHN, M. J., and RAWLINSON, P. A. 'A key to the anuran eggs of the Melbourne area, and an addition to the anuran fauna.' *Vict. Nat.*, vol. 83, pp. 312–5, 1966.

MOORE, J. A. 'The frogs of eastern New South Wales.' *Bull. Amer. Mus. Nat. Hist.*, vol. 121, pp. 149–386, 1961.

PISANI, G. R. 'A guide to preservation techniques for Amphibians and Reptiles.' Herpetological Circular (1), *Misc. Publ. Soc. Study Amph. Reptiles*, 1973.

TYLER, M. J. 'On the preservation of anuran tadpoles.' *Aust J. Sci.*, vol. 25 (5), p. 222, 1962.

TYLER, M. J. *The Frogs of South Australia.* South Australian Museum, Adelaide, 1966.

TYLER, M. J. 'The phylogenetic significance of vocal sac structure in hylid frogs.' *Univ. Kansas Publ. Mus. Nat. Hist.*, vol. 19 (4), pp. 319–60, 1971.

TYLER, M. J. 'An annotated bibliography of the frogs of Papua New Guinea.' *Science in New Guinea*, vol. 1 (3–4), pp. 51–82, 1973.

TYLER, M. J. 'The systematic position and geographic distribution of the Australian frog *Chiroleptes alboguttatus* Gunther.' *Proc. R. Soc. Qd.*, vol. 85 (2), pp. 27–32, 1974.

Index